A Guidebook *to the* NAIS PRINCIPLES OF GOOD PRACTICE

James Tracy, Editor

NATIONAL ASSOCIATION OF INDEPENDENT SCHOOLS

ISBN: 1-893021-68-8
Printed in the United States of America.

The National Association of Independent Schools represents approximately 1,300 independent private schools in the United States and other countries. All are accredited, non-discriminatory, nonprofit organizations governed by independent boards of trustees. NAIS's mission is to serve and strengthen member schools and associations by "articulating and promoting high standards of educational quality and ethical behavior; to work to preserve their independence to serve the free society from which that independence derives; to advocate broad access for students by affirming the principles of diversity, choice, and opportunity."

To find out more information, go to the NAIS website at *www.nais.org.* To receive a listing of NAIS books, call (800) 793-6701 or (301) 396-5911.

Editor: Karla Taylor
Book Designer: Fletcher Design, Washington, DC

CONTENTS

FOREWORD

NAIS's vision for 21st-century independent schools is for them to be transformed into institutions that are sustainable along five continua:

- **Demographic:** Becoming more inclusive and representative of the population—student and faculty—and less unapproachable financially and socially.
- **Environmental:** Becoming more "green" and less wasteful.
- **Global:** Becoming more globally oriented and internationally networked and less parochial in outlook.
- **Programmatic:** Becoming more attuned to developing the skills and values that the 21st-century marketplace will seek and reward, and less constrained by the traditional-disciplines approach to teaching and learning.
- **Financial:** Becoming more affordable and less inefficient and costly.

Fulfilling this vision depends, of course, upon the leaders at the board and school-administration level who have the capacity to address large issues and the will to effect change. There is no better means to manifest that capacity than by developing the respective board and administration teams, each in their own right and together as partners. There is no better means to achieve that goal than a case study approach (used so successfully in pre-eminent business schools such as Harvard, Wharton, Darden, and others and illustrated monthly in the *Harvard Business Review*).

A Guidebook to the NAIS Principles of Good Practice is the product of a case study approach presented by expert practitioners in the field. We are blessed by our industry's penchant for sharing insight widely and freely. Now each independent school has a tool to use to develop the leadership capacity necessary to move the agenda forward.

I recommend periodically taking a case study from this book for administrative and/or board meetings. Doing so will provide the "muscle memory" your leadership needs to plan proactively to deal with the inevitable challenges that emerge in our work. A small investment in this book and the case studies it presents will be rewarded many times over.

Patrick F. Bassett
President, NAIS

May 2007

PREFACE

By James Tracy

James Tracy, who was head of Boston University Academy for six years, became head of Cushing Academy in July 2006. Cushing is a boarding school of 450 students in grades 9-12 in Ashburnham, Massachusetts. He is editor of A Guidebook to the NAIS Principles of Good Practice.

Independent schools have been exemplars of the best of American pre-collegiate education since the colonial era. One of their strengths has certainly been the distinctiveness of culture and pedagogy that marks each school and offers families a wide array of superb options for their children. Although this individuality is key to the flourishing of independent schools (indeed, the concept is imprinted in the very term we use to describe such schools), we who are school professionals nonetheless share many commonalities in the organizational challenges we face and how we surmount them.

Surprisingly, though, there is not a strong tradition of formal and explicit exchange of such experiences among schools. Until recent years, even the best of administrative information flow within the field has often been ad hoc, episodic, and considerably less than optimal. This is especially true when we compare our field to the for-profit or public sectors, which benefit from a vast field of research and experimentation, not to mention the contributions of business schools that develop industry-wide benchmarks and best practices. Many school administrators—especially heads of schools—feel isolated on islands of particularist tradition. Too often, we must reinvent the wheel in a reactive way as administrative needs arise.

Yet the pressures to become more managerially effective are growing monumentally and threatening to bring some schools—and perhaps entire sectors of the field—to their knees if they do not adapt to 21st-century realities. This does not mean we ought to commodify or otherwise debase our vocation to the level of selling, say, toothpaste. Clearly, our first order of business is something that borders on the spiritual: the education, character formation, and nurturance of children.

Nevertheless, it is an inescapable reality that we cannot realize this transcendent mission in the absence of a sustainable business model.

The regulatory environment, our country's changing demographics, the culture of expectation and entitlement, the rapidly shifting economic landscape, and many other exogenous factors increasingly impinge upon our schools in unprecedented ways. In this climate, it is to the benefit of all school administrators to share experiences about what has worked, what has not, why, and how. Precisely because we want to preserve the uniqueness of each school, we must become more committed to sharing our hard-earned experience and disseminating best practices at a national level, among all our schools.

In recent years, NAIS has taken the lead by transforming itself into a research center, locus of discourse, disseminator of information and ideas, resource provider, and advocate for America's independent schools. Of the many benefits that have accrued to all independent schools from these initiatives, one worthy of particular mention is the set of Principles of Good Practice. These are benchmarking practices in 19 areas of independent school administration that provide a guide to how we can survive and thrive despite buffeting from the quotidian vortices of the new millennium. (You can see the entire set by going to *www.nais.org* and searching on "Principles of Good Practice.")

This book's intent is to build upon the framework of the NAIS principles by bringing together national leaders from various areas under the broad umbrella of independent school management. The contributors to the 12 sets of principles featured in this book bring to each chapter a rich tapestry of experience marked by detailed knowledge of the many schools and school practices they have encountered throughout their varied and impressive careers.

It has been a distinct privilege for me to work with so many professionals of such high caliber. They have breathed life into the abstractions within the NAIS principles through their engaging case studies, examples collected from other schools, and—for those readers who wish to learn more—resources for further reading.

My hope is that this book will prove to be an asset to administrators—or aspiring administrators—at all levels of independent school life.

INTRODUCTION
HOW TO USE THIS GUIDEBOOK'S CASE STUDIES
AT YOUR SCHOOL

By Patrick F. Bassett

Patrick F. Bassett is president of the National Association of Independent Schools in Washington, DC.

We at NAIS believe the case study approach the country's leading business schools employ is also useful for training school leaders and boards. Each chapter of *A Guidebook to the NAIS Principles of Good Practice* relates a case study to a set of the Principles of Good Practice. (Additionally, on its website NAIS has more than 30 case studies—in narrative form and in some instances in filmed vignette form—for school leaders and boards. To see these, go to *www.nais.org* and search for "case study.")

For each case study in this book, we recommend that your group read and discuss the case in the context of three questions:
1. What are the leadership issues in play?
2. What are the Principles of Good Practice at stake?
3. In the context of the two questions above, what should we do if this situation arises at our school?

To show you how this can work, here's a brief case related to the Principles of Good Practice for Admission and for Governance, as well as some possible ways to address the dilemma.

CASE STUDY
BANNER YEAR: ONE SLOT LEFT

Bright School is a highly competitive K-12 school in a medium-sized metropolitan area. It has high "reputational value"—so much so that it always has at least three applications for every opening and a long waiting list. A banner year in admissions left Bright School with an outstanding entering class and only one remaining slot available. Lots of qualified candidates would have to be placed on the waiting list, some of them siblings and legacies.

In one 24-hour period, Bright School's head, Bob Hedge, was approached by three parties who missed the initial application deadline but were told they'd be placed on the waiting list and considered with the other candidates there. Bob, knowing the call would be a tough one, decided to share the conundrum with his board chair. The board happened to be meeting that evening, and Bob believed whatever call he made would be second-guessed by some board members.

So Bob called his board chair, Susan Rider, to outline to her the conundrum and to share the facts related to having just one admissions slot left. He explained that those post-deadline applicants were especially important, but to take any of the three would mean jumping them ahead of others on the waiting list. The applicants in question were:

- The third child of a board member. This trustee had initially agreed that the child's testing results suggested another school would be a better match, but upon reflection, he asked for a one-year admit on a trial basis since "we are a family school." The trustee had already signed a contract and paid the deposit for a slot in another local independent school.

- The child of a full-pay "opinion leader" from the Hispanic community. Her admission would drive other families from this demographic pool to the school in future years—a goal that the board had stipulated as a top priority in its strategic plan.
- The "mayor's candidate," the daughter of a CEO who was prepared to move his company headquarters to the city, but only if the mayor could get the kid into this school.

The board chair's first response was "Take them all!" But Bob reminded her that in recent years Bright School had rigidly adhered to its policy on maximum class size (which was useful for consoling families who could not be accommodated). That aside, zoning regulations wouldn't permit a single additional student beyond the one the school had room for.

Bob noted that there were mixed opinions around the management-team table about whom to choose. Taking a page from Dick Chait's *Governance as Leadership,* which recommends that some management decisions that have strategic implications should be shared between management and governance, Susan suggested that Bob should take the case to the board "to test the wind" on where the board might come down, given the competing priorities.

When Bob did so that evening, he had a three-way split among the board members and no clear mandate on which way to go.

Should the head have consulted with the board at all, since now he was sure to disappoint two-thirds of the board members? What decision should he make?

THE CASE IN PERSPECTIVE
How NAIS would address the problem

Leadership Issues in Play

- Where is the line and how clear a demarcation exists between governance and management, especially in the context of the Principle of Good Practice indicating that the board "recognizes that its primary work and focus are long-range and strategic"?
- Is "shared decision-making" possible and prudent in such instances?
- What does a school head do when board policies are contradictory and conflicted, especially in the case of Principles of Good Practice indicating that the board "engages proactively with the head of school in cultivating and maintaining good relations with school constituents as well as the broader community and exhibits best practices relevant to equity and justice"?
- What does a head do when the signals from the board are mixed or in opposition to his or her judgment, or when they will upset the prevailing assumptions among staff?

PGPs at Stake

- How does the admissions director react when a head asks her to "break the rules just this once" because of "special circumstances"? (In this case, the broken rules would be the admission principles on "[ensuring] an appropriate match between a prospective student and family and the mission and philosophy of the school" and on "[operating] under a clear set of practices for gathering, disseminating, and maintaining prospective student information.")
- How does a school handle the conflict with another independent school that believes your school is "poaching" its students?
- How do neighboring independent schools resolve competing Principles of Good Practice that assert collegial relationships are key between the schools but also note the free-market right of parents to shop for the best match for their kids?

NAIS's Take

This case study tests the boundaries between leadership (boards) and management (staff).
- In admissions, the board sets policy (mission-defined priorities of "whom we serve"

and what priorities take precedence), but the staff executes and interprets mandates and policy in terms of which individual students to accept.

- The "constituents" in this case are many. Among them are the faculty on the admissions committee (skeptical about a student who doesn't want to be here and will be unlikely to succeed); the trustee family (whose first instinct is to keep the kids together for all kinds of understandable reasons); and the development office and board members charged with fund raising (eager to leverage an admission for what it can bring in terms of financial support directly and indirectly).

- Best practice would be for the head to make the call. Yes, Bob should confer with at least the board chair (and possibly other board members), who should offer counsel and advice. But this is a management decision, not a board-level decision. Once it's made, neither individual trustees nor the board should second-guess or criticize the decision, publicly or privately.

- The head could easily make a principle-based case for admitting any of the three, depending on which is the "best match" for the school in multiple ways. However, if the trustee's child is chosen, Bob should counsel the trustee that the family would be responsible for meeting any contractual penalty obligations at the other school before the child was admitted to Bright School.

Final note: In all such crisis situations or leadership dilemmas, NAIS recommends a standard operating procedure found in the document "Crisis Decision-making Protocols." You can find these protocols at *www.nais.org.* Just search on the keywords "case study" or "crisis."

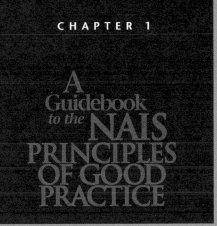

CHAPTER 1

A Guidebook
to the NAIS
PRINCIPLES
OF GOOD
PRACTICE

for

ADMISSION

By D. Scott Looney and Drew Miller

D. Scott Looney is head of Hawken School, which has 950 students in preschool through 12th grade on campuses in Lyndhurst and Gates Mills, Ohio.
Drew Miller is director of admission and financial aid at Cranbrook Schools in Bloomfield Hills, Michigan. Cranbrook is a day and boarding school with 1,630 students in preschool through 12th grade.

NAIS PRINCIPLES OF GOOD PRACTICE for

ADMISSION

Revised and approved by the NAIS board in 2007

Through the recruitment and selection of students, admission professionals play a critical role in their schools' vitality and educational culture. All admission professionals, as well as the head of school, bear the ultimate responsibility for communicating and upholding these Principles of Good Practice to all professional staff and volunteers (including parents, alumni/ae, tour guides, coaches, faculty, and board members) who represent the institution in promotion, recruitment, admission, and retention activities. (Although many of the principles apply to this case study, the ones in **boldface** are the most pertinent.)

1. **The school seeks to ensure an appropriate match between a prospective student and family and the mission and philosophy of the school.**

2. **The school respects and affirms the dignity and worth of each individual in the admission process.**

3. In establishing policies and procedures for student recruitment and enrollment, particularly in the area of non-discrimination, the school adheres to local, state, and federal laws and regulations.

4. The school has available in writing those policies and procedures of the school, member associations, and/or athletic leagues that may affect a family's decision to enroll.

5. **The school operates under a clear set of practices for gathering, disseminating, and maintaining prospective student information, and respects the confidentiality of students, families, and documents in the admission process. Schools will ensure that the admission process and/or transcript have provided sufficient documentation of an appropriate match before offering admission to a student.**

6. **The school maintains an admission process that respects the needs of students and families to learn about school programs and activities, that communicates in user-friendly formats, and that provides clear information, dates, and timeframes for all aspects of the admission process, including expectations around financial aid applications and acceptance of an enrollment offer.**

7. The school recognizes that general advertising, direct mail campaigns, and communications between other schools and current independent school families guarantee the free market rights of the families and the general public to consider all options and that such practices from competitor schools should not be seen as a violation of the spirit of collaboration, collegiality, and professionalism reflected in these principles.

8. **The school recognizes the right of currently enrolled students and families to consider other educational options, and if a transfer is initiated by the family, the school provides appropriate support and documentation in a timely manner, including reminding the family of any policies related to contractual obligations to the current school.**

9. The school shares complete information about the total costs of attending the school and other financial expectations with families before an enrollment commitment is required.

10. The school establishes and furthers collegial relations with neighboring independent schools by undertaking collaborative marketing arrangements to tell the independent school story and to encourage more families to consider independent education.

11. **School representatives apply the same high standards of integrity whether talking about their own school or other institutions.**

12. The school ensures that all recruitment arrangements support the best interests of the student and do not result in a conflict of interest on the part of the school, individual, or firms representing the school.

CASE STUDY
A PROMINENT FAMILY CREATES AN ADMISSION DILEMMA

Jon Raymond, the head of Right School, recognized Sarah Diamond as a rising star, and her first six months as director of admission only enhanced his initial confidence in her. At Sarah's previous school, a well-known private high school on the East Coast, Sarah was known for being wise beyond her years and rose through the ranks quickly, moving from entry-level admission officer to associate director of admission. Jon knew that coming to Right School represented a significant challenge for Sarah, as she not only had to adjust to the added responsibility of being the director but also to living in a new area. He was conscious of the need to mentor Sarah while also making certain not to undermine her authority with her staff, her fellow administrators, and her admission committee. Jon made a point of neither participating directly in the admission committee deliberations nor contradicting the decisions Sarah and the committee made.

In return for this autonomy, Jon gave Sarah one very specific instruction: no surprises. Sarah knew that if an admission decision had the potential to be controversial or problematic, she was to make certain Jon was aware of it.

Sarah prided herself on appearing unflappable, even when self-doubt was raging. But the interview appointment for the Thomason twins, coming up on January 17, tested her resolve. The Thomason family was to Sarah's new city what the Fords are to Detroit or the DuPonts are to Delaware. The Thomasons were the founding family and still owned a controlling interest in America's second-largest retail operation (behind Wal-Mart), and the Thomason Company was the single largest employer in town.

In preparation for this interview, Sarah talked with Jon. He reaffirmed his confidence in her while pointing out how important a positive relationship with the Thomason family could be for their school. Will and Andrew Thomason, fraternal twins, began attending Askew Academy, a nearby K-12 day school, in kindergarten and were now enrolled in the eighth grade. Since Right School was perceived as somewhat more selective and prestigious than Askew, and since Right was a high school, it was not uncommon for Right to receive applications from Askew eighth-graders. But given that the Thomasons served on the Askew board and were known to be its largest benefactors, it was assumed that the twins would simply continue there. Sarah wondered whether the Thomasons' application to her school was serious or just exploratory. She would soon find out.

Sarah spent a good deal of the early morning of January 17 trying to convince herself that the Thomasons were just like other families, wanting what all parents want for their children, so interviewing them would be no big deal. So what if they were billionaires, employed a large portion of the parents whose children attended her school, and could single-handedly fund the school's entire capital campaign? In preparation for this interview, Jon had explained to Sarah how many of the school's current board members had direct or indirect business relations with the Thomason Company. He said he trusted her to do what was right for both the school and the Thomason family, but, he added, "Sarah, this one is 'no fail' … for both of us."

Will and Andrew Thomason arrived at the school admission office with their mother. Sarah welcomed them and explained the agenda for the boys' visit. The boys would each be paired with a ninth-grader and spend the morning touring the school and sitting in on classes. After lunch with the students, Will and Andrew would return to the admission office for a chat with Sarah. Then they would take the admission test.

When Sarah addressed their mother, Mrs. Thomason immediately responded, "Please, call me Claire." Claire seemed gracious, down to earth, and genuinely eager to learn more—even though, Sarah thought, "as the most influential woman in town and someone who grew up here, she probably knows more about this school than I do." Before the boys went off to visit classes, Sarah invited all of the Thomasons to meet Jon.

As delightful as Sarah found Claire, Will and Andrew were enigmas. It was difficult to tell what they were thinking or if they even wanted to visit the school. While introducing the boys to Jon, she noticed that they both looked at the ground when shaking hands and mumbled their responses. Even for eighth-grade boys, they seemed to have somewhat poor social skills.

After some small talk, Jon wished them a great visit and said to Claire, "I am confident that you will find our school to be a good match for your boys."

"Let's just hope we find the boys to be a good match for our school," Sarah thought.

Sarah introduced Will and Andrew to their host students and then sent them off. Once she and Claire settled into Sarah's office, Sarah asked, "So tell me about your boys. What are your hopes for them in high school?"

Claire began by telling Sarah that the boys were having increasing difficulty at Askew Academy, which she attributed to the lack of the right approach to her boys' unique talents. She went on to explain that the past year had been particularly difficult for Andrew. He no longer appeared to be motivated, had difficulty completing his homework on time, and was having a personality clash with his current English teacher—who, Claire added, was notorious for being difficult and playing favorites. Will had that same teacher later in the day without a problem, a disparity that only exacerbated Andrew's troubles. Claire felt that perhaps a change of scenery for Andrew was in order, but she wanted to keep both boys in the same school.

Claire then asked Sarah to compare Right and Askew, adding provocatively, "My child's adviser at Askew Academy once told me that children at Right School are not taught independent thinking skills as thoroughly as they are at Askew."

Sarah knew immediately that it was inappropriate to comment on another school and didn't take the bait. Instead she responded, "Well, I don't know much about the Askew Academy other than its reputation as a fine school. I can only tell you what I know about our school. In the independent school world, it is generally considered bad form to talk about another school in anything but a positive way, so even if I were knowledgeable about Askew Academy, I would restrict my comments to our school. " Sarah then went on to detail the various ways that Right

CASE STUDY
A PROMINENT FAMILY CREATES AN ADMISSION DILEMMA

School worked to develop critical thinking skills and then pointed out the many places in the curriculum guide that referenced the development of critical thinking skills.

At the end of the conversation, Claire asked for two favors: Was there any way that the boys' applications for admission to Right School could be kept confidential from Askew Academy until after an admission decision was reached? And could that decision be made by the beginning of February? The Thomason family had served on the Askew board for many generations, and Claire didn't want to upset the applecart unless the boys were definitely going to attend Right School. Askew's re-enrollment contracts were due on February 15, and if the boys were not going to attend Right School, Claire planned to re-enroll them.

Sarah explained that the normal notification date for first-round admission decisions was March 10, and, normally, all applicants would need to submit recommendations from their current teachers along with a transcript. Claire pleaded with Sarah to use the detailed narrative teacher comments and the parents' copy of the report cards in lieu of recommendations and transcripts "so as not to cause unnecessary stress on the people at Askew Academy or my sons." Being new at Right School and knowing how carefully she needed to handle this admission case, Sarah told Claire she would check on that request with "people who have been here a little longer than I" by the end of the boys' visit that day.

After some small talk, Sarah thanked Claire for helping her know Will and Andrew better and suggested that she return to pick up the boys at about 3 p.m.

Sarah knew she could not both entertain the Thomasons' applications and keep them confidential from Askew Academy. But she did not want to appear to dismiss the request out of hand. So she made a copy of the NAIS Principles of Good Practice—which require that schools be clear and consistent with their acceptance timeframe—and the appropriate page from Right's admission office policies manual—which required that all candidates submit teacher recommendations and a current transcript. Upon Claire's return, Sarah would explain that Right School was bound to live by the NAIS Principles of Good Practice and to enforce admission office policies that Right's own board had endorsed.

Sarah stopped by Jon's office to let him know about Claire's unusual request and her planned response. Jon appreciated the heads-up but asked, "Well, would it really be that much of a problem to waive the teacher recommendations? After all, we do have a full set of written teacher comments with the transcript from Askew."

Sarah was a little taken aback, as she knew this was not good admission practice. "I will do whatever you think is best," she answered, "but you might want to review the NAIS Principles of Good Practice first, because your approach might be in conflict." Sarah then handed Jon the Principles of Good Practice for Admission.

Soon it was time to talk to the boys and administer their tests. Sarah had interviewed hundreds of eighth-graders in her admission career; in fact, interviews were one of her favorite parts of the job. She prided herself on getting even the most nervous or recalcitrant kids to open up. From the little bit she had observed of Will and Andrew Thomason, she knew they would be a challenge, but not one she couldn't handle… she hoped.

Will's tour guide brought him back to the admission office about 30 minutes before Andrew so she could interview them separately. The meeting with Will was relatively routine. Like most eighth-grade boys, Will was monosyllabic at the beginning. But Sarah's knack for finding just the right topic held strong. Learning that Will loved NBA basketball, she got him to open up by staying on that topic for a while. Sarah was left with the impression that he was a nice, good-natured eighth-grader, if a little shy, and would fit in well with the other students at Right School.

Sarah's interview with Andrew started off similarly, although she had a harder time finding the topic that would draw him out. Asked about his current school, he grew sullen and said, "My teachers mostly hate me."

"Why do you think they hate you?" Sarah let the resulting silence stand long enough to force his answer.

"I guess it's because I don't do things the right way."

"Well, why is that, Andrew?"

After another long pause, Andrew said, "Some stuff is hard for me, and my teachers just don't get that I am not like my brother. Everything is easy for him."

Sensing that the conversation was making Andrew really uncomfortable, Sarah guided it in another direction. "Andrew, I'm sure you're good at any number of things. What do you like to do most or think you do well?"

Andrew shifted in his seat, then said, "Well, I like to draw, but I suck at that, too."

Although the interview went on a little longer, Sarah had already recognized that Andrew's self-esteem was pretty low. Claire's sense that Andrew could use a change of scenery was probably right; but was Right School the place? She ended the conversation by saying, "I'll bet you are really good at drawing. I would love to see some of your drawings some time. You have also been a good partner in conversation today. Thanks for talking with me."

After the Thomasons completed their admission testing, Claire returned to the admission office to pick them up. Sarah asked to talk to Claire for a moment alone. Using the admission office policies and the NAIS Principles of Good Practice, she explained that if the boys did apply to Right School, they would have to submit recommendations from their current teachers and a current transcript. Claire appeared to understand. Summoning her courage, Sarah then asked Claire, "Have you and your husband ever considered enrolling Will and Andrew at different schools?"

CASE STUDY
A PROMINENT FAMILY CREATES AN ADMISSION DILEMMA

Claire, a little taken aback, responded, "No, why would we? Did one of the boys have a bad visit?"

"No, both boys had a fine visit, although we won't know the results of their testing until tomorrow. But I had to ask, as it is our admission policy to consider each applicant as an individual."

"Well, it has always been our family's position to offer equal opportunities to each boy, so separating them would seem wrong to us. They have normal sibling issues, but generally they love being together. Please consider their applications as a package deal."

After some small talk, Sarah walked the Thomason family out to their car and thanked them for spending the day at Right School.

The next morning, after scoring the boys' admission test, Sarah briefed Jon on the visit. It was hard to say how the admission committee might vote. But the Thomason boys' credentials looked questionable, with Andrew's more problematic than Will's. Jon would support whatever decision Sarah and the admission committee made, he said—but Sarah had to be certain they were particularly thoughtful in their deliberations. Word of the Thomasons' visit had already made it to some of Right's board members. In fact, one had already called him.

Hitting an application snag

Sarah kept tabs on the Thomason boys' application to the point of making several phone calls to Claire as the deadline for first-round decisions drew near. Claire was perplexed about why Right School had not received all the teacher recommendations and transcripts she had asked Askew to send weeks before. When the materials finally did arrive, several days after the application deadline, there was a notable problem. All the teachers had signed the recommendations, but most of the questions were basically blank. Will and Andrew's applications could not be considered complete.

Given that the Thomasons were borderline candidates, the teacher recommendations were important. Sarah asked Jon to call his counterpart at Askew Academy for assistance. An hour later, Jon told Sarah that the call had been pretty awkward, with the head at first saying that the teachers had done all that was required of them. Jon, wisely, had remembered that the NAIS Admission Principles of Good Practice called upon schools to recognize the right of currently enrolled students to consider other educational options, and he suggested that Mrs. Thomason might not be so happy to learn that Askew Academy was less than cooperative in allowing the family to exercise that right. Askew's head agreed to have the teachers provide more complete recommendations, and Sarah faxed new forms to him.

Because the delay was not the family's fault, the admission committee agreed that the boys could still be considered in the first round of applications after the normal deadline.

The committee decides

This delay had one positive effect for Sarah. It let her get several admission committee meetings under her belt before the Thomasons' applications came up for consideration. She had the chance to size up not only the Right School process but also the composition of her admission committee.

Although for the most part Sarah was pleased with her committee members, two of them concerned her. Jim Wallace, the chair of the math department, was a particularly inflexible character. Jim believed that there were absolute, measurable, minimal standards for admission, and any candidate who failed on any one of those measures was not worthy of admission, regardless of the candidate's other notable strengths. Jill Bosworth, the assistant dean of students, was a counselor by training, which was generally a positive attribute for an admission committee member. However, Jill would occasionally delve more deeply into the psychological meaning behind parts of an application than Sarah felt was appropriate. Well meaning as she was, Jill was prone to over-analysis that sometimes obfuscated the issues rather than clarifying them. Sarah suspected that both Jill and Jim would have a field day with the Thomason boys' applications.

Will's application came first. There was a lengthy conversation about his declining performance over the previous three years and his slightly below-average admission testing. The committee members were generally pleased with Will's admission essay and the teacher feedback identifying him as generally nice, if somewhat undistinguished. Jim Wallace took issue with his score in reading, saying it was several points under what he believed to be the minimal score. Sarah refuted the idea of absolute minimums and pointed out that Will's grades in English and history, two reading-intensive classes, were his

strongest. The admission committee voted to offer admission to Will, albeit without much enthusiasm.

The conversation regarding Andrew was heated and considerably more complex. All of his recommendations were less than stellar, but his English teacher's was particularly damaging because she said he was disrespectful, disruptive in class, and a poor performer. She seemed offended that he and his brother were even applying to Right School. This seemed odd until a committee member pointed out that this English teacher's own daughter had been denied admission to Right School years earlier. The committee discussed the teacher's credibility, particularly since there were no signs that Andrew was disrespectful and disruptive in other classes (nor was there any mention of these traits in written comments the English teacher sent home to Andrew's parents).

Nevertheless, the application did seem to validate Sarah's concern that Andrew had low self-esteem and was not a strong student. The committee discussed the merits of treating the boys as a package but ultimately felt that Right School would not be good for Andrew, regardless of how much the Thomason family might do for the school.

Sarah went to Jon with the decision to accept Will and deny Andrew. Jon supported the decision. He asked her to tell him when she notified the Thomason family so he could then inform his board chair.

To be continued....

EXEMPLARY APPLICATIONS OF GOOD PRACTICE

EXAMPLE 1: Sharing Complete Financial Information

(Relates to Admission Principle 9)

School Y received complaints from parents regarding extra charges for which they were billed, including books, the yearbook, and fees for labs, computers, and special art supplies. So Jane, the director of admission, met with her business manager and head to discuss how to incorporate certain fees into the tuition. The head was concerned that raising the tuition might hurt enrollment. All other local schools followed the practice of suppressing tuition by charging extra fees. Deviating would make School Y look like the most expensive school in the city, even though it was not the most prestigious.

To convince the head to consider covering more expenses within the tuition, she appealed to his sense of what would be best for families and cited the Principle of Good Practice that reads, "The school shares complete information about the total costs of attending the school and other financial expectations with families before an enrollment commitment is required."

Members of the school faculty and staff then formed a task force to look at all items that had been billed to students during the past year. Items that were a central part of the educational experience for most students, such as computer fees and ID cards, were made a part of the next year's tuition. In the spirit of full disclosure, charges that were truly optional, such as after-school snacks and ski trips, were listed on the tuition sheets as typical extra expenses.

To help offset the sticker shock regarding higher tuition, the head wrote to all current parents about the change. Jane made sure that all listings of the school's tuition included an explanation of everything the tuition covered as well as the few optional items.

The result: Parents were pleased to be able to budget properly. The accounting office appreciated not having as many miscellaneous charges to apply to each student's account. And the dreaded competitive disadvantage of having a higher tuition never materialized.

EXAMPLE 2: Refusing to Draw Comparisons
(Relates to Admission Principle 11)

Sally was a veteran admission professional who managed a staff of five, including two young admission officers. By this point in her career, Sally had not only internalized the Principles of Good Practice but had also thought through all the different constituents to whom she owed allegiance. At the top of her list was her school. Its well-being had to take priority over the needs of any individual. But right after her school came the students she served, both those currently enrolled and prospective ones. Also, over the years Sally had come to realize that what is good for one independent school is good for independent schools in general. As competitive as she was, she tried to keep in mind that her work's purpose was to help students find educational environments where they would thrive, which meant that some would be better served elsewhere.

Sally's new hires were bright, eager, and competitive. She was concerned, though, that one of them might be overstepping his bounds with another school that had many cross-applicants each year. To avoid having someone in her office unfavorably comparing another school to her own school, Sally decided to devote the next office meeting to the Principle of Good Practice that states, "School representatives apply the same high standards of integrity whether talking about their own school or other institutions."

At the meeting, Sally outlined her philosophy that those in her office were to talk only about their own school and never compare it to others. When one of the young admission officers—the one she suspected might be tempted to be overly competitive—asked whether it would be all right to make a comparison if a family specifically requested it, Sally was quick to say no. She then handed out a one-sentence statement describing the school's non-comparison policy and asked each staff member to memorize it.

Since then, Sally has heard this statement quoted numerous times to inquiring families. She's proud that her school has taken the high road on this issue.

EXAMPLE 3: Recognizing the Right to Change Schools
(Relates to Admission Principle 8)

Jenni's heart sank when she read the e-mail from the registrar at XYZ School stating that Peter had asked to have his transcript sent elsewhere. Jenni had worked hard to enroll Peter a year before, and, as she expected, he had flourished. Not only had he done well academically, but he also gained the respect of his teachers and his peers.

Jenni took a deep breath, told herself she should not take this personally—but decided she had to react in some way. Her initial instinct was to enlist Peter's favorite teachers and coaches in hopes that they could guilt him into withdrawing his application. But as she calmed down, she remembered that she really did believe in the Principle of Good Practice that states, "The school recognizes the right of currently enrolled students and families to consider other educational options, and if a transfer is initiated by the family, the school provides appropriate support and documentation in a timely manner…."

Rather than mounting a campaign to prevent Peter from transferring, Jenni decided to talk objectively with Peter about his desire to explore other schools. When she did, she learned that although Peter was excelling at XYZ School, he was convinced he would be better served elsewhere. Jenni saw his logic and wrote a glowing recommendation.

CASE STUDY *continued from page 13*
A PROMINENT FAMILY CREATES AN ADMISSION DILEMMA

TELLING THE THOMASONS

When Sarah called to ask Mrs. Thomason to come to the admission office to discuss her children's applications, she knew this would be one of the more difficult and important conversations she would have. But she also believed that the admission committee decisions were the right ones.

When she told Claire of the decisions, Sarah was prepared for an angry confrontation… but not tears. "Why can't you admit Andrew? What am I going to say to him?" Claire cried.

As heartbreaking as it was to watch this mother suffer, Sarah dispassionately explained why the admission committee felt that having Andrew at Right School would, in fact, be a disservice to him. She then noted that Andrew seemed to really love drawing and his self-esteem was an immediate issue. Had the family considered finding a school for Andrew with a focus in the arts?

"That's fine if you only want to be an artist, but those schools are not very rigorous academically," Claire responded.

Sarah looked directly at Claire. "Andrew has more academic challenge than he can handle at Askew Academy, and we fear that would also be the case at Right School. He appears to be a boy in need of tangible success. Perhaps his interest and talent in art might be a good match with the mission of a school like University Arts Academy."

Claire pulled herself together and ended the meeting by saying, "Well, we have a lot of thinking to do as a family. I just don't know what to make of this."

THREE YEARS LATER

Will Thomason did enroll at Right School. Although Will was a less-than-stellar student, he came out of his shell socially and became pretty engaged in student activities, even joining student government.

Andrew enrolled at the University Arts Academy. He apparently didn't "suck" at drawing. He was an honor roll student and planned to apply to Rhode Island School of Design and the Kansas City Art Institute. His self-esteem grew tremendously as he escaped his twin brother's shadow and found success as an artist.

One afternoon Sarah was walking by the front circle of Right School, saw Andrew waiting in the car for his brother, and went over to say hello. "Andrew, I hear that you are doing really well at University Academy!" she said.

"Yeah, I really love it, and I have been on the high honor roll for the last couple of years. Thanks for encouraging my parents to let me go there. It has been really good for me."

Sarah smiled. "Andrew, I am so happy to hear that. I'm glad that turned out to be such a good match for you." They chatted for a few minutes, and then Sarah excused herself to return to work.

"Ms. Diamond, one more thing," Andrew called after her. "I'm sorry you picked the Thomason brother who couldn't make the honor roll. He can't quite live up to my standard, but we'll keep him in the family, anyhow." Sarah and Andrew exchanged a grin. ∎

DISCUSSION QUESTIONS

1. Should a school have a policy that covers how to treat applicants from prominent families? How can the head, admission staff, and other school leaders (such as trustees) be more consistent in their views of how such families should be handled?

2. What kind of training would help admission staff members handle hard questions from families about, for example, how other schools compare, whether applications can be kept secret, etc.? What's the best source of this training, and who should receive it?

3. How should a head and admission staff work together on particularly touchy decisions? If they disagree, how can they come to the best solution?

4. What is the ideal composition of the admission committee? If the composition is less than ideal, what's the best way to remedy it?

SUGGESTED RESOURCES AND READING MATERIALS

BOOKS

Aitken, Peter H. *Access and Affordability: Strategic Planning Perspectives for Independent Schools.* Washington, DC: NAIS, 1994.

Bowen, William G., and Derek Bok. *The Shape of the River: Long-term Consequences of Considering Race in College and University Admissions.* Princeton, NJ: Princeton University Press, 1998.

Breneman, David W. *Liberal Arts Colleges: Thriving, Surviving, or Endangered?* Washington, DC: Brookings Institution Press, 1994.

Grace, Catherine O'Neill, ed. *Marketing Independent Schools in the 21st Century.* Washington, DC: NAIS, 2001.

Ihlanfeldt, William. *Achieving Optimal Enrollments and Tuition Revenues.* San Francisco, CA: Jossey-Bass, Inc., 1980.

Kane, Thomas J. *The Price of Admission: Rethinking How Americans Pay for College.* Washington, DC: Brookings Institution Press, 1999.

Perfetto, Greg, Merida Escandon, Steve Graff, Gretchen W. Rigol, and Amy E. Schmidt. *Toward a Taxonomy of the Admissions Decision-making Process.* New York, NY: The College Board, 1999.

Rigol, Gretchen W. *Best Practices in Admission Decisions* (monograph). New York, NY: The College Board, 2002. (*www.collegeboard.com/research/ abstract/23497.html*)

ARTICLES

"Achieving Diversity: Best Practices." New York, NY: College Board website: *http://www.collegeboard.com/ highered/ad/best/best.html*

Bassett, Patrick F. "Benchmarks for Admission." Washington, DC: NAIS website, 2001: *http://www.nais.org/about/article.cfm?ItemNumber= 145044*

Bassett, Patrick F. "Market Assessment." Washington, DC: NAIS website, 2002: *http://www.nais.org/resources/ article.cfm?ItemNumber=146607*

Braverman, Peter, and D. Scott Looney. "Tomorrow Is Today: Preparing Independent Schools for Greater Accessibility and Diversity." Washington, DC: NAIS: *Independent School Magazine,* Spring 1999.

Looney, D. Scott. "Navigating the Rough Road to Effective Pricing." Washington, DC: NAIS: *Independent School Magazine,* Fall 2003.

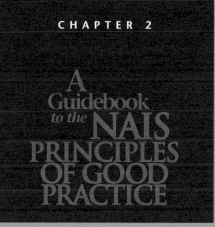

CHAPTER 2

A Guidebook to the NAIS PRINCIPLES OF GOOD PRACTICE

for
ATHLETICS

By Rebecca Reger and David Stone

Rebecca Reger is a science teacher and coach at the Park School, an elementary and middle school of 500 students in Brookline, Massachusetts. David Stone is director of athletics, alumni relations, and governance at Boston University Academy, a high school with 156 students in Massachusetts.

NAIS PRINCIPLES OF GOOD PRACTICE for

ATHLETICS

Revised and approved by the NAIS board in 2006

Athletics can play an important role in the lives of children. The school's athletic program should be an essential part of the education of students, fostering the development of character, life skills, sportsmanship, and teamwork. (Although many of the principles apply to this case study, the ones in **boldface** are most pertinent.)

SCHOOL ATHLETICS

1. **The school's physical health program embodies the mission, philosophy, and objectives of the school.**

2. The school ensures that physical education teachers and coaches have appropriate training and knowledge of the school's mission, philosophy, and objectives.

3. **The school promotes equity in all aspects of its athletic programs, including equal access to athletics, and fair and just treatment within both the curricular and extracurricular program.**

4. **The school's athletic program is an integral part of the school's curriculum.**

5. The school is committed to the safety and physical and emotional health of participants in the athletic program. The school demonstrates this commitment by ensuring that appropriate safety precautions are in place for all physical education activities. Further, the school has appropriate response safeguards in place in the event that a student is injured.

6. The school's athletic program values the dignity and worth of the individual in a context of common purpose and collective achievement.

7. The school educates parents about the philosophy, policies, risks, and appropriate expectations of the athletic program.

SCHOOL TEAM ATHLETICS

1. The school stands firmly in opposition to performance-enhancing drugs.

2. The school and its athletic programs and teams do not tolerate any form of hazing.

3. The school ensures that students, parents, alumni, and others understand the expectations of sportsmanship, civility, and self-control at athletic practices and contests, much as those same characteristics are required within the more traditional academic environment.

4. The school works directly and candidly with other schools to prevent abuses in the following areas: recruitment, eligibility, transfer of student athletes, financial aid, and admission.

COACHES

1. Coaching is teaching: Coaches are, foremost, teachers. In this spirit, coaches have a strong collegial relationship with other educators and contribute to the school's understanding of the whole child.

2. Coaches have an understanding of the developmental needs of the children with whom they work.

3. Coaches design and implement activities that improve the knowledge and skills of all participants.

4. Coaches are aware of the physical abilities of their athletes and do their best to keep the athletes safe while encouraging students to reach new levels of achievement.

5. Coaches maintain the appropriate skills to teach their sport(s) and provide appropriate first aid to an injured athlete.

6. Coaches mentoring athletic teams and events are role models for the behavior expected of all spectators and participants at any athletic event.

CASE STUDY
A SCHOOL CONFRONTS INEQUITABLE SPORTS PROGRAMS

As the Scholars' Academy entered its second decade, its community began to enjoy the feeling that many of the growing pains that came with establishing new programs, procedures, and policies were behind it.

In this relatively short time, the school had established one of the most rigorous academic programs in the area while also raising its arts, athletics, and extracurricular offerings to a level on a par with much older institutions. Its accelerated success was largely due to the school's mission to enroll students who instinctively had a driven yet friendly personality. By purposely admitting students who communicate with, include, and help others, the school had created an atmosphere in which students and faculty were excited about engaging each other both in and out of the classroom.

In addition to committing to the classics and an intense pursuit of academic excellence, the school's mission promised to educate the "whole student." This was the driving force behind mandating that all students study ancient Greek or Latin, perform community service each year, and participate in at least one extracurricular activity each semester. The mission statement made it clear that students should be allowed to pursue activities that interested them while receiving a first-rate secondary school education.

The Scholars' Academy environment inspired many students to join multiple programs, including competitive team sports, drama, robotics, debate, and math club. As a result, students developed skills, knowledge, and friendships and gained all the other benefits of pursuing an education beyond the standard classroom.

What no one intended was for students and teachers to feel that the offerings were less than equal.

The imbalance became noticeable when talk of differences among athletic programs and other extracurriculars started to swirl within the community. The athletic administration took special interest when the topic found its way into a student newspaper article about the fencing team's feelings toward the boys' basketball team. The article claimed that basketball players implied that their efforts and accomplishments were superior to other programs'.

The athletic director talked with the students and coaches involved and found that two factors were creating the structural disparity between the teams.

The first factor was the freedom of each of the school's teams and groups to set its own standards and requirements. In its drive to get new teams and clubs off the ground, the athletic department had from the start given coaches and players flexibility in many areas. For example, they could decide how often and how long they would practice, how many games they would play in a season, and how they would celebrate their accomplishments. Giving teams autonomy, rather than tying them to a set of uniform standards, had been crucial to achieving a robust group of athletic choices in a reasonably short time. However, the approach didn't seem to work as well once programs became school-wide staples rather than occasional offerings.

The second factor concerned the desire of some students—but not all—to become deeply involved in several different activities. Historically, the fencing team was composed of students whose interests crossed over into activities such as robotics, Model UN, and drama. But the students involved with boys' and girls' basketball had chosen to make many fewer commitments to other areas of the school. Thus the boys' basketball coach had no problem getting players to practice five days a week and sometimes on Saturday.

The fencing coach wanted the same commitment from her fencers—but she realized that it would force her students to choose between leaving other groups and leaving fencing. So early on, she had settled for three days of practice instead of five. The group thrived and grew to become the school's largest team sport in less than four years. This might have seemed to be an ideal time to increase the required practice schedule—except that the team's core students continued to enjoy participating in other after-school endeavors. When she tried to increase the fencing practice time, other groups' advisers, as well as

administrators and many parents and students, objected that this would force students to choose between, for example, drama and fencing.

So it was only a matter of time before the students started talking about differences among their teams.

An argument broke out in the student lounge one day when a basketball player claimed that fencers were "lesser athletes" because they didn't practice as long, or as often, as some other teams. This led to an intense debate that drew in fencers as well as members of the girls' basketball team. The girls' team operated under a flexible four-practice-per-week-schedule and so was seen as another example of a group that was less serious or athletic than those who met five days a week. The disagreement grew so heated that students continued to talk about it in the halls and wrote articles about it in the student newspaper.

The old way of determining commitment levels was not going to work anymore. The athletic director knew that if the school was to restore harmony, he had to address the problem. But the solution had to be carefully thought through, as it was bound to set a precedent for all athletic teams as well as extracurricular activities. He began to research both the NAIS Principles of Good Practice for athletics and what other independent schools did in similar situations.

To be continued….

EXEMPLARY APPLICATIONS OF GOOD PRACTICE

EXAMPLE 1: Maintaining the Mission of the School
(Relates to School Athletics Principles 1, 3, and 6)

Citing athletics as a crucial part of the development of the whole student, one school we surveyed takes its athletics program beyond "extracurricular" to "co-curricular." This means that the school sees athletics as an integral part of its program, not just an added option in a student's day. Athletics are used as a way of teaching critical skills and values that students might not otherwise learn within the classroom.

In addition, many schools make athletics programs available to all who want to participate, regardless of their experience, background, or skills. Even when students are not starting members of a team, they're appreciated for showing dedication and determination and thus adding to the overall experience. In this way, many schools show a carryover of their mission statement into athletics.

EXAMPLE 2: Maintaining Equity within the Athletic Program
(Relates to School Athletics Principles 3 and 6)

One school described how its athletic programs display equality when it comes to all aspects of funding, practice space and time, and coaching. Another school cited certain unavoidable and inherent differences among its sports programs, including differing practice facilities, student involvement, and operating costs. This school compensates by determining budgets equitably.

EXAMPLE 3: Integrating Athletics into the Curriculum
(Relates to School Athletics Principle 4)

Several of the schools we examined do not have any sort of physical education classes during the school day. Instead, these schools require participation in a sport during at least two seasons. This way, schools not only integrate athletics into their curricula but also maintain 100-percent student participation, thus creating a culture in which all are student-athletes. Participation is for everyone instead of for a select few who are chosen for their skill or talent.

EXAMPLE 4: Coaches as Teachers

(Relates to Coaches Principle 1)

Although coaches may not be teaching in a classroom in the traditional pedagogical sense, they still serve in an important instructional role. Many schools we surveyed cited examples of coaches' responsibility for teaching life lessons above and beyond sports skills. One school mentioned instances in which coaches speak to students individually on matters of sportsmanship; another spoke of how sportsmanship and other such values are intimately entwined into the coaches' agenda.

EXAMPLE 5: Regarding Standards of Conduct

(Relates to School Athletics Principle 4; School Team Athletics Principles 3 and 4; and Coaches Principle 6)

All of the schools said it is important that students, coaches, and all other members of the community maintain certain standards of behavior within their athletics programs. One school said the league its teams participate in allows them to "grade" teams they play against on matters of sportsmanship. This not only allows students to constantly review and evaluate their own behavior but also to hold other students responsible.

EXAMPLE 6: Managing Parental Expectations

(Relates to School Team Athletics Principle 3)

One school faced an over-eager parent who just would not take a back seat when it came to his daughter's performance at competitions. He constantly challenged referees and officials and went so far as to taunt his daughter's opponents. The head of the school was apprised of the situation by the team's coach, who had tried without success to address the parent directly. The head spoke with the parent and emphasized that, as a representative of the school, the parent had to share the same high standards of behavior the school expected of all its players. Putting the school's full support behind the coach was crucial to solving the problem of a parent who took competition too far.

CASE STUDY *continued from page 23*

A SCHOOL CONFRONTS INEQUITABLE SPORTS PROGRAMS

RESTORING THE BALANCE

The Scholars' Academy athletic director's first move was to deal with the lack of respect shown by the students who got into the argument about the teams. The encounter in the student lounge was clearly out of line with the school's mission to provide an environment in which differences are respected. The athletic director, the coaches, and the school head all spoke to the students about the importance of this ideal. The talks were considered an educational experience, not a disciplinary action.

The next step was to resolve the larger issue. The athletic director wanted to ensure equity among all established interscholastic teams while still recognizing the students' desire to take advantage of several opportunities. The director spoke with the coaches within his program as well as athletic administrators from other schools. He compared the missions of schools that required the maximum time commitment from their teams (five days a week and more) to the missions of schools that restricted all teams to three or fewer meetings per week. Although he gained valuable information by looking at the varying approaches, in the end he used his own school's mission statement to determine how to proceed.

The mission had always been to allow students to achieve a balanced and rich experience. The best way to achieve this, in the community's view, was to have students immerse themselves fully in a select group of endeavors rather than sample in many areas. The director wanted to design a policy that would embrace this mission while ensuring that other school activities could survive if all athletic teams operated under a standard policy.

He began by taking a close look at the other activities' meeting times and goals. Once he and others involved defined which programs had realistic opportunities to allow student-involvement crossover, the dean of students created a schedule that brought some of the more popular extracurricular programs into the academic day so they weren't always in competition with athletics.

The athletic administration then decided to support an across-the-board commitment of four days per week of meetings (practices and competitions) for varsity interscholastic teams. Club and junior varsity athletic groups would be limited to three days or fewer per week. The day off for varsity teams was coordinated with other programs' schedules to make the most of students' time.

The four-day commitment was based upon a number of factors. Teachers and coaches stressed that any interscholastic group would need at least three meeting times per week to be worthwhile and competitive. The school administration, however, felt that the idea behind "worthwhile" fell short of "enriching," a term used in the school's mission statement. So the administration recommended instead a minimum of four days per week. Everyone agreed.

Even with a restructured school-day schedule, there was no guarantee that the school could accommodate all combinations of activities and athletics. However, club members and junior varsity athletes would have enough flexibility in their schedules to participate in other areas. This flexibility would strengthen all the school's offerings while providing reasonable opportunities for students to branch out.

As expected, there were mixed feelings about the new policy. Students who wanted to belong to two groups that required major time commitments felt limited. In addition, the extracurricular programs that had barely enough participation felt pressured to meet quotas.

In the end, however, the students made the choices they had to, and the coaches and activity advisers made the needed adjustments. The school did not lose a single program due to attrition. Many programs did have to re-evaluate their goals, but all groups benefited from an infusion of a more focused and motivated population of participants. Some students even expressed relief that they were no longer performing a juggling act. The community learned a lesson about effective time management, and students still had the benefit of an education that allowed ample participation.

The mission statement of the school was upheld, and the rift between the different teams healed.

Through a thoughtful combination of the NAIS Principles of Good Practice for Athletics and its own mission statement, the Scholars' Academy was able to solve its problems with administering and facilitating athletic programs. The important issues the community kept in mind were equity, fairness, sportsmanship, and opportunity for participation. Equity doesn't mean the same thing to each school, and fairness cannot be justified the same way in every instance; each school's own mission statement will determine how its community will interpret these principles. However, for athletic directors who want the best for their students within their schools' missions, these principles should be sufficient to address nearly every problem that arises in the field of athletics. ■

DISCUSSION QUESTIONS

1. What are the aims of the school's athletic program, and how does the current program meet or not meet these aims?

2. What does the mission statement of the school demand that the athletic director take into account when it comes to competing teams within the school?

3. What other constraints on students' time must the athletic director consider (other sports, clubs, commitments, and schoolwork)?

4. What are the expectations of the students, parents, and other faculty regarding the athletic program?

5. Taking all factors into account, what are the best ways to solve problems of equity within the school?

SUGGESTED RESOURCES AND FURTHER READING

Clifford, Craig E., and Randolph M. Feezell. *Coaching for Character: Reclaiming the Principles of Sportsmanship.* Champaign, IL: Human Kinetics Publishers, 1997.

Koehler, Mike, and Nancy Giebel. *Athletic Directors Survival Guide: Ready-to-Use Techniques and Material for Effective Leadership.* Upper Saddle River, NJ: Prentice Hall Publishers, 1997.

Lombardo, Bennett J. *The Humanistic Coach: From Theory to Practice.* Springfield, IL: Charles C. Thomas, Publisher, 1987.

Lombardo, Bennett J., V.H. Mancini, and D.A. Wuest. *The Humanistic Sport Experience: Visions and Realities.* Dubuque, IA: Brown and Benchmark, Publishers, 1995.

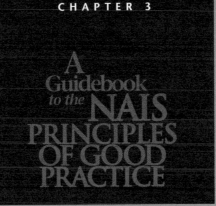

CHAPTER 3

A Guidebook
to the NAIS
PRINCIPLES
OF GOOD
PRACTICE

for
GOVERNANCE:
BOARD OF TRUSTEES
AND
INDEPENDENT
SCHOOL TRUSTEES

By Mary Hundley DeKuyper

Mary Hundley DeKuyper is a Baltimore-based governance consultant to nonprofits who has worked with more than 70 independent schools. She is the author of NAIS's Trustee Handbook: A Guide to Effective Governance for Independent School Boards. As a volunteer, she has chaired 12 nonprofit boards and served on an additional 16. Currently, DeKuyper is a trustee of the Far Hills Country Day School in New Jersey. Formerly, she was a trustee of her alma mater, The Bryn Mawr School in Baltimore, where she was president of the board and the alumnae association.

NAIS PRINCIPLES OF GOOD PRACTICE for
GOVERNANCE

Revised and approved by the NAIS board in 2003

When considering issues like the ones raised in this case study, it is critical to remember, first, that a board is the sole legal entity to have ultimate responsibility for a school and, second, that the board exists only when it is in an official meeting of the whole board.

NAIS has developed two sets of principles that are relevant to governance: 12 Principles of Good Practice: Board of Trustees and 12 Principles of Good Practice: Independent School Trustees. Both sets are reproduced here. (Although many of the principles apply to this case study, the ones in **boldface** are the most pertinent.)

BOARD OF TRUSTEES

The board is the guardian of the school's mission. It is the board's responsibility to ensure that the mission is relevant and vital to the community it serves and to monitor the success of the school in fulfilling its mission.

The following Principles of Good Practice are set forth to provide a common perspective on the responsibilities of independent school boards. The board and the head work in partnership in fulfilling these principles.

1. The board adopts a clear statement of the school's mission, vision, and strategic goals and establishes policies and plans consistent with this statement.

2. The board reviews and maintains appropriate bylaws that conform to legal requirements, including duties of loyalty, obedience, and care.

3. The board assures that the school and the board operate in compliance with applicable laws and regulations, minimizing exposure to legal action. The board creates a conflict of interest policy that is reviewed with, and signed by, individual trustees annually.

4. The board accepts accountability for both the financial stability and the financial future of the institution, engaging in strategic financial planning, assuming primary responsibility for the preservation of capital assets and endowments, overseeing operating budgets, and participating actively in fund raising.

5. **The board selects, supports, nurtures, evaluates, and sets appropriate compensation for the head of school.**

6. **The board recognizes that its primary work and focus are long-range and strategic.**

7. The board undertakes formal strategic planning on a periodic basis, sets annual goals related to the plan, and conducts annual written evaluations for the school, the head of school, and the board itself.

8. The board keeps full and accurate records of its meetings, committees, and policies and communicates its decisions widely, while keeping its deliberations confidential.

9. Board composition reflects the strategic expertise, resources, and perspectives (past, present, future) needed to achieve the mission and strategic objectives of the school.

10. The board works to ensure all its members are actively involved in the work of the board and its committees.

11. As leader of the school community, the board engages proactively with the head of school in cultivating and maintaining

good relations with school constituents as well as the broader community and exhibits best practices relevant to equity and justice.

12. **The board is committed to a program of professional development that includes annual new trustee orientation, ongoing trustee education and evaluation, and board leadership succession planning.**

INDEPENDENT SCHOOL TRUSTEES

The following Principles of Good Practice are set forth to provide a common perspective on the responsibilities of individual members of independent school boards.

1. A trustee actively supports and promotes the school's mission, vision, strategic goals, and policy positions.

2. A trustee is knowledgeable about the school's mission and goals, including its commitment to equity and justice, and represents them appropriately and accurately within the community.

3. A trustee stays fully informed about current operations and issues by attending meetings regularly, coming to meetings well prepared, and participating fully in all matters.

4. The board sets policy and focuses on long-range and strategic issues. An individual trustee does not become involved directly in specific management, personnel, or curricular issues.

5. **The trustee takes care to separate the interests of the school from the specific needs of a particular child or constituency.**

6. A trustee accepts and supports board decisions. Once a decision has been made, the board speaks as one voice.

7. **A trustee keeps all board deliberations confidential.**

8. A trustee guards against conflict of interest, whether personal or business related.

9. **A trustee has the responsibility to support the school and its head and to demonstrate that support within the community.**

10. **Authority is vested in the board as a whole. A trustee who learns of an issue of importance to the school has the obligation to bring it to the head of school, or to the board chair, and must refrain from responding to the situation individually.**

11. A trustee contributes to the development program of the school, including strategic planning for development, financial support, and active involvement in annual and capital giving.

12. Each trustee, not just the treasurer and finance committee, has fiduciary responsibility to the school for sound financial management.

CASE STUDY
A BOARD MEETING VEERS OFF-TRACK

Jane, the head of Superior Academy, and Frank, the chair of its board of trustees, were confident that the agenda for the second board meeting of the school year would go smoothly, as planned. They took their places at the head of the long table and smiled at the 20 trustees assembled before them. Jane leaned over to Frank and whispered, "I do wish we could have better attendance. Ten trustees are missing." Frank replied, "I agree, but I think those who are missing have busy lives, and I trust the rest of the trustees." Frank called the meeting to order.

As the meeting progressed, Jane was pleased that her report and those of the administrators who were speaking on behalf of some missing committee chairs were crisp and well received, eliciting only two questions in total. She let her mind drift during the buildings-and-grounds committee report on deferred-maintenance needs; she thought back instead on the five years of monthly board meetings she had attended as head. "Frank certainly runs a tight meeting, and the year seems to be off to a great start," she mused. "Why, last month's meeting was a record, lasting just one-and-a-half hours, and this one is on its way to being even shorter!"

Frank was equally pleased with the meeting's progress. He believed that the board chair should be a strong manager of the time spent in board meetings. "It is not as if the real work of the board is done in the board meeting," he had been known to remark. "The real work gets done in our eight committees, which seem to be functioning well and producing good reports."

After the last report ended, the board moved on to the "new business" section of the agenda. Frank became uneasy as he saw four or five of the trustees who were also current parents look around at each other and then at Tom, a brand-new board member who was attending his first board meeting. "Something is about to happen, and I do not know what it is," he thought. "From the expressions on some of the trustees' faces, it is not going to be pleasant." He leaned forward to hear what Tom was about to say.

"I have something very critical to the life of the school that I need to bring up," Tom began. "Mrs. Pliny, the new eighth-grade Latin teacher, is a disaster and must go."

Four other heads nodded in agreement.

"In fact," Tom continued, "I have found in conversations with other trustees that at least four of them agree with me. I know first-hand about this problem because my daughter, Betsy, is in the eighth grade and has Mrs. Pliny. Betsy has always done well here at Superior, and now she is struggling with this dreadful woman. Mrs. Pliny just does not understand her. So what is the board going to do about this?"

Tom sat back in his chair and looked around at the other trustees, most of whom looked back at him in disbelief that such a subject had come up at the board meeting.

Sharon, another trustee, said, "I agree with Tom." However, before she could continue, Frank jumped in to say, "Sharon, I am sorry to interrupt you, but it is clear from Jane's reaction that she knows nothing about these concerns. Am I correct, Jane?"

CASE STUDY
A BOARD MEETING VEERS OFF-TRACK

"You are correct," Jane said. "I am completely surprised."

Turning to Tom, Frank said, "I am hoping that the fact that you are a new trustee is the reason you did not understand that a concern about an individual teacher is not an appropriate subject for a board meeting. I am going to rule the matter out of order, and the discussion will end at this point. Tom, if you as a parent have a problem with a teacher, you need to take off your trustee hat and go to the teacher, the division director, or Jane with your concern.

"Now, is there any further business to come before this board? Hearing none, the meeting is adjourned."

Jane immediately sought out Tom to schedule a meeting about his complaint, but he had disappeared. One of the trustees told her he had darted out immediately after Frank closed the meeting—and, she added, "Boy, did he look mad!" Jane then turned to Frank, who looked as exhausted as she felt, and suggested that they meet at 8 o'clock the next morning to discuss what each of them should do next.

The next day, Frank arrived promptly at Jane's office. "I wonder if you have heard what appears to have happened last night after the meeting was over?" he said.

"I know that Tom called a number of eighth-grade parents and trustees to express his anger at the way he was treated, especially as he had the best interests of the students at heart."

"That is only part of it," Frank said. "I got six calls from trustees last night and early this morning. One thought the board should have spent at least a little time discussing Tom's concerns as a courtesy to him. The other five were appalled at Tom's actions at the meeting and after. It appears that Tom has said that the two of us are not responsive to the needs of students and the concerns of parents and neither of us knows what really goes on in the classroom. In fact, the school would be better off if neither of us were in leadership positions. However, there is some good news—all six trustees told him to call me or you."

Frank's voice grew stern. "Jane, this kind of discord is not what I signed on for when I agreed to be board chair. What are we going to do to end this strife and refocus on what really needs to be done?"

To be continued….

EXEMPLARY APPLICATIONS OF GOOD PRACTICE

EXAMPLE 1: A Supportive Board
(Relates to Board of Trustees Principle 5)

Contributed by Neil Mufson, head of The Country School in Maryland

In the spring of my ninth year as headmaster, the board chair told me that, as an extension of my annual evaluation, the board had decided to offer me a sabbatical for some part of the following academic year. The chair said that the board was very sensitive to the fact that my work's demands detracted from my time with my wife and children, who were two and four at the time, and they wanted, therefore, to give us uninterrupted time together prior to my older child's entrance into school. The board also offered me a generous financial stipend to make significant travel possible.

The parameters of the offer were simple: I could decide the amount of time I would take and when in the year I could take it. The only condition was that they didn't want to hire an interim head, so I would have to devise an internal plan to cover my duties.

I decided I would take about two months off, from the day after Parent Night at the end of September until Thanksgiving, and I devised a plan for my two division heads to run things together in my absence. My family and I headed off to London and Tuscany, where we had the experience of a lifetime.

Another example of strong support from my board came some years later in the worst of circumstances. Suddenly and without warning, in September 2002, our seven-year-old daughter was stricken with myocarditis, an inflammation of the heart muscle. She collapsed at school, was eventually airlifted to a Washington hospital, and died 16 days later. My board chair made clear to me from the start of this ordeal that I should worry about nothing other than my daughter and my family, that I should focus only on what I needed to do personally, and that he, along with those same two division heads who stood in for me while I was on sabbatical, would take care of everything at school. I was told I could have as much time as I needed.

EXAMPLE 2: **A Board's Pledge to Communicate and Serve Responsibly**
(Relates to Independent School Trustee Principles 5, 7, 9, and 10)

Contributed by Jayne Geiger, head of the Far Hills Country Day School in New Jersey

Some years ago, the administration of the Far Hills Country Day School developed a communication philosophy that suggests appropriate ways for various school constituencies to have their concerns addressed. The philosophy is spelled out in the *School Handbook* and other publications and is called "A to B Conversation." It states:

> A primary function of education is communication. Some may argue that without communication in some manner or form, there is no teaching or learning. Far Hills Country Day School espouses a philosophy that is based on open and honest communication among all of its constituencies. Through the years, we have come to call this type of direct but appropriate communication "A to B."
>
> What is A to B communication?
>
> In short, A to B is direct, authentic, appropriately stated communication. Sometimes we have concerns, problems, or irritations to communicate about which we may feel uncomfortable. Suppose "A," a parent, feels that "B," a teacher, is not understanding her child. It is far better to approach "B" appropriately and state the concern rather than to discuss the issue with "C," say, another parent or last year's teacher. "C" can't effect a classroom change. Some folks like being "C"—it's a powerful position—they know a lot of the scoop on a lot of people! In short, direct, open communication is the best approach for everyone involved.

This philosophy also applies to Far Hills trustees, who as part of their commitment letter agree to the following: "As part of the formal orientation of new trustees, the committee on trustees stresses the importance of trustees not becoming involved in the concerns of individual parents, students, potential students, or faculty members. Trustees are always 'C.' "

Far Hills goes further with its board of trustees. All members are asked yearly to sign a pledge that they will abide by the very specific items on the trustee commitment list. Some of the items included in the list are:

> I will work hard to understand my own roles and responsibilities as a trustee and those of the head and other administrative staff in order to provide appropriate oversight without interfering or micromanaging in areas that are not the board's responsibility.
>
> When carrying out my roles and responsibilities as a trustee, I will put aside my parent role (or any role I may have in relation to the school) and my personal agendas and

pledge to actively work only toward those decisions and solutions that are in the school's best interest.

I will respect the confidentiality of the board's business at all times because I know that doing otherwise compromises both the head's and the board's authority and efforts on behalf of the school.

In my role as a trustee I will communicate all important issues through the proper channels and thus honor the principle of "no surprises," and expect that my fellow trustees and our head will do likewise.

I will actively support our head and will demonstrate that support within the school community. If I have differences of opinion or concerns, I will address them with the head directly but privately, rather than using inappropriate channels of communication.

I will actively support our chair and will demonstrate that support within the school community. If I have differences of opinion or concerns, I will address them with the chair directly but privately, rather than using inappropriate channels of communication.

When confronted with problems or concerns brought to me by others, I will apprise the board chair or the head of the situation, rather than trying to deal with it myself.

CASE STUDY *continued from page 34*
A BOARD MEETING VEERS OFF-TRACK

STEPS TO RECOVERY

Step 1: Getting ready to meet with Tom

After a long silence, Jane said, "We need to meet with Tom immediately, and we also need a short-term plan to address the current situation. Of course, we will also need a long-term plan to establish policies, procedures, and activities to ensure that such a situation does not occur in the future."

As Frank nodded in agreement, his cell phone rang. It was Tom.

"I've been told by a number of trustees that I need to talk to you," Tom began. "While I'm still angry, I obviously am not clear about my role as a board member and a parent of a current student. We, along with Jane, need to talk, because I really care about the school and want to be a good trustee."

"Well, I am with Jane right now, and we had just agreed that we need to meet with you. We do not doubt that you want to do the best for the school, as do we. So let's set a time when we can get together today."

After arranging to meet with Tom at 4:30, Jane and Frank began their short-term plan, knowing that it might need to be adjusted after they talked to Tom. They decided to talk to some people who had faced similar situations or had broad knowledge of school governance concerns. Jane volunteered to contact Linda, the executive director of the state independent schools' association, and also Fred, the head of Scholastic Country Day School on the West Coast, whom she met five years ago at the NAIS Institute for New Heads. She knew that Fred and others had dealt with issues that come up when current parents serve as trustees and that arise between the board and the head.

Frank had never met other independent school trustees. Could Linda at the state association recommend board chairs whom he could call for advice? Then he remembered that his predecessor as board chair had been well regarded for her knowledge of good governance. He would try to get in touch with Sarah.

Jane and Frank made a pact that they would listen carefully to Tom and not make negative assumptions about his motivations. Jane also planned to talk to the middle school division director about Mrs. Pliny—but, she cautioned, "Tom will need to understand that our meeting this afternoon is about the board's role in the school and not about the specific situation within the eighth grade or with his daughter. I will promise to meet separately with him and his wife as quickly as possible to understand their concerns as parents."

The two school leaders decided to meet again at 3:30 to share what they learned and to plan more specifically for the later meeting. Frank shook his head as he left the school, wondering how he could fit his "real" work into this very stressful day. A sudden realization hit him: "Being chair of the board is difficult work!"

Step 2: Framing the short-term plan

Jane did meet with the middle school director and learned that two parents had come to her with similar concerns that the Latin class was too difficult for their eighth-graders. But Tom was not one of those parents. Mrs. Pliny had worked out a plan of support for the two students she knew were having difficulties. The director had observed Mrs. Pliny in the classroom and found her to be a good teacher, though one who needed more support in understanding eighth-graders. Such support would come from a senior teacher.

Jane also called Linda at the state independent school association and Fred, the head of Scholastic. They both gave her a few names of board chairs Frank could call, suggested possible actions she could undertake, and urged her to check back with them over the days and months ahead. Meanwhile, Frank found the time to talk to the past Superior Academy board chair, who also made a number of suggestions to address the ticklish situation.

When Jane and Frank met at 3:30, they compared suggestions from their contacts and developed a list that could serve as the framework for their short-term plan. They found it interesting that everyone with whom they talked said the same thing: This could be a unique opportunity for the board and head to examine what constitutes good governance, plan for a more effective relationship with the head of school, and improve board performance.

The list they came up with read as follows:

1. Jane and Frank would meet with Tom and use the NAIS Principles of Good Practice for boards and individual trustees as the basis for their discussion.

2. Jane would make an appointment as quickly as possible with Tom and his wife to discuss the issues involving their daughter.

3. Both Frank and Jane would gather more information/suggestions on trusteeship, especially from the NAIS website (*www.nais.org*), the Independent School Chairpersons Association (*www.iscachairs.org*), the state association, and the board chairs who were referred to Frank.

4. Jane would immediately send trustees the NAIS Principles of Good Practice that deal with governance.

5. Jane would immediately order every trustee a copy of the latest edition of NAIS's *Trustee Handbook: A Guide to Effective Governance for Independent School Boards.*

6. The board would dedicate its next meeting to discussing the situation, focusing on how trustees should perform their roles and what the next action steps should be.

7. Frank would meet with the nominating committee chair to talk about an expanded role for this committee.

Step 3: The meeting with Tom

Tom joined Frank and Jane promptly at 4:30 and was the first to speak. "I am truly sorry about what happened at the board meeting last night and my subsequent phone calls to parents and trustees. I was really angry, as I believe it is my trustee duty to bring to the board's attention a situation I see as damaging the education of students and hurtful to the reputation of the school."

CASE STUDY
A BOARD MEETING VEERS OFF-TRACK

"I am sorry that I was so abrupt in adjourning the meeting," Frank replied. "But both Jane and I were greatly surprised, and I believed that it would be damaging to the school and to the relationship between the board and the head to continue the discussion. It seems we both want only the best for the school, which is a great starting point for our conversation."

"I really did want to talk to you at the end of the meeting about your concern for your daughter, but you had disappeared," Jane added. "When this meeting is over, let's set up a time for you and your wife to meet with me and the middle school division director. But this meeting is not the right place to have that conversation. Here we should talk more about governance and why Frank, other trustees, and I had such a strong reaction to your question about what the board was going to do in regard to individual students and their Latin teacher."

Frank handed out copies of the NAIS Principles of Good Practice for Governance and said, "Let's use these principles as the basis of our conversation today."

The three reviewed each principle and found that the discussion helped each of them better understand several things: why trustees need to keep board matters confidential, stay out of administrative matters, keep the head and board chair informed and not spring surprises at the board table, and support the head publicly.

"I wish I had had this conversation before becoming a trustee," Tom said.

"So do I," Frank said, "as I just had to learn about my board role as I went along. I haven't had any orientation or training as board chair, and it is clear I could use some! We are going to suggest that the role of the nominating committee should expand to include board orientation and ongoing professional development. We'll dedicate the next board meeting to governance and set in motion a board governance action plan for the rest of the year."

"I will certainly support you on that and whatever else comes up so that all trustees can be productive members of the board," Tom said.

All three left the meeting feeling that they were back on track—but that there was much work to be done to make the Superior Academy board truly effective in its governance role.

Step 4: The November board meeting

Frank and Jane looked at the 27 trustees gathered for the November board meeting, many of whom were carrying their copies of the *Trustee Handbook,* and realized that this was the beginning of the board's journey to better governance.

After a brief time dedicated to routine business, Frank began. "We are not going to review the specific issue that caused us to examine how this board governs, as it is being handled by Jane in concert with the concerned parents. However, I, along with Jane and Tom, do believe it is an opportunity for all of us to learn about what constitutes an effective board and effective trustees."

Frank went on to explain that the group was going to review and discuss the NAIS Principles of Good Practice for Governance. Then he would suggest establishing a governance task force, under the leadership of Susie, the nominating committee chair, to look at a broad range of governance issues and report back to the board at its April meeting.

After a vigorous and thoughtful discussion on the principles, the meeting drew to a close. Tom spoke up to say, "I have learned so much about good governance these past few weeks, and I realize that my actions last month were inappropriate. Also, you should know that Jane and Frank have been very responsive and helpful. I thank them for working with me and sharing their commitment to our wonderful school."

A motion was made and passed to establish the task force on governance, with the charge to examine at the very least the following items:

- Expanding the role of the nominating committee to give it a more comprehensive charter and changing its name to the Committee on Trustees.
- Facilitating board self-assessment and the performance evaluation of the board chair.
- Developing criteria of needed skills and experiences for new trustees; identifying, cultivating, and recruiting new trustees; renominating eligible and appropriate trustees up for re-election.
- Planning for the succession of officers.
- Planning and implementing board orientation and ongoing board professional development training and education with the board chair.
- Considering a reorganization of the board to focus on strategic issues facing the school now and especially in the future, while continuing high-level fiduciary oversight of current operations.

- Reviewing committee structure and utilization of task forces; meeting agendas and frequency of board and committee meetings; size of the board; and an annual board retreat.
- Suggesting specific board professional development opportunities at the state and national level.
- Drafting a board commitment letter.

Step 5: The task force works to fulfill its charter

The governance task force spent the winter fulfilling its charge to bring its recommendations to the board at the April meeting. However, in February, the task force (1) asked the board to commit to a board retreat in early May to discuss its recommendations in greater depth and (2) suggested undertaking its first-ever board self-assessment in early April so the assessment could be part of the retreat agenda.

The board agreed to both recommendations. The final report was mailed out to the board by the April deadline so that the trustees could come to the retreat ready to discuss the draft governance action plan.

CASE STUDY CONCLUSION: THE MAY BOARD RETREAT

The board gathered for its very first retreat on a sunny day in early May. The agenda covered the recommendations of the task force on governance, the results of the board self-assessment, and the setting of a board action plan for the next administrative year.

CASE STUDY
A BOARD MEETING VEERS OFF-TRACK

Frank opened the retreat for the 28 current and two incoming trustees by saying, "I cannot tell you how pleased I am that we have taken what could have been a destructive event in the life of the board and school and turned it into a positive opportunity to improve our individual and collective effectiveness. I am committed to developing my own skills, and I look forward to my performance evaluation at this time next year. Jane, do you want to say anything?"

"I certainly do," Jane replied. "I want to add my thanks to each one of you for your support of the school and of me personally, as well as for your commitment to excellence everywhere in the school, including the board room."

Susie, the chair of the task force on governance, introduced the professional facilitator who was to lead the board in the day-long discussion. After only slight modifications, the members of the board agreed to the task force's recommendations, but they postponed the official decision until the following month's regular board meeting. The recommendations included:

- Change the nominating committee's name to the committee on trustees and expand its role to cover nominations, board development, succession planning, assessment, and any other governance issues that might arise.
- Take the approved board commitment letter and make sure that current and new trustees understand the commitments and sign their

pledge to fulfill the commitments.
- Refine the new self-assessment process, develop the chair-performance evaluation process, and implement both processes.
- Reorganize the board.
- Reduce the number of committees and establish task forces around critical issues.
- Establish board meetings every other month, with a large portion of the agenda devoted to strategic issue discussion, evaluation, and assessment, or board education and training.
- Put money in the budget for board professional development opportunities.
- Reduce the size of the board to 20 trustees over the next five years by attrition.
- Approve board, trustee, officer, committee, and task force job descriptions.
- Develop a board action plan based on retreat outcomes, the board and individual trustee job descriptions, the Principles of Good Practice for Governance, and the board's role in furthering the school's strategic plan.
- Evaluate the new ways of working at mid-year and at the end of the year.

As the retreat ended, Frank turned to Jane and said, "At the end of the October board meeting, I would never have believed we would be where we are today. It's obvious the trustees care deeply for the school and its mission and truly want to be effective."

To that, Jane said, "Amen." ∎

DISCUSSION QUESTIONS

1. What are the critical components of new trustee orientation that would have helped Tom be prepared to handle the concern about the Latin teacher?

2. How can all trustees take ownership of ensuring that trustee behavior—both within the board and committees and with all school constituencies—is appropriate?

3. How would you describe the optimum relationship between the head of school and the board chair?

4. How can you balance the importance of in-depth strategic discussion at all board meetings with trustees' time constraints?

5. How can all school constituencies learn about the role of the board and individual trustees?

6. What should the incoming board chair's orientation include? Where are the resources for such an orientation? Who should conduct it?

SUGGESTED RESOURCES AND FURTHER READING

INSTITUTIONAL RESOURCES

Association of Governing Boards of Universities and Colleges
One Dupont Circle, Suite 400
Washington, DC 20036
(202) 296-8400 *www.agb.org*

AGB is dedicated to strengthening the performance of boards of public and private higher education. Offers workshops and publications that may also be useful to independent schools.

BoardSource
(Formerly the National Center for Nonprofit Boards)
1828 L St., NW, Suite 900
Washington, DC 20036-5114
(202) 452-6262 or (877) 892-6273 *ww.boardsource.org*

BoardSource is considered the authority on nonprofit governance. Plans an annual conference for nonprofit leaders each fall and offers a number of publications and consultative services designed to help boards improve. Publishes the magazine *Board Member* 10 times a year.

Independent School Chairpersons Association
PO Box 418
Cazenovia, NY 13035
(315) 655-3561 *www.iscachairs.org*

ISCA is a nationwide organization of chairpersons of independent school boards of trustees. Membership is open to current, past, and newly elected chairs of elementary and secondary schools. ISCA holds an annual conference and facilitates networking among its members through its listserve.

Independent School Management
1316 N. Union St.
Wilmington, DE 19806-2594
(302) 656-4944 *www.isminc.com*

ISM is a research, analysis, and consulting firm devoted to the management needs of independent schools. ISM produces two advisory publications, *Ideas & Perspectives* and *To the Point,* and offers administrative workshops.

National Association of Corporate Directors

Two Lafayette Centre
1133 21st St., NW, Suite 700
Washington, DC 20036
(202) 775-0509 *www.nacdonline.org*

NACD is the only membership organization devoted to improving the performance of corporate boards. In addition to publishing a newsletter, *Director's Monthly,* NACD conducts educational programs and standard-setting research on board governance issues and practices. Most members are for-profit corporate directors.

National Association of Independent Schools

1620 L St., NW, Suite 1100
Washington, DC 20036-5695
(202) 973-9700 *www.nais.org*

NAIS is a membership organization for more than 1,300 member schools and associations in the United States and abroad. It is the national institutional advocate for independent precollegiate education. NAIS has numerous publications, monographs, reports on research and statistics, and conferences dedicated to issues of governance and leadership. It also provides assessment services for boards of trustees. Publishes the quarterly magazine *Independent School.*

GENERAL NEWSLETTERS AND MAGAZINES

The Head's Letter and *The Trustee's Letter,* published nine times a year by Educational Directions, Inc. (401) 683-3523 or *www.edu-directions.com/.*

ARTICLES AND BOOKS

Bobowick, Marla J., Sandra R. Hughes, and Berit M. Lakey. *Transforming Board Structure: Strategies for Committees and Task Forces.* Washington, DC: BoardSource, 2001.

Chait, Richard P. *How to Help Your Board Govern More and Manage Less.* Washington, DC: BoardSource, 2003.

Chait, Richard P., William P. Ryan, and Barbara E. Taylor. *Governance as Leadership: Reframing the Work of Nonprofit Boards.* Hoboken, NJ: BoardSource and John Wiley and Sons, Inc., 2005.

DeKuyper, Mary Hundley. *Trustee Handbook: A Guide to Effective Governance for Independent School Boards.* Washington, DC: NAIS, 2007.

Dietel, William M., and Linda Dietel. *The Board Chair Handbook.* Washington, DC: BoardSource, 2001.

Gale, Robert L. *Leadership Roles in Nonprofit Governance.* Washington, DC: BoardSource, 2003.

NAIS, *The Source. Twelve Principles of Governance That Power Exceptional Boards.* Washington, DC: NAIS, 2005.

"Parents and Independent Schools: Roles, Relationships, and Boundaries." Glen Burnie, MD: Association of Independent Maryland Schools, December 2001.

Taylor, Barbara E., Richard P. Chait, and Thomas P. Holland. "The New Work of the Nonprofit Board." *Harvard Business Review,* September-October 1996. Cambridge, MA: Harvard Business School.

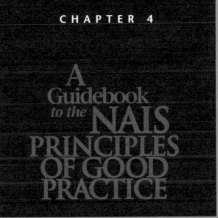

CHAPTER 4

A Guidebook
to the NAIS
PRINCIPLES
OF GOOD
PRACTICE

for
EQUITY
AND JUSTICE

By Caroline G. Blackwell

Caroline G. Blackwell *is director of multicultural affairs at University School of Nashville, a K-12 school of 1,000 students in Tennessee.*

NAIS PRINCIPLES OF GOOD PRACTICE for

EQUITY AND JUSTICE

Revised and approved by the NAIS board in 2004

Creating and sustaining an inclusive, equitable, and just independent school community requires commitment, reflection, and conscious and deliberate action, as well as constant vigilance based on the overarching principles of inclusivity, diversity, and multiculturalism. The following Principles of Good Practice for Equity and Justice provide the foundation for such a community. (Although many of the principles apply to this case study, the ones in **boldface** are the most pertinent.)

1. The school establishes the foundation for its commitment to equity and justice in its mission statement and strategic planning.

2. The school respects, affirms, and protects the dignity and worth of each member of the school community.

3. The school establishes, publishes, implements, and reviews policies that promote equity and justice in the life of the school.

4. The school supports the ongoing education of the board, parents, students, and all school personnel as part of the process of creating and sustaining an equitable and just community.

5. The school ensures an anti-bias environment by assessing school culture and addressing issues of equity and justice in pedagogy, assessment, curriculum, programs, admission, and hiring.

6. The school values each and every child, recognizing and teaching to varied learning styles, abilities, and life experiences.

7. The school uses inclusive, anti-bias language in written and oral communication.

8. The school complies with local, state, and federal laws and regulations that promote diversity.

9. The school provides appropriate opportunities for leadership and participation in decision-making to all members of the school community.

10. The school includes all families and guardians as partners in the process of creating and sustaining an equitable and just community.

11. The school expects from its students and all members of the community an appreciation of and responsibility for the principles of equity and justice.

CASE STUDY
AN UNEASY FIT

Looking up from her desk, phone propped against one shoulder, Pam signaled to her advisee, Julian, who was pacing just outside her door. "Give me just a minute," she said, mouthing the words softly while reaching for a sticky note on which to jot down the caller's number. Minutes seemed like hours before she could finally put down the phone and stand up to greet the lanky teen, whose signature Red Sox cap was repositioned for sentry duty. It had been more than a year since Julian entered Urban River School and almost that long since she'd seen him look so ill at ease. Sure, when he first arrived at Urban River, he wore his "safety cap" throughout the week-long freshman orientation. But he lifted the brim a bit each day, finally turning it completely backward on the bus ride home. Pam couldn't help smiling at the memory of her first real look at Julian's deep hazel eyes and open smile—neither of which he offered up for view today.

"I didn't want to go on that stupid trip, anyway. It's just a bunch of losers," Julian blurted out. "And who decided that you need to spend $1,100 to help a bunch of poor people in Mexico? Don't they know there are poor people everywhere?" His voice trailed off.

One of the qualities Pam valued most in Julian was the compassion he demonstrated so effortlessly—at least when he wasn't shielding it beneath a carefully crafted street-wise persona. "What kind of person would I be if I didn't care about my 'peeps'?" Julian had explained when, during a recent advisee meeting, he was recognized for his active involvement in Urban River's community service programs. "Helping people is the way I roll, you know. I can't look like a punk about it." He winked and bumped fists with his buddies in the group—the latest adaptation of the high-five.

It was during that same meeting that advisers announced the service club's Alternative Spring Break trip to Mexico. For 10 days, students would help renovate the only school serving several remote, impoverished villages; they would also tutor and otherwise care for dozens of children while living at nearby farms. The estimated cost of the trip was $1,100, including airfare.

Pam's advisees immediately began nominating Julian for the trip: "You're going to go, aren't you, Julian?" "You'll be great!"

"Hold on, everybody," Pam interrupted, watching Julian shift in his seat. "Each of you needs to discuss this trip with your families first. There are lots of ways to spend time during spring break, including staying home."

"You can stay home, Ms. P, but a bunch of us are going to St. Croix, Max is going on the awesome senior trip to Jamaica, and Julian can represent our advisee group in Mexico," Sean said happily as they filed out for class.

"Yeah, represent," Julian mumbled, darting into the crowded hall. The look on his face that morning left little doubt that he believed the trip was out of reach. Still, maybe his family could get access to some resources of which he was not aware.

In Pam's office today, however, Julian's guarded veneer made it clear that hope may spring eternal, but it fades nevertheless with time.

Watching Julian swallow what surely tasted of humiliation and untrustworthy dreams caused Pam to reflect on the social distance she had traveled since her own prep school days. The daughter of a domestic and an unskilled factory worker with a fourth-grade education, Pam had scored a "free ride" to boarding school, a trip similar to the one that now nearly brought Julian to tears. For a moment, she remembered how each day's promise of the highest-quality education was tinged by her awareness of the habits and trappings of advantage. School was a world largely foreign to a rough-edged girl who carried her family's hopes through the campus's old stone gates. "Study hard, pay attention to your teachers, and don't get in trouble" was her parents' oft-repeated formula for success.

"Simple, but not easy," she sighed, remembering lessons learned in dorm rooms and dining halls, in casual conversations, and in crowds when no one seemed to notice she was there. Troubling tests and pop quizzes for which she had little preparation littered her memories.

"I wonder what advice Julian received when he began his journey?" Pam thought. "What besides books and binders are stuffed in his backpack?"

Pam's tenure as assistant head of the K-12 Urban River School, centrally located in a bustling city, had begun three years before. The position carried with it a fair degree of influence with respect to school operations—curriculum oversight, discipline, community relations—but little authority to stop the buck that Julian had just placed on her desk. She was first drawn to Urban River because of its far-reaching reputation as an academically challenging, progressive, coeducational community that prized student initiative and involvement as well as faculty-staff innovation and collaboration. It did not take long to see that the school's reputation was well deserved.

But Pam's allegiance to the institution was actually forged while observing the head of school, Robert Wilder, who regularly challenged faculty and staff to exercise the school's mission-driven commitment to valuing and leveraging diversity. Although Pam had once viewed limited authority as an unwelcome constraint on her ability to bring about change, she now embraced the opportunity to help lead Urban River and work cooperatively to advance a model of shared responsibility for building and sustaining an inclusive school. Often it was neither easy nor expedient to pass responsibility and accountability for diversity-related issues to and through the school's wider circle of influencers and decision makers. But, over time, faculty experienced the change brought about by such a process more positively and expectantly. Pam knew her ongoing effort helped ensure that Urban River's mission served as both a beacon and a measure of educational excellence and community well-being, even when a process or outcome did not mesh with her own preferred course or goals.

So, what of Julian's problem? Certain that "his" issues were systemic failures that only masqueraded as personal problems, she knew she needed to do some thinking before sitting down with Robert.

To be continued....

EXEMPLARY APPLICATIONS OF GOOD PRACTICE

EXAMPLE 1: **Investing in the Future**
(Relates to Equity and Justice Principles 2 and 3)

Nestled in the verdant hills of Marin County, California, the Branson School reaches throughout the San Francisco Bay area for the leaders of tomorrow.

"We're investing in our alumni now—current students who, after Branson, are going to graduate and go on to college and graduate school, students who want to, and will, change the world," says Bridget Anderson, who was admissions director for 11 years before becoming director of alumni relations in July 2006. "It is not acceptable for students to just come to school, read, write, and leave."

As a measure of Branson's commitment to socioeconomic diversity and inclusion, the high school focuses on policies and practices that create what Anderson describes as a "full education," inside and outside the classroom, for its 320 students. Branson's need-based financial aid program supports that philosophy, not only by funding tuition but, in some cases, also covering the cost of books, other educational materials and supplies, and expenses related to a student's quality of life. For example, travel abroad, music lessons, appropriate clothing—even orthodontia—have been covered for some students who qualify for 100-percent need through a student fund.

Still, with more than 15 percent of its student body receiving some type of aid, Anderson says, the pool is not limitless.

"Every year, many more families qualify for financial aid than we are able to fund," Anderson says, especially as families in the Bay Area experience what has been described as "the middle class squeeze."

"We know there are middle class families out there who are barely managing to cover tuition and whose needs are not being met. That middle class group raises a lot of questions, questions for which we have not yet found all the answers."

EXAMPLE 2: **On Becoming Green and White**
(Relates to Equity and Justice Principles 2, 3, and 4)

Following a selection process steeped in tradition, shrouded in secrecy, and performed by candlelight, "new girls" and "old girls" of varied ethnic, racial, and cultural backgrounds are transformed. "They're inducted into a green or white team—our school colors," explains George Swope, head of Oldfields School outside Baltimore. "After that, there are no new girls or old girls, just Oldfields girls."

Swope believes it is especially important to transmit Oldfields' core values, and the normative behaviors associated with them, when new students and faculty enter the school community, which is for grades 8 to 12. Thus, the school's orientation programs—and the activities that flow from them—have been completely redesigned to inculcate its central tenets and beliefs throughout the year. Daily opportunities to incorporate those values help students ameliorate some of the unconstructive tensions that can occur in diverse school settings, Swope says. This helps the institution to better adjust to the unique challenges facing boarding schools.

For example, Oldfields is employing net-tuition discounting as one tool to create greater socioeconomic diversity on campus. Tuition discounting is a financial aid practice schools and colleges use to help meet a range of enrollment objectives. Discounting reduces the out-of-pocket costs families must pay for tuition—an acknowledgment of the fact that matriculation decisions are influenced as much by a family's ability to pay as by its willingness to do so. Swope says he helped the board understand that tuition is both "real and philosophical" and that, with proper management, empty beds can be filled in ways that meet multiple objectives. Similarly, Oldfields is expanding its experiential education programming to include an array of stimulating, high-quality, affordable options—and informing students about these choices early on—to help girls and their families plan and participate more fully.

EXAMPLE 3: An Educational Imperative
(Relates to Equity and Justice Principles 1, 3, and 4)

To Frank Garrison, president of University School of Nashville's Board of Trustees, the institutional imperative is clear. "The educational experience of all students will be enhanced if we have families that include the entire socioeconomic spectrum—those who have 100 percent need, those who have 0 percent need, and those who fall everywhere in between," he says.

"While we don't know yet what all the right yardsticks are, we do know that we want to avoid the 'barbell effect.' We are committed to a school that looks more like the rest of the world, and that means more than a handful of ZIP codes."

Embracing the role and responsibility to champion a just and inclusive K-12 learning community, University School's board has primed itself to consider a series of benchmarks and long-range goals that will help ensure access for children from all socioeconomic strata. Based in part on research compiled by the trustees' ad hoc Committee on Affordability, the board is weighing a series of bottom-line targets over the coming months. These questions include: In the near term, how rapidly can the school become truly need-blind in its admissions processes? In the long term, how much will it cost for USN to achieve and sustain its optimal socioeconomic profile? Still a third key set-point board members hope to determine: What is the nexus between the rate of tuition increases and the effect such changes have on the number of families who would correspondingly qualify for aid?

Tantamount to the board's need for reliable information is the necessity that current and prospective families be able to understand, accurately count, and ultimately plan for the costs associated with private schooling. As one support for meeting this objective, every year University School's Office of Multicultural Affairs sponsors a free public workshop on financing independent education.

Analyzing and effectively addressing affordability issues is a mission-driven exercise, integral to sustaining the school's unique culture as well as its academic and institutional vitality, Garrison says. By leading in this area of diversity, the board affords USN's administration maximum resources and flexibility to design and manage a qualitative experience for students that gives them a wider lens, and thus a comparative advantage, in today's changing world.

EXAMPLE 4: Leveling the Playing Field
(Relates to Equity and Justice Principles 2, 4, and 11)

It is not unusual for an afternoon visitor to find a student pushing a sturdy vacuum cleaner across an office floor, washing windows, loading a dishwasher, or gathering bucket and brush to attend to a nearby classroom. At Wooster School in Danbury, Connecticut, each day ends with all of its K-12 students on "a level playing field."

"It's countercultural in general, and for independent day schools in particular, but it's an aspect of our culture that we're most proud of," says Headmaster George King about Wooster's Self-help philosophy and jobs program. "It doesn't matter what race or religion you are, or how wealthy you are. Everyone participates."

Wooster's jobs program, which dates back to the school's founding in 1926, invests students with the responsibility for cleaning and maintaining the campus. King believes the program is the nexus of several common denominators that embody Wooster's longstanding commitment to educational equity. "We were committed to racial, ethnic, and socioeconomic diversity long before it was trendy. It is a way of being and a way of life here," King says. The first New England boarding school to integrate in 1956, Wooster maintains traditions that support a mission of inclusion. Among them are ecumenical chapel programs, family-style lunches, and required service learning.

Students participate in a variety of small-group activities, including athletics, fine and performing arts, and clubs, King says. But the beauty of the school's senior-led jobs program is that at the end of each academic day, the entire student body works together.

"I make it a point to tell prospective students and their parents that everyone participates; there are no exceptions," King continues. "Wooster's Self-help philosophy and the jobs program definitely provide students with a level playing field."

CASE STUDY *continued from page 49*
AN UNEASY FIT

MORE THAN A NUMBERS GAME

Notwithstanding the compassion and enviable financial resources at Urban River, indulging any impulse to "solve or fix" the problem couched in Julian's present circumstance could easily amount to an $1,100 mistake with interest. What was it he said? "Who decided that you need to spend $1,100.... Don't they know there are poor people everywhere?" Giving Julian the money would buy him a place on the trip, Pam thought, but would it address his questions, unlock their underlying values, or help students like him feel secure?

She picked up a legal pad and began making notes. "Socioeconomic diversity—as with all forms of human difference—is more than a numbers game," she wrote.

For Urban River to benefit from the socioeconomic differences within the community, the school would have to acknowledge and understand the powerful role class plays in society, generally, and within the institution, particularly.

Socioeconomic class is a cross-cutting dimension of diversity. Commonly though not exclusively, it's measured as a function of education, wealth, occupation, or social position and income. Like its umbrella concept—culture—class provides and transmits to its members a sense of identity, belonging, common language and experiences, political and social views and preferences, aesthetic interests, and consumption patterns. Class is evident everywhere, even in Urban River's outcomes, Pam thought, allowing her awareness to encompass the school's vast facilities, resources, and inhabitants; its governance and leadership structure; its history and public perception.

Ironically, however, the markers and meanings ascribed to the obvious (and less obvious) class differences that exist at Urban River are so illusory, so intractable, or so misconstrued that honest conversation among faculty, staff, and parents and guardians about this aspect of diversity is almost as rare as the school's milieu.

"Rarified air," Pam scratched on the pad. "Does that description match UR's institutional self-perception?"

As one of approximately 1,300 NAIS independent schools in the United States that in total educate just over 500,000 students (around 1 percent of the school-aged population), Urban River occupied a privileged position. Among schools of its type and size, Urban River averaged an application-to-acceptance ratio of 5 to 1, making it one of the country's most competitive schools—or, as some prospective parents say, "one of the right schools." Urban River's growing financial aid endowment allowed the school to award need-based aid to just over 15 percent of its student body. But the lion's share of UR students—approximately 85 percent—came from households with incomes no less than $88,000, placing them in the highest quintile of income earners in the country. And, Pam thought, that's just one measure of economic prosperity.

"Yes, we're a private school, but…," Pam wrote, this time making mental note of an expanding list of attributes, programs, and services that schools like Urban River undertake to carry out a "public" mission and help counter perceptions of elitism and exclusivity.

Yet the very ability of Urban River and other independent schools to act in the public good is most often a direct function of the affluence that established and sustained them—affluence wrought in a widely accepted economic system that engenders have-nots, have-muches, and have-much-much-mores. Independent schools often mirror the ambivalence about class that pervades our national consciousness. It's a feeling that seems to necessitate a language and culture of class relativism to militate against the discomfort of owning up to our institutional "lot" with the assertion, "We're a private school and…."

Pam played with a list of statements that completed an accurate, but perhaps less liberal, reflection of schools like Urban River, schools that are sought after by families across the economic spectrum precisely because they are the symbols and slices of the American Dream.

"We're a private school and… we teach habits of achievement and advantage, including personal responsibility and accountability, competition, and perseverance…. We value individual industry, self-reliance, and cooperation…. We support and actively participate in America's economic and political system to help ensure our livelihoods and long-term survival…. We acknowledge that this same system confers unearned advantage on some and unwarranted disadvantage on

others…. We are committed to developing positive self-concepts, critical inquiry, and compassion in all members of our learning community…. We value difference but not at the expense of our core values and mission…."

Pam kept a watchful eye out for Julian throughout the rest of the day, but he did not come back to her office. She checked e-mail and voicemail. No reports from teachers or coaches.

"Good, he made all of his scheduled appointments," she thought. "I'll check in with Robert tomorrow morning." In the meantime, she finished the notes and recommendations she would bring to the meeting.

PRACTICE AND PRINCIPLED ACTION

Robert's door was rarely closed, and Thursday was no exception. His imposing desk was perpetually stacked with piles of files, the contents of which he could find without a second thought. Pam had learned quickly that as the head of school, Robert had a style of inquiry that was more than an educational practice; it was how he approached the world. She was prepared to strategize with him about how Urban River could benefit from an exploration of the issues and questions that had been raised by the Alternative Spring Break trip.

But, more significantly, Pam knew that if she helped the school stay its course and apply the standards set by its mission to the diversity challenges the trip raised, then the unique needs and best interests of all Urban River students and families would be served, including Julian's.

CASE STUDY
AN UNEASY FIT

One of those standards is adherence to the NAIS Principles of Good Practice for Equity and Justice. When Pam brought up these principles, Robert wasted little time asking about faculty and staff familiarity with the principles or offering an answer to his own query. "We published the principles, and we asked administrators and diversity council members to review them, but as a community, would you agree that we have a ways to go?" he asked.

"Absolutely," Pam replied. "And what far-reaching issue is more appropriate to deconstruct using these principles than our effectiveness in the area of socioeconomic diversity?"

For the next hour, Robert and Pam reviewed the 11 principles, noting how each could be used to help illuminate the complex of issues socioeconomic diversity raises.

Acknowledging that Urban River had met Principle 1 by establishing the foundation for its commitment to equity and justice in its mission statement and strategic planning, they quickly began translating Principle 2 into a series of questions aimed at raising awareness of the complex class issues in school and opening dialogue on the topic among parents, faculty, students, and staff. Productive questions could include:

- In what ways are class differences evident in the school community? In what ways does the school demonstrate respect for and affirmation of these differences?
- How does Urban River protect and promote the dignity and worth of each member of the community?

- Do all members of the community feel valued and included, regardless of income, wealth, education, or occupation? If not, what are some of the barriers?

The next three principles could be used to help answer the questions Julian had posed haltingly and perhaps even rhetorically earlier that week. Undoubtedly but ironically, the Alternative Spring Break trip was planned and sponsored "by the school" with the best intentions of supporting Urban River's ongoing commitment to service and global awareness, both of which are critical elements of its diversity initiatives. Another aspect of the trip's appeal (at least for some parents) was its riposte to a chorus of demands that "everyone goes to the beach during spring break."

Applying Principle 3, Urban River could explore how inclusive or representative of all school constituencies are the key decision makers who establish, publish, implement, and review policies that promote equity and justice in the life of the school. This principle could be mined to determine which perspectives and experiences inform such decision-making processes and to create a mechanism for ongoing assessment of these processes' relevance and impact.

Similarly, the call for ongoing education of the board, parents, students, and all school personnel, as suggested in Principle 4, would allow Urban River to move the subject of class and classism from the unstated to the stated curriculum. In thoughtful examination, the school could expose the norms, values, behaviors, expectations, and other influences attending socioeconomic difference. And the school could accomplish this while increasing understanding of privilege and power and its differential impact on individuals, groups, and the organization itself. Once unveiled, this knowledge could be accessed in age- and experientially appropriate ways to strengthen relationships and interconnectedness throughout the community.

Finally, grounding all of Urban River's teaching, learning, assessment, policy-making, and procedural activities in an anti-bias, anti-discriminatory framework, as addressed in Principle 5, would underscore the shared democratic ideals on which both NAIS's principles and Urban River's mission were founded.

Looking up from the notes and diagrams they had drawn, Pam and Robert smiled in unspoken accord.

MAKING THE PASS

Pam was continually impressed with the thoughtful ways in which Urban River's 15-member diversity council had wrestled with a range of complex topics since she had arrived three years before. Group members disciplined and leveraged their distinct personalities and divergent political views by adhering to dialogic guidelines for all meetings. Wise counsel, Pam thought, when it came time for her report, which she began by forecasting both the opportunities and challenges a new initiative in socioeconomic diversity would bring.

Over the next month, Pam helped the council develop a multi-year plan that focused on a systematic application of the Principles of Good Practice to an exploration of class differences at

the 84-year-old school. Divided thematically and based on the four most common markers of class in America, the initiative would annually address issues related to:

- **wealth** (including how the school builds, manages, and uses its endowment);
- **income** (including affordability, financial aid, and demographic trends);
- **education** (how socioeconomic diversity and its attendant values are defined and expressed in the community); and
- **occupation/status** (including quality of life issues, relationships, hierarchies, and conflict).

The plan began with a climate study and series of schoolwide conversations aimed at benchmarking key variables while increasing awareness and understanding of the impact of class differences on campus. Council members laid the groundwork for that study by interviewing school administrators, department chairs, supervisors, and parent leaders. Their initial findings reinforced the need for additions to the curriculum and the professional-development program to provide for more direct instruction on class and socioeconomic diversity as well as to help craft shared meaning and understanding about terms such as affordability, fairness, equity, and privilege, to name a few.

During the formative stages of the initiative, the diversity council took inventory of its own composition and expanded its membership to include two additional representatives from the school's maintenance staff, one of whom was bilingual, and a second upper school student representative, nominated at large. The council's trustee representative volunteered to seek board

CASE STUDY
AN UNEASY FIT

leadership and endorsement of an ad hoc committee on affordability to address internal and external pressures and trends and to clarify or recommend policy guidelines with regard to costs and school-sponsored activities.

Lastly, Robert agreed to feature the initiative periodically in his regular newsletter column. This would make clear his support for the plan and encourage widespread involvement to ensure that it reflected both the school's fundamental and emergent values.

Four months after Robert and Pam's meeting, the first schoolwide parent forum on socioeconomic diversity was held.

AHEAD OF THE CLASS

Two long-term diversity council members fussed with the placement of danish and sweet rolls on the crowded refreshment table. "We could end up with a lot to take home," one commented, still oblivious to the steady line of cars making their way to the parking lot. Across the hall, a handful of middle- and upper-school community service club members began to assemble. Free child care would be offered at all forums; squeals of laughter from runaway toddlers suggested the morning was off to a good start.

When Julian stood to speak, Pam couldn't help admiring the poised and unaffected way he

moved through the crowd toward the podium. The decision to ask Julian to welcome participants and introduce Robert was a testament to the leadership Julian had displayed since being selected by his peers to serve on the council. Pam watched as the still-lanky young man scanned the room; he then smiled openly but waved discreetly to his parents, who were sitting a few rows from the door. After the previous Friday's advisee meeting, Julian had confided that the forum was the first meeting his mom and dad could attend together because they worked different shifts at the automobile plant 40 miles away. "My parents said they were coming to check on what I do. But you know, Ms. P, I think they're coming to help their 'peeps,' " he had said, winking and adjusting the brim of his cap so the "B" was in clear view from behind.

Once in front of the assembled group, Julian began reading from the preamble to the NAIS Principles of Good Practice. " 'Creating and sustaining an inclusive, equitable, and just independent school community requires commitment, reflection, and conscious and deliberate action, as well as constant vigilance....'

"Good schools—no, great schools, like Urban River—include all families and guardians as partners in that process as recommended by item 11," he continued, holding up a copy of the document. "That's why each of you was invited here today." ■

DISCUSSION QUESTIONS

1. Access, expectations, and outcomes in education vary with social class. How much do you know about the socioeconomic profile of your school community? What data do you collect and why?

2. In recent years, much has been made of a "middle class squeeze." What percentage of families in your school constitutes the true versus emotional middle income? How are the needs of this group being met?

3. Are income and race conflated in discussions about financial aid, diversity, or affordability in your school? How can you help to de-couple these conceptions?

4. How are differences in social-class status experienced in the school community? Does class reside in the "hidden" or "stated" curriculum?

5. Which does your institution value more: equality or equity? What evidence points to this conclusion?

6. What concrete (next) steps should the head of school, board of trustees, division and department heads, and classroom teachers take to help create or sustain a respectful environment relative to socioeconomic difference?

SUGGESTED RESOURCES AND READING MATERIALS

Adams, Maurianne, Lee Ann Bell, and Pat Griffin. *Teaching for Diversity and Social Justice.* New York: Routledge, 1997.

Center for Research on Education, Diversity & Excellence (*www.cal.org/crede/*).

Class Matters, a New York Times Special Series. Available at *www.nytimes.com/pages/national/ class/?8dpc*

Freire, Paulo. *Pedagogy of the Oppressed.* New York, NY: Continuum International Publishing Group, 2000.

hooks, bell. *Teaching to Transgress: Education as the Practice of Freedom.* New York, NY: Routledge, 1994.

Jones, Rebecca. "Defining Diversity," *American School Board Journal.* Vol.189 (10), October 2002. Alexandria, VA: National School Board Association.

Kozol, Jonathan. *Savage Inequalities: Children in America's Schools.* New York, NY: Crown Publishers, Inc., 1991.

Kugler, Eileen Gale. *Debunking the Middle-Class Myth: Why Diverse Schools Are Good for All Kids.* Lanham, MD: Scarecrow Education, 2002.

Lee, Steve. "Dean Pushes for Socioeconomic Diversity." *The Harvard Independent,* May 5, 2005. Cambridge, MA: Harvard University.

Loewen, James W. *Lies My Teacher Told Me: Everything Your American History Textbook Got Wrong.* New York, NY: New Press, 1996.

Nieto, Sonia. *Affirming Diversity: The Sociopolitical Context of Multicultural Education.* White Plains, NY: Longman Publishing Group, 1996.

Orfield, Gary, and Chungmei Lee. *Why Segregation Matters: Poverty and Educational Inequity.* Cambridge, MA: Civil Rights Project, Harvard University, 2005 (*www.civilrightsproject.harvard.edu/research/deseg/ deseg05.php*).

Reardon, Sean, and John T. Yun. *Private School Racial Enrollments and Segregation.* Civil Rights Project,

Harvard University, 2002 (*www.civilrightsproject. harvard.edu/research/deseg/Private_Schools02.php*).

Rothstein, Richard. *Class and Schools: Using Social, Economic, and Education Reform to Close the Black-White Achievement Gap.* Washington, DC: Economic Policy Institute, 2004.

UNC Center for Civil Rights. *The Socioeconomic Composition of the Public Schools: A Crucial Consideration in Student Assignment Policy.* Charlotte, NC: University of North Carolina School of Law, 2005.

U.S. Census Bureau Home Page (*www.census.gov/index.html*).

U.S. Department of Education, Office for Civil Rights, *Achieving Diversity: Race-Neutral Alternatives in American Education.* Washington, DC: 2004.

Weis, Lois, and Michelle Fine. *Beyond Silenced Voices: Class, Race, and Gender in United States Schools.* Albany, NY: State University of New York Press, 1993.

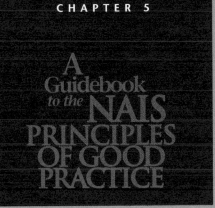

CHAPTER 5

A Guidebook
to the NAIS
PRINCIPLES
OF GOOD
PRACTICE

for

FINANCIAL AID ADMINISTRATION

By Mark J. Mitchell

Mark J. Mitchell *is vice president for school information services at NAIS in Washington, DC.*

NAIS PRINCIPLES OF GOOD PRACTICE for

FINANCIAL AID ADMINISTRATION

Revised and approved by the NAIS board in 2003

Recognizing that each family bears the primary responsibility for financing a student's education costs, NAIS's Principles of Good Practice for Financial Aid Administration are designed to serve as guideposts in the development of professional policies and orderly procedures among schools. Through these principles, NAIS affirms its belief that the purpose of a financial aid program is to provide monetary assistance to those students who cannot afford the cost of attending an independent school. Furthermore, these principles reflect the standards of equity and fairness NAIS embraces and reassert NAIS's ongoing commitment to access and diversity. (Although many of the principles apply to this case study, the ones in **boldface** are the most pertinent.)

1. The school adheres to local, state, and federal laws and regulations that require nondiscriminatory practice in the administration of its financial aid policies.

2. The school operates within the context of both short- and long-range financial aid budget and policy goals.

3. The school uses objective research to measure the effectiveness of its progress toward its goals, and communicates the outcomes as appropriate.

4. The school provides outreach, education, and guidance to students and families on all aspects of its financial aid process and options.

5. The school determines eligibility for admission without regard to a student's application for financial aid.

6. The school commits to providing financial aid dollars to applicants who demonstrate that their family resources are insufficient to meet all or part of the total educational costs.

7. The school continues to provide support to students as long as financial need is demonstrated.

8. The school maintains the same standards of behavior and academic performance for recipients of financial aid as it does for non-recipients.

9. The school enacts documented procedures that ensure a fair, consistent, and equitable assessment of each family's ability to contribute toward educational expenses.

10. The school makes and communicates financial aid decisions in a manner that allows families to make timely, careful, and fully informed enrollment decisions.

11. The school establishes administrative and accounting procedures that distinguish the school's need-based financial aid program from tuition-assistance programs that are not based on financial need.

12. The school safeguards the confidentiality of financial aid applications, records, and decisions.

13. The school supports collaboration between the financial aid office and other offices within the school.

CASE STUDY
PONDERING FINANCIAL AID'S ROLE IN A DIVERSE STUDENT BODY

As a founding board member of the five-year-old Brand New School, Jane became concerned with the seemingly "elitist" posture that the school was already taking relative to socioeconomic diversity. Because the board worked hard from the start to establish the tuition at a reasonable level for a K-6 school of about 300 students, the school did not offer financial aid. But Jane noticed that applications were coming only from well-to-do students, not from broad segments of families across various income levels.

BNS's mission statement proclaimed (among other things) that the school is dedicated to "educational excellence for a diverse student body." So at the spring board meeting, Jane and the director of admission gave a brief presentation for the entire board to discuss. Although some board members saw the fact that all families were full-paying as a positive sign for the school's fiscal health, the group embraced Jane's assessment of the situation and appointed her to chair a task force on expanding economic diversity at the school. The task force's charge was to deliver a set of recommendations by July 1 to guide the following year's enrollment management efforts.

Lamenting the fact that she did not heed the famous warning to "be careful what you wish for," Jane found herself lying awake at night and grappling with questions such as:

- Is the lack of economic diversity a perception problem, a financial issue, or both?
- Do people of different income levels have different perspectives about what our school is like?
- Is there something about our image or reputation that keeps lower- and middle-income families from considering us?
- Is our tuition not as reasonable as we thought?
- Do we need to offer financial aid?
- If so, how do we determine who should receive how much of it? How do we fund it? What is the ultimate goal of having it?

To get a handle on both the big-picture aspects of the dilemma and the practical implications of designing a financial aid program from scratch, Jane decided to attend one of the NAIS/SSS Financial Aid Workshops, sponsored by NAIS and its School and Student Service for Financial Aid. Jane was particularly intrigued by a presentation about "affordability range." Given a school's tuition price, what is the income range of families who would be unable to afford that price in full?

Jane realized that her board had never thought about tuition-setting in these terms and began to wonder how and why board members discerned that their tuition was "reasonable." In fact, they had based the decision mostly on comparisons to similar schools and had never considered it in the context of families' ability to actually pay it. The working presumption was always, "If they're paying that much or more for other schools, then they can pay it for ours, too."

At one of the session breaks on the workshop's first day, Jane introduced herself to the presenter and explained her school's situation. Would the presenter be willing to discuss how she might gather information and strategies for determining the hows, whats, and whys of investing in financial aid?

As they talked, it became clear to Jane that her task force members had to tackle their issue from three distinct angles:

1. **Learn more about BNS's affordability.** The school needed to know how much a family had to earn to pay its tuition and fees and had to collect objective, reliable data about its economic diversity.

2. **Learn more about BNS's broader community.** The school had to know whether its drawing area had the economic diversity BNS sought and needed to gather the facts about the income ranges of families within a 30-minute drive of the school.

3. **Learn about best practices for setting up and managing a financial aid practice.** The school had to have a clear and realistic estimate of how much funding BNS needed to commit and had to know how to distribute the dollars effectively.

Additionally, BNS needed to study various parents' perceptions about the school. This knowledge could have an impact on strategies the school needed to take to become more affordable and could inform methods for enhancing the school's value proposition.

Back at school, Jane thought hard about how to lay the right foundation for a new financial aid program. A logical first step, she decided, was a visit to the NAIS website, where she could review the NAIS Principles of Good Practice for Financial Aid Administration.

To be continued….

ANALYSIS OF THE PRINCIPLES AND EXEMPLARY APPLICATIONS OF GOOD PRACTICE

PRINCIPLE 1: **Nondiscriminatory Policies**

Nobody wants to break the law. Schools have to be conscious of any local, state, and federal laws and regulations regarding assessing financial aid eligibility and offering financial aid dollars in a nondiscriminatory manner. In the administration of financial aid, discriminatory policies are most likely to put the school at risk when race or gender plays a part in the final determination of whether to award a grant or scholarship. It is critical to be aware of when such a determination might expose a school to liability and when it might not.

In the brief called "Race Consideration in Admission and Financial Aid," NAIS provides the following suggestions to help avoid some of the pitfalls of establishing race-based awarding policies.

1. Review your school's consideration of race in the admission and financial aid process.
2. If you give such consideration, create a policy statement articulating the reason for such consideration.
3. Consider the following questions in reviewing your policy:
   - Is race considered in a way that puts minority students outside the realm of equal competition?
   - Are there other non-race-based traits that might achieve the same objective?
   - Does the school consider each applicant individually?
   - Does the school consider other diversifying traits besides race?
4. Build in a durational element of the program—in other words, a set time frame for it—or schedule a periodic evaluation to ensure that considering race is still necessary to achieve diversity within the student body.
5. Have the school's legal counsel determine applicable state law and review the policy regularly.

Issues like these are typically not on the table when it comes to need-based financial aid. Indeed, the Principles of Good Practice spelled out in this chapter reinforce the ideal that only financial need (not race, gender, or any other personal characteristic) should matter in decision making. In some situations, donors wishing to provide scholarships to students of color will approach a school to establish an endowed fund. According to "Race

Consideration in Admission and Financial Aid," a school would be wise not to accept donations for administering race-based scholarships. Instead, the school should work with the donor to set up scholarships having race-neutral characteristics that might achieve the same goals.

Alternatively, a school can help donors find ways to administer the funds themselves, directly to students, without involving the school. And the school could take steps to inform the community about the availability of and application process for the awards.

PRINCIPLE 2: Short- and Long-term Goals

Many independent schools' financial aid offices run in predictable and cyclical patterns, and it is not uncommon to find them operating in a "we've always done it that way" mode—particularly when the director is part-time or wears several other hats (admissions, business office, teaching, coaching, etc.). Under these circumstances, short-term concerns get most of the attention. However, it is vitally important for schools to attend to long-term considerations when planning for future financial aid.

Consider Friends School of Baltimore, which took an important step by placing the direction of the admission and financial aid program in the context of the changing demographic landscape. Not content to do what it had always done, the school established an Admissions and Financial Aid Task Force to study internal enrollment trends compared to external demographic changes in the city of Baltimore and Baltimore County. The task force developed a briefing on a five-year projection of the school-age population and its potential effects on Friends School's enrollment. Its conclusions and recommendations covered implications for policy and budget-making decisions in admissions and financial aid to carry the school into a data-driven planning posture through 2008.

In this way, Friends School of Baltimore exemplified the spirit of NAIS Financial Aid Principle 2 by clearly placing its program in a context of both short- and long-term budgetary and policy goals. Furthermore, the school embraced the concept of Principle 3 by using objective research and data to identify its directions, possibilities, and priorities. By establishing specific enrollment and financial aid targets based on these projections, the school will be able to monitor its progress toward its goals in a dispassionate way.

To articulate short- and long-term goals effectively, a school should clearly state the purpose and/or philosophy of the financial aid program in printed materials (policy manuals, brochures, etc.) and on the school's website. Of course, it takes longer to make some changes (such as building endowment so that more can be drawn to support financial aid) than others (such as revising a policy to require noncustodial parents to submit financial aid documents). So schools must think purposefully about the strategic and tactical steps they need to take relative to appropriate financial aid policy and budget setting in time frames of one, three, five, and 10 years, if not longer.

PRINCIPLE 3: Institutional Research

Using data to inform financial aid policies and practices is a critical step all independent schools must take. Many schools keep important and useful statistics on the percentage of the student body receiving aid, average aid amounts, and percentage of the budget allocated to financial aid. These statistics are helpful to families because the data present an accurate picture of the aid program's reach, and they're helpful to schools in establishing trends and benchmarks related to their commitment to financial aid.

This "snapshot" brand of institutional research, though, is only part of the charge for independent schools. At Albuquerque Academy, engaging in a broader sort of institutional research yielded valuable information in the 1990s when the school was deciding how to shape financial aid policy to address a perceived dearth of middle-income families.

Like many independent schools, AA was concerned that middle-income families were under-represented in the school community. So the financial aid staff was charged with developing policies to further the reach of the aid program to increase the enrollment of middle-income students. Seeking to make data-driven decisions, the school conducted a survey of the entire student population to discover first whether the perceived dearth was a real one. After defining the middle-income range, the school worked with an outside research firm to develop a survey of current parents' opinions on strengths of the school, areas needing improvement, and other parent-satisfaction measures. The survey also collected demographic information, including income information. Instead of asking "What is your income?" the survey asked parents to select the range in which their family income fell. Among the choices was the school's self-defined middle-income band.

When the survey results were tabulated and confirmed as statistically valid, the school found that the middle-income band that was thought to be under-represented was in fact represented in about the same measure as all other income bands. Not one of the five or six income ranges was significantly higher or lower than any other. As a result, the school learned that it did not need to change its financial aid policy.

In this way, AA used institutional research to find out if it had a perceived problem.

The research results saved the school thousands of dollars in financial aid monies that it didn't actually need to extend to a less-than-needy group of families.

PRINCIPLE 4: Outreach, Education, and Guidance

In 1999, NAIS conducted a public opinion poll in which it asked respondents to rank 20 possible words to describe independent schools. "Approachable" ranked 17th on the list. So on top of a general unwillingness to talk about personal finances with almost anyone, the public at large is reluctant to seek out information from independent schools in particular. This means that to get the right messages to the right people about a school's affordability, it's essential to provide information about tuition and financial aid options in proactive and comprehensive ways.

These are among the most common means to communicate with mass audiences:

- **In print, especially through affordability brochures.** Many schools create financial-aid-specific brochures that describe the general policies and expectations of which families need to be aware. Schools provide these materials in varying ways—to all current financial aid recipients, to prospective families indicating that they want to receive financial aid information, or to the entire school population at re-application time.

- **Online.** Independent school websites are notorious for burying financial aid information. Typically, school websites will have a tab or link labeled "Admission," and the financial aid piece will be a subset of that. Too often, though, schools fear that the term "financial aid" has a negative connotation and instead use a label such as "Affording an XYZ School Education," "Tuition Assistance," and "Flexible Tuition Plan." But in a drop-down list of choices, it's easy to skip right over other phrases in the search for the term "financial aid."

  Families should be able to find information about price and financial aid options within two clicks of the mouse. At the website of the Key School in Maryland, one click is all it takes. The Key School has a front-page link to "Admission" that produces a drop-down box that says, "Admission to Key" and "Financial Aid"—all of which are direct, easy-to-understand words that parents use routinely and will naturally look for.

  So remember that less is more. Be direct with language you choose for links, and use alternative phrases only for webpage subtitles or within the copy describing the program.

- **In person.** Large-group presentations provide another great opportunity to deliver a single message to a mass audience. Many schools provide hands-on "how to complete your application" forums or general information sessions focused on financial aid. Typically, these are part of an open house program or a separate meeting near the start of the financial aid season. For example, each December, Landon School in Maryland offers a financial aid clinic to give prospective families step-by-step guidance for completing the forms and to answer questions about the aid process.

Schools do not have to engage in such outreach alone. There are many successful models of joint sessions for families interested in several schools. In Cincinnati, Richmond, New York, Nashville, Philadelphia, and elsewhere, three to five schools (or even more) have issued invitations to a financial aid seminar for current and prospective parents. Such collaboration reduces replication of effort, provides convenience to parents, and helps spread the cost of hosting across several schools.

In the Cincinnati case, the Queen City Foundation provides support and mentoring to under-represented students seeking access to private school education. The foundation's network connects families with scores of private schools locally and around the country. On the students' placement-testing day, usually held at a local independent school, parents are required to attend a four-hour financial aid workshop while the children are taking tests. This arrangement connects schools, families, and organizations for mutual benefit.

PRINCIPLE 5: Separating Aid Decisions from Admission Decisions

The NAIS principles assert that an applicant's financial aid status and his or her admission status should bear no relation to each other. That is, an admission offer must not depend on a student's financial need. Likewise, the amount of a student's need-based financial aid should not be a measure of his or her "quality" as an admit.

Nonetheless, when schools have more eligible students than available funding, they often have to make such decisions. Admission professionals are constantly forced to ask themselves, "Why admit a student I know we can't fund?" or "Which of these students is most deserving of our last $5,000 grant?" Answering these questions inevitably mingles admission decisions with financial aid decisions to some degree.

A typical problem for which schools must make and articulate a clear policy concerns "need-blind" admission. Many schools feel they should not admit a student for whom the gap in funding will be so large that the family cannot afford to enroll. But often the underlying problem is either that the school has inadequate funding or plans poorly when anticipating admitted students' full need. In these cases, the school should carefully consider whether there's an alternative to denying admission to qualified students. For example, families may want the chance to decide their capabilities on their own; they may be able to pay the tuition by borrowing, finding outside scholarships or sponsors, getting support from family members, etc.

Another problem arises when competitive factors that influence admission decisions also play a part in decisions to award grants. Some factors are objective (such as GPAs), and some are subjective (such as leadership ability). The student who shows need but doesn't get the grant is placed on a waiting list for financial aid and may get the award if another student with financial aid chooses not to enroll.

Many schools separate admission decisions from financial aid decisions by separating the financial aid director from the admission office. Like many colleges and universities, Kamehameha Schools in Hawaii have a distinct financial aid office that handles financial aid applications separately from admission decisions. More commonly, a school's business officer manages financial aid to eliminate the direct (and sometimes conflicting) connection between an admissions function and financial aid decision-making.

Typically, allowing admission criteria to mingle with financial aid decisions is less than optimal. Like the tail that wags the dog, the lack of funding, not sound policy, drives decision making.

PRINCIPLE 6: Aiding Those Demonstrating Need

Principles 5 and 6 are intrinsically related, though they have slightly different emphases. Of all the financial aid principles, Principle 6 is most central to the notion of need-based aid because in it, NAIS affirms that schools' financial aid dollars should focus on providing tuition relief first to those families who show that they need it. Furthermore, this principle also implies that schools should meet the full financial need that families demonstrate. But due to demands on funding, meeting full need is a relative rarity. Schools with a broader base of income sources—particularly endowment draw or investment income from endowed sources—are more likely to be able to fund families' full financial need from the schools' own coffers.

In deciding how to stretch their financial aid dollars, schools usually struggle with the fact that they cannot meet the financial need for all students. So the choice boils down to two options: Meet a larger percentage of need for fewer students, or meet a smaller percentage of need for more students. The 2002 NAIS Attrition Study found that schools with lower attrition rates tended to have a smaller percentage of students receiving aid but on average gave a higher discount off tuition, probably because they were meeting a greater percentage of need. Although we can't be sure of the cause and effect in such cases, this pattern may be one of the more telling indicators in many schools' retention experiences.

In addition to weighing the effect of grant size, schools must resist the constant pull to provide financial aid to those who do not demonstrate need. Particularly in the admission process, it is easy to justify offering "only" a couple of thousand dollars to families and students "we just don't want to lose." In these situations, schools have a difficult time saying no—and an even more difficult time losing the family to a rival school with cheaper tuition (or the willingness to offer some sort of aid package).

However, providing aid to such families doesn't just siphon much-needed funds from those who've shown they need it. It also creates serious challenges to the integrity of your program. Quickly, peer schools will hurl accusations of "buying students." Furthermore, word will spread rapidly throughout the parent community that the school can be "bargained with" if the child is desirable or if the parent is vocal or influential enough. At that point, the school is no longer in control of its aid program.

In some locales, the willingness to bargain can put even students in a bad spot. An example of how this can happen comes from the Tennessee Secondary School Athletic Association, which dictates that students receiving financial aid in excess of their demonstrated financial need will be deemed ineligible for varsity athletics, although they may participate at the junior varsity level. Other states have similar restrictions.

PRINCIPLE 7: Continuing to Meet Need as Long as It's Demonstrated

This principle is designed to prevent schools from placing families in the untenable "bait and switch" position. No school should promise to give a family financial aid indefinitely; the aid process must be a yearly one since a family's situation may change at any given moment. However, the school should commit to meeting a family's demonstrated need as long as that family shows need. In this way, the student can access the school in a reliable and predictable manner throughout his or her tenure there.

Most independent schools find it fairly easy to embrace the spirit of this principle. But problems arise when unforeseen budget pressures build the concomitant yearning to restrict aid to students who are perceived as "not pulling their weight." If they have to tighten the purse strings on the financial aid budget, schools and boards may weigh return on investment and withhold or restrict aid to students who do not meet certain criteria for academic, athletic, artistic, or leadership success. In these cases, such schools and boards neither value nor honor the principle of continuing to meet need as long as it is demonstrated by the family.

Once financial aid is restricted or withheld due to factors unrelated to need, one likely consequence is that the student will be unable to return to the school and improve his or her performance—creating an indirect form of suspension or expulsion. This jeopardizes another Principle of Good Practice for Financial Aid because the aid recipient is held to a different standard of behavior, since an underperforming student without financial aid would not face a similar sanction. If a school would normally allow an underperformer to return, then it must provide the same opportunity to come back by continuing to offer financial aid as long as there is a demonstrated need.

In a need-based program, this principle reaffirms that the only determining factor in offering (or, particularly, re-offering) financial aid is the need of the family. If it truly matters whether the student's performance or behavior is a major factor, then the school must be clear and upfront about the expectations and the consequences of not meeting them. In these cases, schools should carefully consider labeling the monies as a scholarship or award, since they are based on or driven by non-need factors.

It is equally important to be stalwart and consistent by suspending aid when a family no longer shows eligibility. Often, schools struggle with the notion of denying aid to a family that received it before, even when it is clear that the family no longer qualifies. Some schools "wean" the family off of financial aid over one or two years; others grandfather a family in; still others just continue to approve the aid (particularly if the student has only one or two years left in school). However, schools must recognize that extending their limited resources to those who do not show financial need has an impact on those who do.

PRINCIPLE 8: Using the Same Standards of Behavior and Performance

Since the principles of need-based financial aid center around the critical concept of demonstrated need, this principle emphasizes that the only factor that should matter in assessing aid eligibility is financial need. Students who receive financial aid should not be held to standards of behavior or performance that are more (or less) stringent than those for students who do not receive such support. As noted in our discussion of Principle 7, this is sometimes easier said than done at schools facing pressure on their financial aid budgets.

Nevertheless, it is imperative to resist the urge to expect a higher standard of return simply because a student receives a need-based grant. Clearly, if a student is underperforming or badly behaving in any respect, he or she needs to be either (1) counseled on how to improve and by when, or (2) counseled out of the school by attrition or dismissal. In neither of these cases does the fact that the student receives financial aid come into play.

If the student's behavior is not so bad as to warrant dismissal or denial of re-enrollment, then the student should be given every opportunity to remain enrolled, including extending financial aid if the need is still demonstrated. If a school denies aid because the student is receiving Cs (not low enough to be dismissed but not high enough to make some people regard the aid money as well spent), the student may not be able to stay enrolled. Indeed, it is the need-based grant that enables the student to be there, and as long as he or she meets the same standards as full-pay students, the resources and support must continue on a financial-need basis.

PRINCIPLE 9: The Importance of the Policy Manual

Once (or, better yet, before) a school establishes an aid program, it must recognize that consistency and continuity are essential to the program's long-term effectiveness. To this end, developing written policies and procedures is an important part of good practice. A well-written policy and procedures manual is not just an effective training tool for new staff who are responsible for managing a financial aid program. The manual is also the school's voice in ensuring objective and fair treatment of applicants and a statement of what it finds important when administering aid dollars.

Some of the best examples of effective policy guides are at the McCallie School in Tennessee, Rye Country Day School in New York, and the Oregon Episcopal School. Each is comprehensive in the breadth of topics and policies it covers but also appropriately succinct in describing the policies themselves. Starting with the purpose and goals of the aid programs, these manuals cover important areas such as:

- office timelines and calendars;
- types of aid available;
- special considerations of financial need;
- documentation requirements;
- financial aid committee structures;
- budget and reporting;

- special family situations;
- international students;
- divorced, separated, and unemployed parents;
- business owners;
- merit award policies;
- wait-list approaches;
- appeals process;
- payment plans;
- co-curricular expenses (books, sports equipment, field trips, etc.);
- sample applications and letters;
- glossary of terms;
- other resources available (tuition loans, tuition insurance, etc.);
- and much more.

Although the policy manual is an internal document, it should be written clearly and directly enough to be meaningful to an outsider. In fact, many schools create an external version of the policy manual to share with families and other constituents, if needed.

Of course, the manual should also be considered a living document that must be updated and revised frequently as conditions, funding, staffing, and other circumstances warrant. Developing the policy manual provides an excellent opportunity for a school's leaders to deliberate, discuss, and decide what the policies should be and which procedures and resources are needed to enact them.

Furthermore, an effective manual assures everyone involved that decisions are made according to the institution's rules, not the individual whims or preferences of a particular administrator.

PRINCIPLE 10: Timely Communications

Optimally, schools should send their notices about financial aid decisions and letters of acceptance at the same time. The aim is to give families as much time as possible to evaluate their financial responsibilities and sort out their various options. Sending acceptance letters without the requisite financial aid information is not helpful to families who depend on tuition assistance.

The problem with coordinating the two notices often lies in the struggle to get the necessary documents from families in a timely enough manner to provide a financial aid decision by early to mid-March (if not sooner). The major complication is the receipt of required tax forms. Typical financial aid application deadlines in early January or February fall well before federal tax-filing deadlines (and sometimes before parents receive their W-2 forms).

One common solution is to allow the family to submit the most recently completed tax form even if it's not from the current year. This lets the school make a decision based on the prior-year's facts (since most people's income picture does not change dramatically on a yearly basis). It also provides the opportunity to collect current-year tax forms by April or May. The school has the right to make a preliminary decision and then adjust it if the current form comes in showing income that's significantly different from the amount on which the aid offer was based. But the school must be clear about this "provisional" status and its consequences when allowing applicants to submit tax information from a year other than the current one.

PRINCIPLE 11: Distinguishing Need-based from Non-need-based Aid

The "middle-income family" dilemma has plagued many independent schools around the country for years. Anecdote, observation, and "gut feelings" have created a sense that the middle-class family is being squeezed out of attending NAIS schools. The dilemma is that the families appear (on paper) to be wealthy enough to afford most or all of the cost of attendance. But in reality (based on daily expense experience), when the families are told of their ineligibility for financial aid, they cannot attend. The question that schools then struggle with is "How do we make it possible to help more middle-income families?" One solution some schools consider is offering tuition-assistance programs specifically geared toward middle-income families. The difficulty in doing this is balancing the integrity of a strictly need-based aid program with a more incentive-based program that is not completely based on demonstrated need.

At St. Mark's School of Texas, the middle-income aid program was created to address this dilemma in a way that honors the NAIS principle of distinguishing need-based aid from non-need-based aid. St. Mark's engaged in research to identify the school's self-defined "middle-income family." The school wanted to find out whether any segment of income earners was relatively absent from the student body. The research yielded a specific "St. Mark's Middle-Income Family" group that was under-represented. When families from the middle-income range applied for financial aid, the school would assess a portion (say, 75 percent) of the family contribution derived by the School and Student Service for Financial Aid and fund the adjusted financial need with a "middle-income grant." In this way, the middle-income program operates distinctly from the standard need-based aid program, with separate funding sources and separate (though related) methods for determining eligibility.

This principle touches squarely on guidelines for offering merit awards and tuition-remission benefits. Most schools do not offer merit-based scholarships due to limited funds (only about a quarter of NAIS members reported doing so in 2006-07). It's important to keep these non-need-based dollars separate and distinct in accounting and delivery methods so as not to confuse how much financial aid is truly available for applicant families. Non-need-based grants are given in recognition of some talent or characteristic, not in recognition of inability to pay.

Of course, it's possible to help many needy students with either merit-based awards or some combination of need- and merit-based awards. McCallie School in Tennessee offers a few merit-based scholarships in addition to its need-based program (most of them endowed by outside donors). Its Honors Scholarship Program is a prime example. The Honors Scholarship allows candidates to apply for need-based aid. If a student selected for a scholarship is also eligible for need-based aid, the financial aid will be applied first and then the merit scholarship will be added, up to but not exceeding the full tuition.

Tuition remission is, indeed, a benefit, not a grant, and schools should not include the value of this benefit in reporting financial aid granted. Often, schools provide tuition remission in combination with need-based aid for faculty and staff who qualify for both. That is, a school might offer a 50-percent remission to a faculty member, and the faculty member might apply for need-based aid to help cover the difference. In many schools, faculty and staff are given preference in or exceptions from certain financial aid procedures (such as guaranteeing to meet full need for faculty—when the guarantee for others might be capped at 50 or 75 percent—or getting priority status when available funding is limited).

The intent of the merit aid and tuition-remission guidelines is to encourage schools to be clear about how much money comes from each type of assistance and to emphasize that providing merit-based awards should not detract from the school's ability to provide the most generous need-based aid program possible.

PRINCIPLE 12: Confidentiality

Maintaining families' privacy is essential to making sure they can trust the financial aid process enough to participate with the full disclosure required. Confidentiality doesn't only mean safeguarding personal and financial information (applications, tax forms, etc.). It also extends to the "output" of the process as well (lists of recipients and their grant amounts, public announcements of "financial aid kids," etc.). Most schools do not have work-study programs for students receiving financial aid so that the students don't have to be identified publicly as aid recipients. (However, some schools address this by offering work programs to all students, not just aid recipients.)

To reduce the risk of misusing sensitive family information and financial aid results, many schools limit the number and types of people who serve on financial aid committees. One of the best methods to get the work done while limiting the potential for leaks may be to create a working committee made up only of the director of financial aid, the director of admission, a business officer, and perhaps the head. Committees that include board members, parents, alumni, or other volunteers are better suited for discussing broad financial aid policy and strategies than for assessing individual applications.

Protecting confidentiality in operations doesn't stop with "not telling." A school should take additional security measures, including building in password-protected access to financial aid-related databases and storing documents in lockable filing cabinets or off campus.

One confidentiality dilemma involves deciding whether to provide financial aid workshops despite the risk that some may feel there's a stigma attached to being identified as a "financial aid family." However, it is not a violation of confidentiality to offer families an opportunity to learn more about how to finance the education they seek. Indeed, such sessions are not about disclosing who gets how much financial aid but how the school goes about providing it. When confidentiality concerns trump the school's ability to deliver important information to parents, neither the school nor the families are well served.

PRINCIPLE 13: Collaboration with Other Offices

Confidentiality is essential, and most schools protect it very well. However, schools should not get to the point where the subject of financial aid becomes too taboo to discuss openly or where it jeopardizes Principle 13, which involves supporting collaboration with other offices at a school.

A typical challenge involves policies regarding when and with whom it is appropriate to share lists of financial aid recipients when requested. One common source of such requests is the development office. For example, donors may want to invite recipients of named scholarships to a recognition luncheon. Although many schools bristle at the notion of providing such disclosures, they can be handled with the tact necessary to maintain positive relationships with donors. At McCallie School, the financial aid office provides an agreement through which the student and parent(s) give permission to the school to release general information to a scholarship donor about the student's activities and accomplishments.

Sometimes development officers want to know which families they should avoid soliciting for a specific fund-raising effort. (The reasoning goes that if families are receiving a significant amount of aid, the school should not solicit them since the chances of giving are slim.) However, many financial aid professionals argue that development offices should solicit all families for giving, regardless of their financial aid standing. Also, some financial aid officers prefer providing a list of prospects to the development office instead of sharing financial aid information.

Collaboration extends beyond the tactical considerations noted above to include strategic partnering as well. At schools like Lick-Wilmerding High School in California, Columbus School for Girls in Ohio, and Campbell Hall in California, the financial aid directors and the heads of school work closely to strategize on creative ways to think about affordability, to ensure that the schools meet their goals for socioeconomic diversity, and to highlight success stories that may spur greater investment in financial aid from board members and the community. The financial aid office oversees a piece of the budget that's larger than most other areas (larger, typically, than everything except salaries and benefits). As a result, tactical collaboration must go hand in hand with strategic collaboration to make sure that the financial aid program is as effective as possible.

CASE STUDY *continued from page 65*

PONDERING FINANCIAL AID'S ROLE IN A DIVERSE STUDENT BODY

BUILDING THE AID PROGRAM FROM THE GROUND UP

Brand New School began the task of developing a brand-new financial aid program by articulating its long-term financial aid mission and policy goals: to create socioeconomic diversity by removing financial barriers that accepted and re-enrolling students might face. From this philosophical starting point, grounded in Principle 1, the school defined the parameters of its budget- and policy-setting approaches.

To create a starting point for a reasonable year-one financial aid budget, BNS used objective research about the community at large. The school started by determining the average income of families in its drawing area (within a 15-mile driving radius). Using SSS methodology, the researchers discovered that a family would need to earn $110,000 to be able to manage one full-paying tuition—and that about 70 percent of the families in the drawing radius did indeed earn that much. On average, the remaining 30 percent who qualified for aid would be eligible for approximately $6,200 of the school's $14,500 tuition.

By extension, if 30 percent, or 150, of BNS's enrolled students qualified for aid at this level, the school would need $930,000 to fund its financial aid program. But where would this money come from? How could this affect the school's overall financial position?

To answer these questions, Jane assembled the admission and financial aid director, business manager, development director, and herself. Together, they determined that the school could afford to fund about half of the needed budget ($450,000) in the form of forgone tuition revenue; that endowment income could cover an additional $100,000; and that about $20,000 of the proceeds from annual giving could be earmarked for financial aid grants.

They also agreed to set more ambitious fund-raising goals to support financial aid even as they monitored the evolving need for dollars and the capacity to raise funds for this purpose. For now, they proposed that BNS could deliver on $570,000 of the $930,000 projected budget.

This inter-office collaboration (Principle 13) ensured that all interested and important parties were aware of the goals and resources needed to advance a critical part of the school's mission. It also illuminated the reality that the school would have a limited budget in the short term, which helped prompt a longer-term view of what would be necessary to achieve a fully funded budget (Principles 3 and 4).

The next task was to establish parameters for allocating the aid budget, especially since the budget might be significantly lower than the eventual requests for aid might dictate. They realized that an underfunded budget would mean making a choice between meeting a higher need for fewer students and meeting a lower need for more. Either the target of 30 percent of enrolled students had to go down or the average grant target of $6,200 had to drop.

The school agreed that, since funding was limited, Principles 6, 9, and 11 were the critical ones to implement. Financial aid would be granted according to demonstrated financial need, and the school subscribed to the NAIS SSS program to help ensure objectivity and acquire the training and resources needed to carry out effective decision making.

To develop specific decision-making policies, the school created a financial aid committee consisting of the director of admission and financial aid, the business manager, and the head of school. The committee members used resources available on the NAIS website, information gleaned from Jane's attendance at the NAIS financial aid workshop the prior fall, and queries and conversations on the NAIS listserves.

Then BNS crafted a simple but important policy-and-procedures manual outlining the key considerations for reviewing financial aid applications. The committee made sure that the specific policies lined up with Principles 5, 7, 8, and 12 in particular. As a result, families could be certain that financial aid eligibility did not jeopardize admission status, that the school would not "bait and switch" them with a one-year guarantee of aid, that aid recipients would not be held to different expectations, and that sensitive family and financial information would be handled confidentially. Regarding the last point, the group agreed that only committee members would have access to the students' financial aid files and records, which would be kept in lockable, fireproof filing cabinets and destroyed one year after the student left the school.

"Now that we have a budget and a plan for allocating the aid, how do we let parents know about it?" Jane asked her colleagues.

BNS made a point of including information about the new financial aid program at open houses and created a brochure that it mailed to all current and prospective families. The school revised its admission application and information request card to give families the option of specifying whether they would like to have financial aid information sent to them. Later in the year, the committee members planned to hold a financial aid kick-off meeting to help answer questions or concerns from families who would be going through the process.

Launching the program took a great deal of time and effort and was fraught with a considerable amount of uncertainty. But BNS was able to use the NAIS Principles of Good Practice for Financial Aid Administration to help frame the whys and hows behind the aid program. As a result, the board and staff were able to establish a solid starting point for what they wanted to accomplish and create specific goals to measure the success of their efforts. ■

DISCUSSION QUESTIONS

1. When developing financial aid budget, policy, and strategies, what is the best way to distinguish the board's role versus the staff's role?

2. What kinds of data and other research are important to collect in depicting the school's financial aid reach?

3. How would you describe the optimum relationship between the head of school and the director of financial aid?

4. How can you balance the importance of in-depth strategic discussion about financial aid at the board level with trustees' time constraints?

5. How can all school constituencies learn about the role of financial aid in advancing the school's mission?

6. What should the head and/or director of financial aid do to receive effective training in financial aid administration? Where are the resources for such training?

SUGGESTED RESOURCES AND READING MATERIALS

Research and publications on independent school financial aid practices are in fairly short supply. Nonetheless, there are a few books and journals that can help shed more light on this topic at the K-12 and at the college and university levels.

FOR FURTHER READING, TRY THE FOLLOWING NAIS PUBLICATIONS:

Aiken, H. Peter. *Access and Affordability: Strategic Financial Planning.* This book provides a broad look at independent school finance with discussion around pricing and discounting through financial aid. Washington, DC: NAIS, 1994.

Grace, Catherine O'Neill, Ed. *Marketing Independent Schools in the 21st Century.* This guide covers a wide variety of topics including branding, image development, technology, and market research. It also includes a chapter on trends and issues in affordability and their bearing on a school's marketing strategies. Washington, DC: NAIS, 2001.

Jamison, Patricia P., and Rachel Countryman. *Financial Aid Administration for Schools.* This manual offers a broad look at the topics and issues all financial aid administrators need to consider in managing their financial aid office. Washington, DC: NAIS, 1999.

OTHER READING INCLUDES:

Publications from the National Association of Student Financial Aid Administrators
(www.nasfaa.org)

Although written for the higher education community, these publications often have articles of interest and applicability for independent school administrators. Though rare, some independent school administrators join NASFAA for access to publications, resources, and some training opportunities. Note that the following publications are available only to NASFAA members:

*   *Student Aid Transcript.* Published quarterly, NASFAA's official magazine contains articles that help shed light on practices and procedures of college-level financial aid offices. Visit *www.nasfaa.org/publications/2006/ transcript/vol17n1/indexv17n1.html.*

*   *Journal of Student Financial Aid.* NASFAA's journal presents mostly research-based articles and essays on a variety of financial aid issues and topics. Visit *www.nasfaa.org/Annualpubs/Journal/vol36N1/ index36n1.html.*

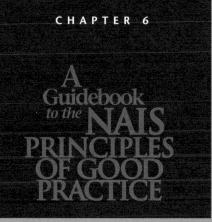

CHAPTER 6

A Guidebook to the NAIS PRINCIPLES OF GOOD PRACTICE

for

FUND RAISING

By Travis J. Tysinger

Travis J. Tysinger is senior development officer and director of planned giving at Woodberry Forest School in Woodberry Forest, Virginia. Woodberry Forest is a boarding school with 400 boys in grades 9-12.

NAIS PRINCIPLES OF GOOD PRACTICE for

FUND RAISING

Revised and approved by the NAIS board in 2006

The advancement program of the school should exemplify the best qualities of the institution and reflect the highest standards of personal and professional conduct. The following Principles of Good Practice are addressed to those involved in the school's advancement operation, including trustees, school heads, development and alumni/ae officers and staff, volunteers, consultants, and business officers. (Although many of the principles apply to this case study, the ones in **boldface** are the most pertinent.)

1. **The school establishes a well-constructed development plan to guide its fund-raising activities.**

2. The school is mindful and respectful of the cultural and economic diversity of constituent supporters.

3. The school accepts only gifts that support its mission, character, integrity, and independence.

4. The school understands that accepting a gift is accepting the obligation to honor the donor's intent.

5. **The school advocates stewardship (preserving and growing the resources of the school), as well as nurtures, appreciates, and sustains an ongoing healthy and effective relationship with its constituents.**

6. The school clearly articulates roles and responsibilities for volunteers.

7. **The school safeguards its constituents' privacy and all confidential information.**

8. The school encourages donors to consult with their own professional tax advisers when making charitable gifts.

9. The school complies with all provisions of the United States Tax Code that affect charitable giving.

10. **The school, as appropriate, discloses to its constituents gifts received through philanthropy.**

11. To ensure financial sustainability, the school makes certain that income earned from endowment is spent wisely and equitably. In doing so, the school ensures that endowments maintain their real value over the years so that future generations benefit as much or more from endowment as current and past generations.

12. The school adheres to accepted standards concerning the management and reporting of gift revenues and fund-raising expenditures, and seeks to promote the profession by sharing its data with relevant professional organizations, such as the Council for Advancement and Support of Education (CASE), Council for Aid to Education (CAE), and NAIS.

CASE STUDY
A CRISIS TESTS BOTH TRUSTEES AND FUND RAISERS

Founded in 1938, Mountain Heights Academy has enjoyed steady growth and progress; maintained a history of solid, if unimaginative, leadership; and garnered adequate support over the years. It's a nondenominational, co-educational K-12 day school of 575 students, situated in a reasonably diverse, economically viable city of 200,000 people.

Shortly after concluding a comprehensive long-range plan that identified the program's most recognized strengths and critical needs, the school's much-respected head of 13 years was diagnosed with a terminal illness and forced to retire. A vibrant and well-credentialed new head was hired soon after. But after just five months, he was charged with shoplifting in a local department store. So the board of trustees determined that his appointment had to be terminated.

Clearly, this situation presented Mountain Heights with many challenges. But none were more pivotal than those placed upon the school's governing board and development office. Although fund raising seemed a distant consideration at this critical moment, the school's legitimate financial needs could hardly be put on hold. How would the trustees and development staff respond to this challenge? How could they keep this vital component of the school's program on track during a period of great uncertainty?

At such a pivotal time, it is vital to maintain focus, and institutional focus must always be driven by the institution's mission statement. The mission statement of MHA is brief but compelling:

It is the mission of Mountain Heights Academy to provide a secure, supportive, and stimulating educational environment, where intellectual curiosity is encouraged; where diversity, civility, and cooperation are honored; and where moral integrity is an imperative. Students are encouraged to be active in every area of school life—athletic, artistic, and extracurricular—to respect things spiritual, and to explore avenues of service to their fellow human beings, both in their own communities and beyond.

At such a time, it is also wise to revisit the NAIS Principles of Good Practice for Fund Raising. The principles proved helpful in guiding both John, the head of the board's development committee, and Ian, Mountain Heights' director of development.

The board's first steps

Immediately after the new head's arrest, the board met to formulate plans to convey the decision to terminate him to the school family. The board president, Jay, was careful to be objective and professional with his remarks. The trustees fashioned two messages: the first for the faculty and student body, and a second for all other constituents. The board also named an ad hoc administrative team and a subcommittee to renew the search process for a head of school.

The next step was to strengthen the administrative team. John, the development committee chair, was a recently retired college vice president for external affairs who remained well connected to higher education. He had a close friend, Cassandra, who had recently stepped down as dean of the school of education at a nearby university. Earlier in her career, Cassandra had headed the upper school division of a fine day school in the state's capital city. Knowing that Cassandra was now on sabbatical, John—with Jay's blessing—called to ask if she might be willing to serve on Mountain Heights' interim administrative committee. After meeting with John, she agreed to visit the campus and, at the end of that day, tentatively agreed to serve as an ad hoc member of the interim committee.

At the same time, John turned his attention to Mountain Heights' development office, which had existed since the 1960s and now had four staff members.

The office's principal initiative was the annual fund, which employed the club-level system of recognition and used the slogan "Sustaining the Mission." Its other major fund-raising efforts had been two modest capital campaigns. It had no formal planned giving program, although the staff had made sporadic attempts to educate its constituency about the basic planned gift options, and the school had been pleasantly surprised by several generous estate gifts over the years. The biannual alumni magazine, the *Spotlight,* was the only publication aimed at external constituents.

The office had done an excellent job of keeping up with its graduates and past parents, and many constituents came to view Mountain Heights as an extension of their family. It helped that Ian, the development director, was an admired and capable former classroom teacher who kept things running smoothly.

John and Ian worked together to form several development office strategies for the near term, including:

- **Bring major donors and key volunteers into the inner circle.** John knew it was crucial to meet with key donors and volunteers as quickly as possible, both to dispel half-truths and to personally assure these friends that the board was moving quickly to stabilize the school's leadership and daily operation. Once these best-connected constituents were well informed, they would provide the school with an influential second tier of goodwill ambassadors.

  By empowering these good friends with the truth from Day One, and by personally asking for their thoughts going forward, the school also made them partners in the ultimate resolution of this challenging situation. This is where Ian proved his great worth. Because of his knowledge of the school's donor family and his reputation for integrity and good judgment, he was able to accompany various trustees on their personal visits with these faithful friends, which sped up the process of transforming an atmosphere of crisis into one of expectation.

- **Keep the school's annual fund on track.** The news of the head's termination put everything else on the back burner. In December—the month when Mountain Heights usually received almost 40 percent of its annual fund support—gifts dropped off dramatically. To make things worse, many of the gifts that did come in were not acknowledged.

  Because Ian had to be away from school so often and on such short notice, he called on his assistant, Beth, to bring the annual fund back on track. Working with key volunteers, she moved quickly to acknowledge all gifts.

CASE STUDY
A CRISIS TESTS BOTH TRUSTEES AND FUND RAISERS

Along with the gift receipts, she included a special printed thank-you note from the chair of the board. She also gave class agents specially drafted material to use with their notes to their classmates. Similar enclosures were included with the thank-yous signed by chairs of the annual fund drives for parents and grandparents.

Ian and John decided that if the annual fund was not back on track by mid-April of the next year, the development office would try to enlist a challenge grant from one of the school's key donors.

- **Enhance the external publication.** As she took on her new responsibilities, Beth's energy and creativity seemed boundless. For some time, she had wanted to revamp the alumni magazine's format and broaden the topics it covered. Now the time was right. She planned feature stories focusing on program excellence and the school's many accomplished graduates. She also wanted *Spotlight* coverage to include parents and grandparents. Working with a senior faculty member who taught 12th-grade honors English, she initiated these changes and assigned students from the honors class to do research and write for the magazine.

As dedicated and hard-working as the development staff members were, they still confronted several urgent questions. How would the school's next leader affect their fund-raising efforts? And until that leader was found, how could staff members maintain donor confidence even as they undertook new initiatives to sustain financial support—or, better yet, help that support grow?

To be continued....

EXEMPLARY APPLICATIONS OF GOOD PRACTICE

EXAMPLE 1: Graduates from Long Ago Rise to a Challenge
(Relates to Fund-raising Principles 1 and 5)

Contributed by Chip Spencer, retired director of development and director of planned giving at the Taft School in Connecticut

The capital campaign the Taft School launched in the early '90s started off well, with major commitments from trustees and a number of other leadership-level donors. Soon we were more than halfway toward our ambitious goal of $75 million—by far the largest in the school's history. Then, about halfway through the second year, things slowed down.

For many years prior to this campaign, we had followed the "rifle shot" approach, raising capital funds annually from a small group of selected prospects. Though these efforts were successful, they failed to cultivate the rest of our constituents or to educate them about the school's ongoing needs. One group that needed more work was our older graduates. They had been at the school long before co-education, and many of the program and facility improvements seemed to have caused something of a disconnect. How could we re-energize this vital segment of constituents and motivate them to give— and give generously?

The answer came when an alumnus from the Class of 1935 agreed to make a $5 million gift. We asked him to offer this as a challenge gift targeted at our oldest alumni— up through the Class of 1940, the years that encompassed the tenure of our founder and first headmaster.

The challenge was outlined in a special brochure geared toward our older alumni. It contained a primer on planned giving along with sample gift illustrations. Gifts from alumni in these classes were to be matched dollar for dollar up to $5 million. In addition to cash gifts, the match was to include various planned gifts, which we agreed to count at their full face value.

The challenge captured the attention of the older alumni. It also gave the director of planned giving an excellent talking point and another reason to call on these constituents. As before, our first ask was for an outright gift, but a planned gift could be an alternative or addition to the outright gift. Interestingly, many alumni contributors to the challenge had never been regular donors. They viewed this as a one-shot opportunity to participate in the school's biggest-ever campaign as well as to double their gift.

The overall capital campaign went extraordinarily well. We reached the $75-million goal three years ahead of schedule. When we closed the books after five years, the total was $134 million! The challenge raised more than $15 million—three times the original goal. The challenger was so pleased that he supplemented his original $5 million gift in his estate plan.

Is a challenge a gimmick? To a certain extent, yes. But it energizes prospects while it gives a solicitor an additional talking point to couple with the overall campaign goal of enhancing a school that has added greatly to graduates' lives. Additionally, a challenge can be restricted to smaller groups, such as a reunion class or first-time donors in younger classes. A school that tries a challenge will almost certainly be pleasantly surprised.

EXAMPLE 2: **Recent Graduates Respond to Tailored Techniques**
(Relates to Fund-raising Principles 1 and 5)

Contributed by Cathy Coleman, director of development at the Westminster Schools in Atlanta

After graduating, alumni go off to college for adventures in a great new phase of life. The here-and-now becomes so much fun, so complicated, and so absorbing that alma mater often becomes an afterthought.

As elusive as they are, young alumni are vital to overall alumni participation rates. So we have redoubled our efforts to engage them with the following multifaceted approach.

- **Segment them.** It may seem obvious, but we don't communicate with or solicit recent graduates in the same way we do our older alumni. Messages must be short, catchy, and clever to get their attention. We consult with young people the same age about what to say and how to say it, because if our ideas of "cool" are very different from theirs, our messages could fall flat.

- **Find them.** This is the biggest challenge. Often a college postal address is ineffective. Mail sent to a parent's address rarely gets forwarded and, even if students see it when they get home, paying attention to it may not make their to-do list. So we find it essential to get e-mail addresses, which, unlike housing addresses, students usually keep throughout college and sometimes beyond. We try to get e-mail addresses during the summer before they leave for college. E-mail with a link to our giving page has the added benefit of prompting students to make a gift right then, while it's on their minds.

- **Time carefully.** It's often easier to reach recent graduates during the summer and school holidays, when young alumni are more likely to be at home. We also send postal mail and do targeted phonathons during those times. If we plan special on-campus events for this age group, we hold those during school vacations as well.

- **Try different media.** We invest in videos or slide-style presentations to send to young alumni at school via e-mail. We fill these with images of campus, their teachers, and sports/arts activities; use a current senior to do any narration; and choose meaningful music, such as school groups playing or singing the alma mater or special songs. At the end, we ask for a gift that supports the people and activities they just saw or heard.

- **Keep their budgets in mind.** All college-age alumni are broke. So, over and over, we emphasize that what matters is not how big a gift is. The important thing is to make a gift as an affirmation of their school, their teachers, and their teams. To help them relate to a reasonably sized gift, we've sent messages in the shape of a pizza with a request that they forgo a pizza and, instead, send the cost of it to the school. Or we ask them to reach in their wallets at that moment and send what they have to the school. Many actually do it!

- **Make it personal.** Our greatest success comes from asking young alumni to give in honor of their favorite teacher. This makes the giving process real to budding philanthropists. We then let each teacher know that a former student made a donation in his or her honor and provide the teacher with the student's e-mail address. This circle of affection not only fosters stewardship but also builds a relationship that becomes the foundation for ever-greater involvement.

EXAMPLE 3: A School Reforms Its Endowment Reporting Process
(Relates to Fund-raising Principles 3 and 5)

Contributed by Joe Flynn, assistant head and chief development officer at Woodberry Forest School in Virginia

"What is the value of the endowed fund my family established a number of years ago, and how much income is it generating annually for the financial aid program?" the donor inquired shortly after my arrival at the school. The donor was a major benefactor of our program and a savvy philanthropist. As I soon discovered, he had asked the question before without receiving a prompt response. Other organizations to which he had made endowment gifts sent him regular reports. Our institution was suffering by comparison.

His question was simple and straightforward. Finding the answer was more complicated. The inquiry led me to the school's vice president of finance. Although we had a $40-million endowment and scores of named endowed funds, our endowment reporting was sporadic and reactive. Only when a donor asked did we run the calculations and share the information with the donor.

Recognizing a need to build the school's endowment reporting and stewardship, the development and business offices worked together to create policies and implement procedures for processing and sending regular donor reports. The process was neither easy nor quick, and it required fundamental changes to the accounting system. These changes permitted the allocation of investment returns to individual funds as well as the tracking of annual spending from these funds.

At this school, like most other educational institutions, the majority of endowed gifts are restricted for specific purposes (such as financial aid, faculty enrichment, and program support). Cultivating and maintaining relationships with these donors requires substantial time. In addition, the cost of this tailored reporting is considerable. Time will tell if the labor and dollars devoted to this reporting initiative will have a widespread impact on our institution's fund-raising efforts, but the initial results have been encouraging. Donors who have received reports on their funds responded favorably, and, in more than one instance, reporting has helped us rekindle a dormant relationship.

CASE STUDY *continued from page 88*

A CRISIS TESTS BOTH TRUSTEES AND FUND RAISERS

MOVING FORWARD ON ALL FRONTS

Although Cassandra's presence on the Mountain Heights administrative committee was somewhat awkward at first, she had such an understated and thoughtful manner that she quickly became an integral part of the group. Her influence on the committee, and on the entire school community, was felt and appreciated.

In the weeks after Christmas, the interim administrative team worked to keep daily operations on track. Meanwhile, the head search committee moved forward under the leadership of the board vice president, Kim. Because of the shortened timeline, the group had agreed to use a head search consultant, but the preliminary list of candidates he submitted to the committee was not promising. As the weeks sped on, Jay became increasingly concerned about the search process timeline.

A solution occurred to Kim and quickly spread throughout the search committee. They should hire an interim head: Cassandra. Taken by surprise, Cassandra felt both flattered and conflicted by the offer. She really had enjoyed working in her advisory capacity at Mountain Heights, but her sabbatical would soon end, and she had a job to return to.

The next day Cassandra called her former faculty adviser from graduate school. "You'll be professionally stimulated in either role," she told Cassandra. "Ask yourself where you will have the greatest positive impact, be certain that you have a passion for the task you choose, and then go with your heart."

Cassandra returned to Mountain Heights for an upper school faculty meeting on Monday. At the end of the meeting, a young first-year teacher came up to her and said, "I just want you to know that in the opening months of classes, I wasn't at all sure that teaching was for me. But the recent mentoring sessions you conducted for new faculty have helped me feel increasingly connected to my students and to their progress. I still have a lot to learn, but I feel really good about my work, and I am grateful for your help."

The following Monday, Cassandra called to ask the president of her university for a leave of absence for the remainder of the academic year. That evening, she called Jay to say she would like to be the interim head of Mountain Heights.

Carpe diem: Planning to take action

Having named a highly capable interim school head, the board and administration focused on an important question: Which program issues and initiatives should they undertake in this interim period, and which policy decisions should they leave to the school's next permanent head?

Both Cassandra and the board agreed that a number of vital initiatives could be advanced now. Even so, she was determined to keep the focus on the program, not her, and to restrict her role to more of a facilitator than a creator.

They agreed on another point as well. Although the administrative and program-oriented initiatives should be diverse enough to attract a broad cross-section of interest and support, the initiatives should not be so numerous as to seem random or fractured.

CASE STUDY
A CRISIS TESTS BOTH TRUSTEES AND FUND RAISERS

To Ian's delight, Cassandra was keenly aware of the vital role that development plays in independent education. Although she confessed to a lack of knowledge regarding the specifics of the development art, she expressed determination to be a key player in moving Mountain Heights' development efforts forward.

"Once you've identified specific donor prospects for a board-approved program need, count on me to make any calls necessary," Cassandra told Ian. "Give me as much notice as possible, prepare for me a one-page overview on the prospect and what we are seeking from the call, and tell me what part you want me to play." She was eager to learn the "art of asking."

This was a development director's dream. Just hearing her express this kind of support gave Ian the courage to dust off ideas he had been considering for some time. Specifically, he wanted to focus more creatively on the annual fund, capital and endowment giving, and planned giving. Although these were the most basic areas of the development art, his knowledge of the Mountain Heights family persuaded him that this trying time in the life of the school might actually create an opportunity to improve a well-entrenched development program. He also wanted the Mountain Heights community to begin thinking about the school's long-term financial strength.

Among the specific development initiatives Ian had in mind:

Introducing new annual fund gift clubs. The last time the annual fund had added an upper-level gift club was in 1988, when the $1,000-plus Founders Circle was instituted. That gift club now numbered more than 350. Ian and John agreed that it was time to move the Founders Circle to the $2,500 level. Although the new level would not become official until fall, several members of the Development Committee increased their gifts to that level right away. Soon, most members of the board increased their gifts as well, giving the annual fund an immediate boost.

Increasing alumni participation. As is typical with day schools, parent participation had always been strong at Mountain Heights. Grandparent giving was also a good source of support, but it dropped off dramatically once the grandchildren left the school. Alumni participation was respectable —around 30 percent—but given the fondness most graduates professed for MHA, Ian felt it should be much higher.

Occasional annual fund challenge grants seemed to create only temporary improvement and often diverted funds that might be better used for critical capital needs. In addition, Mountain Heights had only a few donors capable of donating a big enough challenge gift to make a real difference.

But what if Mountain Heights created a special permanent gift club called the Challengers? As Ian envisioned it, the Challengers would pledge a set number of dollars (over and above their normal annual fund gift) for each percentage point of participation that alumni reached beyond a designated benchmark. Challengers did not have to be super-wealthy. One might pledge $50 for every percentage point of participation above the goal while another pledged $2,500. Each year the development committee could recruit a different group of challengers to spread the responsibility around. If successful, this challenge idea might push participation to the 35- or 40-percent level, giving the school that many more donors who had formed the habit of giving annually. John liked the idea and asked Ian to present a simplified version of the proposal to the entire committee.

Taking a fresh look at reunions. Homecoming weekend reunions at Mountain Heights were all-class affairs—not particularly difficult to orchestrate, but not terribly effective for fund raising. Ian knew that other schools used reunions as a major giving opportunity. However, because his staff was already stretched thin, he decided to focus initially on just three key classes: the 25th-, 40th-, and 50th-anniversary years. He and Beth would personally select the steering committees for these classes and ask the committee members to not only adopt a stretch goal but to make their own lead gifts toward that goal.

To increase interest, the school would invite these selected classes back to campus a day early as honored guests at a gala reception and dinner. In state-of-the-school remarks, the head would detail the MHA program, its needs, and their opportunities to play a part. The talk was not to be a heavy-handed solicitation but a thorough

and unapologetic picture of what it would take to make Mountain Heights' future as noble and productive as its past.

Revisiting planned giving. Since Ian had neither the time nor the expertise to launch a full-blown planned giving program, he and John agreed they would emphasize bequests. But unlike previous attempts, this time around the staff would give the planned giving initiative greater focus and follow-through. After Ian and John fleshed out the basic strategy for this initiative, the development committee lent its enthusiastic endorsement.

Among the steps: an article in *Spotlight* on what bequests had meant to MHA, and a concerted effort to identify constituents who had made a provision for the school in their estate plans. These constituents would become charter members of a new recognition society named for the school's earliest known bequest benefactor, Eleanor Chesterfield Leland. John vowed to be the first charter member of the Leland Society, and he pledged to recruit other board members as well.

Auditing the development office. Ian knew the development office needed additional staffing, but he also knew he would have to build a strong case for it. John agreed with Ian that a departmental audit was in order, especially since the school would almost certainly go into a full-blown capital campaign as soon as the new head came on board.

The development committee endorsed the audit idea, but the problem was money. Fortunately, a former board member who had recently sold a family business expressed interest in funding the

CASE STUDY
A CRISIS TESTS BOTH TRUSTEES AND FUND RAISERS

project. She ultimately committed $25,000—which Ian felt might pay for the consultant's fees for the audit plus an assessment of the new development initiatives.

The audit took almost a month. It included one-on-one interviews with staff followed by a review of existing programs, proposed initiatives, and the office's support systems. The final report had two principal recommendations.

1. The school's website needed a major overhaul to permit online admissions applications, reunion registration, and so on. In addition—and this would be key going forward—the school needed the capacity to solicit and process online gifts in a way that was simpler and more transparent.

2. The department needed additional staff. The consultant suggested adding a full-time position in support of annual giving, creating a half-time position to support the website, and contracting with a firm to manage the website. To free up Ian to concentrate on major gifts and learn more about planned giving, the report suggested giving Beth more responsibility, particularly for the annual fund and external publications.

The consultant endorsed each of the other development initiatives Ian and John had outlined. While she shared John's hope that the Challenger program could be packaged in the simplest possible format, she very much liked the concept.

Progress with the new head of school

Although head search procedures remain more an art than a science, they must also be thorough and deliberate. In the process, timelines often get stretched, scheduling conflicts occur, and search committees have to face the fact that no candidate ever has all the strengths they seek. This was the case with Mountain Heights' search as well, and time was definitely not on the committee's side.

Nevertheless, by early March, most conversations around the school were not about the search committee's progress but about the school's progress under Cassandra's leadership. When the March meeting of the search committee was called to order, John surprised his colleagues by saying, "I think we already have our new head of school, and I think it's Cassandra. When have we ever seen the school healthier or happier? I would like to move that we ask her to be our new head."

After a brief moment of stunned reflection, the committee agreed by acclamation to offer the headship to Cassandra.

Some things seem meant to be. Before John could set up a meeting with Cassandra, she called him. "I realize this may seem off the wall," she said, "but I would like to be considered as a candidate to head Mountain Heights. I have come to love MHA, its people, and its mission. So much of what I have studied and taught and dreamed about seems to be coming together in the work of this fine faculty and staff. The value of the school is not just in the outstanding product it produces. The true value of Mountain Heights' program is its process, and it is the challenge of continuing to refine this vital process that so intrigues me."

This news made its way to the school family as if by magic, and the entire community seemed to respond with a collective sigh of relief. In the months that followed, Cassandra organized her administrative team and began to meet with every constituency. She was officially installed as Mountain Heights Academy's seventh head of school at the May board meeting. At that same meeting, the board approved additions to the development staff and the hiring of outside fund-raising counsel to help position MHA for a major capital campaign.

The challenges were great, but the leadership of Mountain Heights Academy had never been stronger—and the alumni, parents, past parents, and friends of MHA had never been prouder of their school. ∎

DISCUSSION QUESTIONS

1. What, in your opinion, are the unaddressed stumbling blocks that the Mountain Heights development office will face during the period this case covers?
2. Would you have chosen to emphasize different development initiatives? If so, what would you do differently?
3. List, in priority order, the constituents you would take Cassandra to visit if she were your new head of school.
4. Write an introductory paragraph for a letter of invitation to all former trustees of Mountain Heights Academy, enlisting their membership in the school's new bequest society.
5. What three pieces of advice would you give to a new head of school who came to the task as Cassandra did?
6. What would be the ideal composition of Mountain Heights' capital campaign steering committee?

SUGGESTED RESOURCES AND READING MATERIALS

BOOKS AND E-PUBLICATIONS

ADVANCEMENT MANAGEMENT

Buchanan, Peter McE., ed. *Handbook of Institutional Advancement.* Washington, DC: Council for Advancement and Support of Education (CASE), 2000.

Phair, Judith, and Roland King. *Organizational Charts and Job Descriptions for the Advancement Office.* Washington, DC: CASE, 1998.

ALUMNI RELATIONS

Alumni Administration (selected chapters from CASE's *Handbook of Institutional Advancement* in electronic format). Washington, DC: CASE e-publications, 2004.

Taylor, Gordy, and Cathy Onion. *Alumni Relations: Launching Your Program.* Washington, DC: CASE, 1999.

COMMUNICATIONS AND MARKETING`

Harris, April. *Etiquette and Protocol: A Guide for Campus Events.* Washington, DC: CASE Books, 1999.

Harris, April. *Special Events: Planning for Success.* Washington, DC: CASE, 1998.

Sevier, Robert A. *An Integrated Marketing Workbook for Colleges and Universities: A Step-by-Step Planning Guide.* Hiawatha, IA: Strategy Publishing, 2003.

DEVELOPMENT

Ashton, Debra. *The Complete Guide to Planned Giving.* Mansfield, OH: Atlas Books, 2004.

CASE Report of Educational Fund-raising Campaigns: 2004-2005. Washington, DC: CASE e-publications, 2006.

Colson, Helen A. *Philanthropy at Independent Schools.* Washington, DC: NAIS, 2002.

Craig, Donald E., Johanne E. Hall, and Royster Hedgepeth. *Askophobia: A Guide for Anxious Fund-Raising Volunteers.* Washington, DC: CASE, 1991.

Elliott, Deni, ed. *The Ethics of Asking: Dilemmas in Higher Education Fund Raising.* Baltimore, MD: Johns Hopkins University Press, 1995.

Independent School Advancement series (electronic format): *www.case.org/Publications/ Detail.cfm?ProductID=3100.* Washington, DC: CASE e-publications, 2005.

Kihlstedt, Andrea. *Capital Campaigns: Strategies That Work.* Sudbury, MA: Jones and Bartlett, 2002.

Management and Reporting Standards: Standards for Annual Giving and Campaigns in Educational Fund Raising. Washington, DC: CASE Books, 2004.

Matheny, Richard E. *Major Gifts: Solicitation Strategies.* Washington, DC: CASE, 1999.

Prince, Russ Alan, and Karen Maru File. *The Seven Faces of Philanthropy: A New Approach to Cultivating Major Donors.* San Francisco, CA: Jossey-Bass, 2001.

Rosso, Henry A. *Achieving Excellence in Fundraising.* San Francisco, CA: Jossey-Bass, 1991.

Savage, Tracy G., et al. *Donor Relations: The Essential Guide to Stewardship Policies, Procedures, and Protocol.* Washington DC: CASE, 1999.

Schroeder, Fritz W. *Annual Giving: A Practical Approach.* Washington, DC: CASE Books, 2000.

Seymour, Harold J. *Designs for Fund-Raising: Principles, Patterns, Techniques.* Farmington Hills, MI: Taft Group, 1992.

Worth, Michael J. *New Strategies for Educational Fund Raising.* Washington, DC: ACE/Praeger, 2002.

MISCELLANEOUS

Collier, Charles W. *Wealth in Families.* Cambridge, MA: Harvard University Press, 2006.

Drucker, Peter. *Managing the Nonprofit Organization.* New York, NY: Harper Collins, 1992.

Geever, Jane. *The Foundation Center's Guide to Proposal Writing.* Washington, DC: The Foundation Center, 2004.

Hesselbein, Frances, Marshall Goldsmith, and Richard Beckhard, eds. *The Leader of the Future: New Visions, Strategies, and Practices for the Next Era.* San Francisco, CA: Jossey-Bass Books, 1997.

Hesselbein, Frances, Marshall Goldsmith, and Richard Beckhard, eds. *The Organization of the Future.* San Francisco, CA: Jossey-Bass, 2000.

ORGANIZATIONS

BoardSource, *www.boardsource.org*

Council for Advancement and Support of Education, *www.case.org*

Indiana University Center on Philanthropy, *www.philanthropy.iupui.edu/*

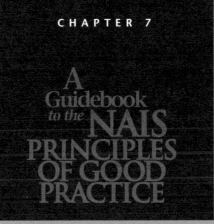

CHAPTER 7

A Guidebook
to the NAIS
PRINCIPLES
OF GOOD
PRACTICE

for

HEADS OF SCHOOLS

By Patricia T. Hayot

Patricia T. Hayot *is head of school at the Chapin*
School in New York City, which has 650 girls in
kindergarten through 12th grade.

NAIS PRINCIPLES OF GOOD PRACTICE for

HEADS OF SCHOOLS

Revised and approved by the NAIS board in 2003

The primary responsibility of the head of an independent school is to carry out the school's stated mission. While there are profoundly different ways to accomplish this goal, NAIS offers the following principles as guideposts for all heads engaged in this rewarding, complex job. (Although many of the principles apply to this case study, the ones in **boldface** are the most pertinent.)

1. The head works in partnership with the board of trustees to establish and refine the school's mission; articulates the mission to all constituencies—students, faculty and staff, parents, alumni/ae, and the community; and supports the mission in working with all constituencies.

2. The head oversees the shaping of the school's program and the quality of life in the school community.

3. **The head establishes an effective manner of leadership and appropriately involves members of the administration and faculty in decision-making.**

4. The head is responsible for attracting, retaining, developing, and evaluating qualified faculty and staff.

5. **The head is accessible, within reason, and communicates effectively with all constituencies.**

6. The head is responsible for financial management, maintenance of the physical plant, strategic planning, and fund raising.

7. **The head ensures that every element of school life reflects the principles of equity, justice, and the dignity of each individual.**

8. The head is alert to his or her role within the broader networks of schools, school leaders, and the community.

9. The head cooperates with heads of other independent schools to ensure that the principles of good practice of all school operations, especially those of admission, marketing, faculty recruitment, and fund raising, demonstrate integrity at all levels of the school.

CASE STUDY
AN ALTERNATIVE PAPER ROILS THE COMMUNITY

One extraordinary morning at the Elliot Academy, an alternative student newspaper appeared in upper-school classrooms, faculty workrooms, offices, and the assembly hall. The alternative paper blasted the existing (and award-winning) student paper as "an instrument of the administration"—one that failed to give voice either to the real concerns of the students and community or to global concerns. The established paper was accused of being out of touch with issues facing the school, out of date by the time it was published, and hampered by the watchful eyes of faculty and administration.

The alternative paper was not signed. Nor did it give any indication of whether its author was a current student or even associated, directly or indirectly, with the school.

The Elliot Academy community felt collective pride in the century-old institution, which enjoyed a reputation for placing equal value on academic rigor and core values that guided decision-making, curriculum, and programs beyond the classroom. Visitors and new faculty alike marveled at how consistently the message echoed from the youngest grades to those in the graduating class: *Academic excellence and respect for one another have defined the learning community for many decades and are central to the school's programs and practices.*

The first edition of the alternative paper, therefore, engendered enormous controversy among students and concern among the upper school faculty and administration. The student newspaper staff felt attacked but confused about how to respond. Some upper school students expressed dismay that the paper was not signed; others claimed that the publication did indeed point up some authentic concerns about the lack of vibrancy in student-community dialogue.

Because there was no way to determine who was responsible for the paper, the faculty and administration, including the head of school, adopted a wait-and-see attitude.

As the week unfolded, two further editions appeared, still unsigned. Both editions seemed to respond to criticisms that swirled about the school that the first edition was poorly written and edited and its arguments were sophomoric and emotional. The fact that the subsequent editions contained fewer grammatical errors and presented opinions more thoughtfully led to a shift of opinion among some students. Some were now prepared to support the "ghost writer" in his or her effort to raise issues that would gain the attention of the adults in the community.

A growing sympathy for the publisher roused the indignation of the students when the head of school, upper school director, and faculty advisers interviewed several assumed editor(s); the students felt that the interview subjects were being harassed and embarrassed. The fact that an investigation was underway became, for some students, a *cause célèbre.*

As always, the head of school found the NAIS Principles of Good Practice helpful in developing a response plan. In this case, the principles for school heads provided a strong reminder of the value of open, transparent community dialogue. Recognizing also that "respect for all" is a central tenet of the Elliot Academy's community, the head invited a representative group of students to discuss their views and share their concerns with her and the director of the upper school. The students wanted to be reassured that the administration would maintain confidentiality and discretion during all student conversations.

With the publication of the fourth edition of the alternative paper, the editor—a current upper school student—finally stepped forward and acknowledged her role to the head of school. Emotions ran high among both students and faculty as they waited in anticipation to see how events would unfold.

To be continued....

EXEMPLARY APPLICATION OF GOOD PRACTICE

EXAMPLE: A Board Crosses the Line
(Relates to School Head Principles 1, 2, 4, and 5)

A recently founded school in a thriving urban center represented the hopes and dreams of parents who could not find an appropriate school for their children. A group of families had worked tirelessly for years to secure a site for the facility, to raise funds, to attend to the extensive legal work required of all new schools, and to build awareness in the community of the academy's mission.

The head of the new school was charged with hiring the faculty and, with faculty participation, developing the curriculum. The founding parents applied for 501(c)(3) nonprofit status and appointed themselves members of the board of trustees.

The first three years presented many challenges, such as a lower-than-anticipated enrollment, higher expenses, and some founding parents who believed it was both their responsibility and their obligation to challenge the head's decisions about hires and programs, as well as admissions practices. These blurred lines between the head and trustees generated tremendous angst among members of the small faculty. Several indicated they would be leaving by the end of the third year because of what they perceived as an inappropriate level of involvement by board parents.

The head expressed her growing concern about faculty morale to members of the executive committee. After listening patiently, most concluded the head's concerns were ill founded and somewhat overstated. They encouraged her to be patient and understand that the board's intentions were honorable and appropriate, given the level of dedication and sacrifice the board members had demonstrated in those challenging, nascent times.

As the months unfolded, tensions increased. The proverbial last straw, however, was not a major crisis but an issue concerning the academy's Appropriate Technology Use Policy, which both parents and students had been required to sign at the beginning of the year. Included in the policy was a provision about the way families should use e-mail to communicate with the faculty:

> The use of e-mail by parents in communicating with faculty or staff should be limited to emergency situations or to conveying information that will help us in our work with your child(ren). It should not be used for philosophical discussions concerning programs or school policy. Parents are urged to make an appointment with the appropriate professionals so that our commitment to thoughtful home-school partnership and dialogue is realized.

On several occasions, one founding trustee-parent used e-mail to express his outrage to a teacher about discipline issues involving his child. The second time, he followed up with an e-mail copied to the head and board chair because, as his message explained, five hours had passed without a reply from the teacher. The head conferred with the board chair who, after reflection, was loath to intervene because the parent in question was the school's single largest donor.

The head thus decided to meet with both the trustee-parent and the teacher. Believing that the chair might disapprove of, or even forbid, such a meeting, the head didn't tell the board chair; seeking forgiveness in this case seemed more prudent than asking permission. The head also believed the teaching staff had every right to expect her to support the core values of the school and to express her respect for the faculty. Refusing to confront the situation would itself represent a decision—one at odds with her own definition of her responsibilities as the educational leader of the school.

The head opened the meeting by presenting the conflict's history from various perspectives: the parent's, the teacher's, and her own. She then invited the trustee-parent to explain his view. The parent expressed his outrage at being "called into the principal's office to be raked over the coals in front of his child's teacher, who, like the head of school, was an employee of the board." He said he had never agreed with the board's decision to appoint the present head and would work to unseat her as soon as possible.

Soon the entire board received an e-mail message from the trustee-parent, demanding that an executive session of the board be held within the next three days. He made clear that his financial support for the school was in jeopardy if the board did not take immediate action.

The members of the board's executive committee, recognizing the gravity of the situation, decided to engage an outside consultant to guide them through the crisis. The board chair, who by this time had also been informed by the head of the meeting's outcome, decided she must inform the trustee-parent that no full board meeting would be held until the executive committee had a chance to discuss the situation.

Four days later, the consultant attended a preliminary executive session to gain a better understanding of the school's history, the procedures and policies that guided the trustees' work, and the board's relationship with the head of school. The conversation revealed deeply conflicting views within the board about what constituted effective head-board partnerships. Executive committee members were particularly eager to better understand the role and responsibilities of the head of school. Two committee members suggested it might be time to force a vote of no-confidence for the head.

The board chair and the consultant faced a serious challenge. Together, they agreed that the executive committee must re-examine its own behavior, practices, and policies; its expectations and requirements of all trustees; and its collective expectations of the head. Making progress would require great skill and patience.

A first step was to invite the head to meet with the executive committee and the consultant to discuss her experiences as founding head and her perspective on the present crisis, and to explain her reluctance to seek the board chair's advice about the meeting. The board chair and consultant both reiterated their belief in candid and respectful communication.

The head then explained how demeaning it was to receive signals from the board indicating that it was not her responsibility to oversee the shaping of the school's program and quality of life. She spoke of low morale among members of the faculty, who felt discounted by parents and board members alike—some of whom, it appeared, felt entitled to seek board intervention if they did not agree with an educator's decision. The faculty lived in constant fear and thus did not feel they could be present for the children in meaningful ways.

What followed were many challenging, soul-searching conversations among the members of the executive committee, the full board, and the head of school. As an anchor for these deliberations, the consultant drew upon the mission and values of the school and suggested that major decisions of the previous three years be revisited within the context of the school's guiding principles. Clearly, this work would require patience and a willingness to engage in intelligent, thoughtful reflection. Nothing less than the future of the school was at stake.

In recognition of the seriousness of the situation, the board chair proposed a two-and-a-half-day retreat. She stipulated that attendance at the retreat was an acknowledgment of the critical work at hand and suggested that those who were not able to participate in compromise may wish to rethink their engagement as trustees. Feeling increasingly isolated from his fellow trustees, the trustee-parent resigned his position on the board and intimated that he would withdraw future financial support.

Ultimately, this crisis provided the school's leaders with a powerful new way to think about the meaning of their work on behalf of young people. It helped the school's board and head to develop policies and practices, the value of which was measured not in short-term gain but in the context of integrity of purpose.

The impact of these events transformed the climate of the professional community. The head of school re-established her credibility with the faculty and the majority of the trustees, and she was able to deal more effectively with parents.

With some new policies in place, the board functioned more effectively and predictably. Though many challenging situations continued to test the leadership of this nascent school, its future became more secure each time the trustees recommitted themselves to the school's mission and to the Principles of Good Practice for both heads and trustees.

CASE STUDY *continued from page 105*
AN ALTERNATIVE PAPER ROILS THE COMMUNITY

THE COMMUNITY DEBATES THE CRITIC'S CHARGES

After the student responsible for the alternative paper came forward, the head of school and the upper school director met with her several times. In addition to probing the discontent the young woman felt with the school's newspaper, structure, and policies, the three analyzed the entire situation's impact on the school, the faculty, and the student body.

In discussing with the student editor why she believed the form, style, and substance of the alternative paper caused such turmoil, the head drew on the school's mission and values. She noted that the academy not only valued but required mutual respect. She pointed out that the alternative paper represented the voice of one anonymous student who presented criticism that the head believed disparaged fellow students, the administration, and the faculty adviser of the school's official paper. The form of criticism did not promote thoughtful, respectful school-wide debate.

The administrators spoke of the rupture in the community that occurred when the members of the paper's editorial board came under attack but had no one with whom to discuss their concerns. Because it was published anonymously, the alternative paper was in opposition to the academy's commitment to encourage students to take responsibility for their opinions and perspectives.

After several challenging but fruitful discussions with the responsible student, her adviser, and other faculty leaders, the head of school decided that she should provide an all-school forum to allow this complex situation to be examined and understood more thoroughly by students and faculty. Without this open airing of viewpoints, she recognized that some of the same student concerns that led to the creation of and support for the alternative newspaper would remain unresolved and could, in the future, undermine the school's commitment to cohesiveness and transparency.

Before scheduling the assembly, the head and assistant head met with elected student government leaders to hear their views and reiterate that any forthcoming resolution concerning school-wide forums for debate or dialogue would succeed only if student leaders got involved. The student government leaders agreed that, even though they concurred with some of the premises of the alternative paper, they were committed to generating solutions that would strengthen school communication going forward.

The all-school assembly opened with the head of school explaining why, in her opinion, the alternative newspaper had created such a rupture in the community. Because the clandestine paper's anonymous author openly challenged the official student newspaper—which a significant group of community members worked hard to create—the action threw into question the prized values of open dialogue and thoughtful debate. Given that a defining principle of the school was the belief in and expectation of civil discourse, the alternative newspaper represented a challenge to beloved traditions.

The head further explained that in a series of private meetings, the editor of the alternative paper, who was present at the assembly, had provided thought-provoking arguments for her decision to publish the paper. In addition, the head shared the editor's willingness to help generate new ways to promote authentic dialogue in the future. This acknowledgment was meant to alleviate uneasiness among those who may have thought the assembly's purpose was to extract the proverbial "pound of flesh" from the editor or her supporters.

After these remarks, the head opened the floor to questions. Hands flew up. Students from every class seized the opportunity to express their opinions—all strongly held and representing every conceivable perspective. Many respondents offered passionate counter-arguments, and the assembly provided an outstanding opportunity for everyone to witness the power of debate and dialogue in action.

Several students agreed with the opinions expressed in the alternative paper; the school would be strengthened, they suggested, by a more transparent and immediate vehicle for public student debate. One student pointed out that because everyone communicates electronically today, the lag time between editions of the school paper resulted in a far less engaged readership.

In the charged atmosphere of the assembly, it became clear that a growing number of students came to see the publisher of the alternative paper as a kind of folk hero who, in a dramatic way, gave voice to what some others had thought of, if only fleetingly.

During the assembly, anyone who wished to speak had the opportunity to do so. The editor of the alternative paper spoke up several times, reiterating her original message of discontent about school publications and communications, while also acknowledging the disruptive nature of the form of her message. She acknowledged as well that her actions had been hurtful to the editors and contributors of the school's paper and expressed her hope that they could work cooperatively together in the future. The frank and lively exchange helped revive the faith of those who had doubted the school's willingness to support meaningful dialogue, particularly in such a charged atmosphere.

Following the assembly, the student leaders met with the head and assistant head of school, the upper school director, and the faculty adviser to reflect on the opinions and suggestions expressed. All agreed that the dialogue in the assembly served as a catalyst for creative problem-solving among the student leaders. What just a few hours earlier seemed to be an adversarial climate was transformed into one in which civil discourse unleashed imaginative ideas and solutions.

CASE STUDY
AN ALTERNATIVE PAPER ROILS THE COMMUNITY

The student leaders were charged with working with all members of the student self-government to develop an entirely new concept: an electronic message board that would allow upper school students and faculty to debate important topics, such as the platforms of political candidates and international events, and permit them to share opinions about plays, assemblies, speaker programs, and school policies.

This site, ultimately known as "Post-It," was overseen by two faculty members and three upper school elected student leaders. They reviewed all entries for appropriateness of language and tone and, as needed, worked with a student to explain why a particular entry might be considered inappropriate. Post-It became a vibrant part of school life. Students and faculty alike felt pride in their roles as architects of a

vehicle that responded to the realities of 21st-century technology while being grounded in school values that had guided the community for decades.

For the head of school, this situation represented one of those teachable moments that, if seized, could lead to "good fortune," to paraphrase Shakespeare. Good fortune in this kind of situation depended on being able to place trust both in the students and in the faculty, and in the dynamics that gave meaning to the relationships between the two. It meant suspending control over the outcome with the hope that when facing uncertainty, good minds and dedicated hearts would merge to create a brighter tomorrow for the community. ■

DISCUSSION QUESTIONS

1. How can a head of school ensure that all constituents understand and commit to the school's mission and philosophy?

2. How can the head and board chair communicate their mutual understanding of roles and responsibilities in ways that will generate confidence among faculty?

3. What steps can the head take to ensure a full understanding of complex situations before decisions are made or action taken?

4. In times of crisis, how can the head ensure the understanding and support of trustees and faculty?

5. What practices and procedures might the head introduce to ensure that the relationships with the board chair, the executive committee, and the full board are grounded in respect and driven by a common vision?

SUGGESTED RESOURCES AND READING MATERIALS

de Bono, Edward. *Six Thinking Hats.* Boston, MA: Little, Brown and Co., 1999.

De Pree, Max. *Leading Without Power.* San Francisco, CA: Jossey-Bass, 2003.

Gardner, John W. *On Leadership.* New York, NY: The Free Press, 1993.

Goleman, Daniel, Richard Boyatzis, and Annie McKee. *Primal Leadership.* Boston, MA: Harvard Business School Publishing, 2002.

Harvard Business Review on Leadership. Boston, MA: Harvard Business School Publishing, 1998.

Lambert, Linda. *Building Leadership Capacity in Schools.* Alexandria, VA: Association for Supervision and Curriculum Development, 1998.

O'Toole, James. *Leading Change.* San Francisco, CA: Jossey-Bass, 1996.

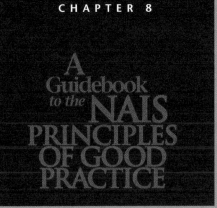

A Guidebook to the NAIS PRINCIPLES OF GOOD PRACTICE

for

MIDDLE SCHOOL EDUCATORS

By Ruth Glass

Ruth Glass is head of The Wesley School, a K-8 day school of 200 students in North Hollywood, California.

NAIS PRINCIPLES OF GOOD PRACTICE for

MIDDLE SCHOOL EDUCATORS

Revised and approved by the NAIS board in 1993

Recognizing that middle school students experience a variety of significant changes, middle school educators respond to and provide for the unique developmental needs and characteristics of their students. (Although many of the principles apply to this case study, the ones in **boldface** are the most pertinent.)

1. Middle school educators affirm the dignity of each individual and promote equity and justice.

2. Middle school educators and all personnel who interact with middle school students have a thorough understanding of the patterns of physical, intellectual, social, and emotional growth of their students.

3. Middle school educators actively engage parents as partners in recognizing the implications of the significant changes affecting middle school children.

4. Middle school educators work to ensure a smooth transition experience for students and parents entering and leaving the middle school years.

5. **Middle school educators provide programs that support each student's need to develop a distinct self-concept and to be recognized as an individual and as a member of a group.**

6. **Middle school educators create an environment that fosters respect, understanding, and acceptance of differences.**

7. Middle school educators help students learn to make responsible choices and understand the consequences of their actions.

8. **Middle school educators create opportunities for students to develop a sense of belonging to and responsibility for the multiple communities in which they participate.**

CASE STUDY

A TEAM CONFRONTS QUESTIONS OF WHO GETS TO PLAY

The coach of the middle school softball team at Canyon Country Day School pored over the roster of girls, selecting who would play what position and when at that afternoon's league championship game. Frankly, given the history of the team in other years, it was a surprise to all concerned that this championship match was even a possibility. Over the previous three years, despite the fact the school won many games, both the players and their parents had frequently expressed dissatisfaction with the former coach's interpretation of the school's philosophy regarding playing time, and a lack of team spirit had kept the team from achieving real success.

Prior to this year, in fact, it seemed there was no clear policy or philosophy. Theoretically, the eighth-grade girls were picked as starters, with seventh-graders filling holes and the bench. But the previous coach had clearly had his favorites, so it was never possible to anticipate how much playing time individual girls would have. Some rode the bench game after game and were never included in play. Others started and were kept in the entire seven innings, regardless of how poorly they might be fielding or hitting. Some eighth-grade girls played only part of one inning. One year, a fifth-grader had been "imported" from the junior varsity and started every game.

The CCDS student handbook stated there was a "no-cut" policy, so every girl who tried out was included in the official roster. But a playing-time minimum was clearly lacking.

More than one irate parent approached the head of school to complain. But most gave up in discouragement. The head, not an athlete himself, looked at the win-loss records of the softball team and noted the rave reviews of a few parents whose daughters played frequently. So he retained his faith in the coach. Plus, many sports banners lined the gymnasium walls, and prospective parents on admissions tours responded with enthusiasm.

The middle school division head, Christy Stuart, was relatively new to Country Day. When she attempted to discuss the athletic department's philosophy and goals with either the athletic director (who was also the coach) or the head, she felt their resistance. It was clear that nothing was going to change unless she found a way to become involved personally with the situation.

For Christy, the situation had come to a head following a softball game the previous spring. Country Day had won handily, but four girls had not played at all. On her way back to the office, Christy heard someone crying softly and came upon Joy, one of the four who hadn't played. Although aptly named for the indomitable spirit she demonstrated, Joy was not really considered "team material." No. 1: She suffered from cystic fibrosis. No. 2: Because of her illness, she was both a bit overweight and slow of foot.

When Christy asked Joy what was bothering her, Joy looked straight at her and said softly, "I know I will never be good enough to represent Country Day on any team. I will never be able to play for my school, no matter how hard I try."

To be continued....

EXEMPLARY APPLICATIONS OF GOOD PRACTICE

EXAMPLE 1: Confronting Racist Jokes

(Relates to Middle School Principles 1, 3, 6, and 7)

On a long bus ride home after a soccer game and cross-country meet, a group of middle school boys from a Massachusetts school started rating each other's jokes. The situation grew inappropriate when a few hunkered down, got quiet, and told several racist jokes. An African-American cross-country runner on the bus heard the jokes and got angry, but she kept her feelings to herself. Two boys spoke up almost immediately and told the offenders to stop.

The middle school division head, Stephen, found out about the incident later that night when the girl's mother called him about it. He convinced her to come to school the next morning with her daughter, who was feeling unsafe and needed to be reassured. But in addition to her insecurity, the girl felt a righteous sense of anger.

Stephen met with the members of the soccer and cross-country teams as well as the coaches. They discussed what happened; what it means to be a stand-up person; why the girl felt unsafe in school; what happens when others don't do anything and what that means regarding their role in the incident; and what needed to be done next.

Happily, the other students on the bus spoke up for the two boys who had been stand-up people. They understood the courage those two had demonstrated and acknowledged both their individual actions and the positive self-concepts that enabled them to be proactive.

In keeping with the school's zero-tolerance policy for bullying or harassment, the boys who told the racist jokes were suspended. One of the suspended boys had an uncle who was black and a mother who was an immigrant. When her son was required to tell her, word for word, what he had said, she was so incensed that she cried, and the boy could not look her in the eye. When Stephen asked why he avoided his mother's gaze, the boy said he knew what he had done was wrong and that it hurt her. An important lesson was learned about accountability for actions.

Several parents, however, felt the school came down too hard on the joke-telling boys. Stephen spoke personally to every parent who wished to have a conference. He explained that his bottom line was not just the moral issue—how important it was to "walk the walk" regarding the school's inclusion statement. This was also the first time in his 18 years there that a child had felt unsafe—which he could not tolerate. The parents rethought the situation and supported Stephen's actions.

Stephen also laid into the coaches (one at a time, and in private) for sitting in the front of the bus instead of spreading out so they would know what was happening around them. By their inaction they had set the kids up—something that must never happen in school.

At the end of that first tough day back, Stephen met with the girl to ask if she felt safe again. She replied, "Mr. H., I know you love me. "

In short, the school responded with vigor to a potentially volatile situation, exposing the issues rather than hiding them. In this way, the incident was transformed into a lasting lesson. Throughout, Stephen framed and asked the right questions, and the kids responded in ways that made them feel they were doing the hard work.

EXAMPLE 2: Age-appropriate Admissions Preparation
(Relates to Middle School Principles 4 and 7)

In many parts of the country, middle schools encounter intense pressure not only to prepare students for high school but to ensure they get accepted at their schools of choice. To enhance that process and involve students and parents more directly, many NAIS schools begin the placement process in seventh grade.

In one Western school, the director of placement (who is also the admissions director) teaches a spring course that requires seventh-graders to review, as a group and individually, exactly what is covered on the recommendation forms that teachers will fill out on their behalf six months later. The placement director also asks all students to fill out recommendations for themselves from a teacher's perspective. In this way, they look at the questions high schools ask on their recommendation forms with an eye toward the skills and accomplishments high schools value.

Within that class, students spend considerable time discussing the differences between life in middle school and high school. Students begin to realize that how they perform in eighth grade will affect their choices in ninth grade—and that they have considerable control over that performance. Students create their own, very private, lists of strengths and things they wish to do better. From the latter, they select the three most important and then formulate goals and an action plan to meet their goals.

When school starts in September, the eighth-graders create their own resumes and supply copies to the faculty and administration, all of whom will be writing letters of recommendation on their behalf. Just before off-campus visits commence, eighth-graders meet with the head of school in groups of three or four for mock interviews to prepare them for both format and content. After the visits, they spend more time with their advisers to talk about the choices that confront them, including the advisability of selecting a school just because that's where their friends are applying. Because of the ongoing, close counseling and discussion, students from this school make remarkably smooth transitions into a refreshingly wide range of secondary schools.

EXAMPLE 3: Creating a Mutually Beneficial Buddy System
(Relates to Middle School Principles 5, 6, and 8)

Like many other strong independent schools, a Virginia school for students in preschool through eighth grade has discovered the value of using middle school students as mentors for younger children. In this particular case, eighth-graders are assigned preschool and kindergarten buddies each year. The teachers on both levels consult to arrange the best match-ups. Precious time is carved out of the weekly schedule for buddy interaction. In addition, eighth-graders are responsible for accompanying their little buddies to all-school functions.

In some schools, similar programs include sixth- and seventh-graders as buddies and incorporate grades K-2 for the partnerships. During those occasions, buddies read, play, and work together. Sometimes they may also participate in appropriate service-learning experiences. One K-8 school in California sends its entire student body off, organized into buddy groups, to various locations around the city to volunteer in community service projects.

Something about those relationships breaks through the defensive exterior of even the most recalcitrant, confused adolescent. The older students recognize their responsibilities to the younger ones and quickly realize how important they are in those young lives. Most of them remember vividly their own buddies from when they were little and anticipate with great pleasure this wonderful opportunity.

Through the program, the schools help students develop a sense of belonging to and responsibility for multiple communities. The initial challenge is to convince faculty members that they won't miss valuable instruction time. Proving the value of the program sometimes takes a year or two, but the feedback from graduated students indicates how much the program contributed to their sense of confidence and self.

EXAMPLE 4: Easing the Trials of Adolescence
(Relates to Middle School Principles 2, 5, 7, and 8)

Adolescence has never been easy. But due to increased exposure to topics and situations that used to be reserved for much older students, many schools have created ethics courses.

Under the tutelage of experienced teachers who understand students' patterns of physical, intellectual, social, and emotional growth, these classes provide a formal opportunity to explore what is on middle school minds. By taking the time to talk and write about topics such as heroes, peer pressure, cheating, what constitutes honor, and random acts of kindness, schools ensure that they at least have some sense of what is important to their students. In the presence of a teacher they trust and who assures them of confidentiality, middle school students can and will be remarkably open and honest. Most crave the opportunity to share what worries them most and to find help in seeking solutions. Although parents hope their children will talk to them about everything—and certainly it is a good school's job to refer issues home—all youngsters should know they have receptive advocates at school.

One middle school teacher reported a fascinating conversation about peer pressure in an eighth-grade ethics class. The topic evolved from the stereotypical "just say no to drugs" message to very real questions about how to deal with far more subtle situations. For instance, what should you do if, at the end of a baby-sitting job, the parent about to drive you home has clearly been drinking too much—and your parents aren't available?

"I would call a teacher," announced one boy, much to the amazement of the ethics teacher. As the rest of the class nodded in agreement, he continued, "Teachers have always told us we could call them if we were in trouble."

That particular school has created a remarkable level of trust between its faculty and students. Part of the key, it appears, is a mentor/adviser program in which students feel they are heard and respected as individuals. Another key is hiring faculty who do, indeed, understand and respect their charges.

In that same course, students periodically draw from a hat the name of a faculty or staff member. In groups of two or three, the students are assigned to create a random act of kindness for that person and carry it out anonymously. Often the participating students are not only inspired to levels of surprising creativity but also take great pride in remaining anonymous. At an age and stage when kids can be very self-absorbed, this activity again reminds them of both their greater school community and also the positive impact each one of them can have.

EXAMPLE 5: Promoting True Teamwork

(Relates to Middle School Principles 1 and 6)

At an annual middle school swim meet in Southern California, School W was in the lead, but the last relay was up. The coach, who was just getting on board with the school's no-cut policy and the "middle school concept," knew she could structure the relay team so the meet would be W's all the way.

To do so, however, would mean rearranging members of the relay team. If Emily swam "anchor," the team would definitely sink. Emily could barely swim the 25 yards, racing or not. If the coach dropped Emily and substituted someone else, the school would win.

The coach knew how the middle school division head felt—so well that she later said that in her mind she could actually hear the division head's voice, reminding her of the school's policy.

Emily stayed in as anchor. Sure enough, the team lost. The next worry, of course, was what the other kids would say. They were fine. Because they understood and accepted the school's policy, they showed good sportsmanship and completely supported each other and Emily.

CASE STUDY *continued from page 118*

A TEAM CONFRONTS QUESTIONS OF WHO GETS TO PLAY

A NEW COACH TAKES INCLUSIVE ACTION

Joy's misery stuck with Christy Stuart throughout the summer and into the fall. Her school's mission statement included references to inclusiveness, the whole child, and helping individuals reach their potential. She did not believe the girls' softball team was supporting this mission.

In January, Christy met again with the head of school to share her concerns—and propose a solution. Christy stressed the mission statement as well as the NAIS Principles of Good Practice for Middle School Educators, which emphasize the need for every child to be recognized as an individual and a member of a group. She reminded the head of the school's responsibility to create an environment that fosters respect, understanding, and acceptance of differences.

Then Christy said she would like to assume responsibility for coaching the girls' softball team. As an athlete herself, she had played numerous sports, including softball. As division head, she would find coaching to be time well spent on a number of levels. As the only woman coach in the school, she would be a unique role model for all students.

Coincidentally, another coach had expressed a desire to step down from his responsibilities, which added to the athletic director's load. Fortunately—and somewhat surprisingly—the athletic director was amenable to the situation, given his own schedule for the spring. The head of school agreed, albeit reluctantly.

On the first day of softball practice that spring, the seventh- and eighth-graders were surprised to find that Ms. Stuart was to be their coach. To their even greater surprise, she asked all of them to sit in a circle on the grass and said they had things to discuss. First, Coach Stuart asked each girl to tell why she wanted to play.

"My father loves baseball, and he wants to play catch with me."

"I love Country Day and want to be on a team."

"Baseball is my favorite sport. I want to be on the Olympic team some day."

"My friends are playing, and I want to be with them."

"High schools like it if you play sports."

"I was on the team last year, but I never got to play. I want a chance."

Next, Coach Stuart led a discussion related to playing time. She made it clear that, although it was her responsibility to determine who played when, it was up to the team to determine whether everyone should play an equal amount. The girls decided that everyone should be guaranteed at least half a game. Since the roster had 15 players, that meant a few girls might play an entire game, but most would be in for three-and-a-half of the seven innings. In addition, anyone who missed practice would not be allowed to start the next game, regardless of skill level.

Joy suggested that, if the game were close or critical, maybe only the best players should play. The team disagreed: Policy would prevail.

The season progressed surprisingly well. At the end of each practice, the girls were not dismissed until everyone shared something specific that she had done well that day and something she needed to improve upon. Initially, team members often had to help point out the good, but by the end of the season, everyone had learned to—and allowed herself to—recognize even small assets. Everyone's confidence grew.

So in May, there they were, in the championship game.

In the bottom of the sixth, with a runner on first and the opposition's strongest batter up, Coach Stuart caught the eye of her finest player, Jenny, at short. Jenny, who played on a summer league team highly ranked in the state, understood the message. She called to Joy, who was waiting eagerly at second, "Be ready. I'm coming to you." Joy planted her body, positioned as she had been trained throughout the season.

Taking the first pitch, the batter smashed a hot grounder to Jenny. Jenny fielded it flawlessly, turned, and, taking off just a touch of heat, tossed it to Joy for the out. Most incredibly, Joy pivoted and threw to first, not quite in time for the double play but clearly proving her development as a player and her value to the team. Jenny—she who played with all-stars in the summer—looked at coach and smiled the smile of someone who had just been part of something very valuable.

At the end of the day, this Cinderella team did not win the championship. But one of the miracles of the season was that the members of the team—all of them—believed they could. ■

DISCUSSION QUESTIONS

1. What are the critical components necessary to create a middle school athletic program that is both inclusive and competitive? How should such a program differ from one on a high school level?

2. What specific programs within your school help develop a climate of mutual respect for individuals of varying abilities and stages of development?

3. How do middle school administrators become involved appropriately in the mentoring of individual students and teachers?

4. Given the huge range of maturation that occurs within the middle school years, how do middle school administrators and teachers hold students accountable in a fashion that is developmentally appropriate and consistent?

5. Middle school is a time when students need to begin to make decisions about themselves and choices about their future that might vary somewhat from their parents' desires. How do educators help students reflect on their own strengths and needs and learn to articulate them responsibly?

SUGGESTED RESOURCES AND READING MATERIALS

Atwell, Nancie. *In the Middle: New Understanding About Writing, Reading, and Learning.* Portsmouth, NH: Boynton/Cook Publishers, 1998.

Barbieri, Maureen. *Sounds from the Heart: Learning to Listen to Girls.* Portsmouth, NH: Heinemann, 1995.

Chapman, Anne. *A Great Balancing Act: Equitable Education for Girls and Boys.* Washington, DC: NAIS, 1997.

Chasnoff, Debra, and Helen S. Cohen, Co-Directors. "Let's Get Real." Video and accompanying curriculum guide. *www.womedia.org,* 2004.

Finks, Harry. "Remember the Middle Schooler in You." *Independent School Magazine,* Summer 2002, Washington, DC: NAIS.

Goleman, Daniel. *Working with Emotional Intelligence.* New York, NY: Bantam Books, 1998.

Meier, Deborah, Nancy Sizer, and Theodore Sizer. *Keeping School.* Boston, MA: Beacon Press, 2004.

Sizer, Theodore R., and Nancy Faust Sizer. *The Students Are Watching: Schools and the Moral Contract.* Boston, MA: Beacon Press, 1999.

Thompson, Michael G., and Teresa Barker. *The Pressured Child: Helping Your Child Find Success in School and Life.* New York, NY: Random House, 2004.

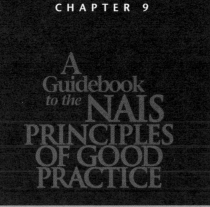

CHAPTER 9

A Guidebook
to the NAIS
PRINCIPLES
OF GOOD
PRACTICE

for

SECONDARY SCHOOL EDUCATORS

By Peter Gow and Debi Ellman

Peter Gow is director of college counseling and special programs and **Debi Ellman** is director of counseling services and associate director of college counseling at Beaver Country Day School, which has 404 students in grades six to 12 in Chestnut Hill, Massachusetts.

NAIS PRINCIPLES OF GOOD PRACTICE for

SECONDARY SCHOOL EDUCATORS

Revised and approved by the NAIS board in 2003

Secondary school educators are committed to helping their students move from adolescence to young adulthood. (Although many of the principles apply to this case study, the ones in **boldface** are the most pertinent.)

1. Secondary school educators help students to become passionate, serious scholars capable of effective communication, sustained work, independent thought, meaningful collaboration, and original expression.

2. **Secondary school educators use their training and knowledge of their disciplines to design programs appropriate to the developmental characteristics of this age.**

3. **Secondary school educators employ a range of teaching and assessment strategies that invite students to learn and to demonstrate their learning in a variety of ways.**

4. **Secondary school educators teach to the learning styles, abilities, and life experiences of their students.**

5. **Secondary school educators develop and sustain relationships with colleagues that benefit their students and further their own professional growth.**

6. Secondary school educators develop and sustain relationships with parents that support each student's well-being and increasing autonomy.

7. **Secondary school educators take responsibility for being role models.**

8. **Secondary school educators affirm and defend the dignity and worth of each member of the community and maintain an environment that fosters respect.**

9. **Secondary school educators help students take more and more responsibility for themselves and the multiple communities in which they live.**

10. Secondary school educators prepare students to take advantage of subsequent opportunities for learning and to take their places as members of a democratic society and the global community.

CASE STUDY

A NEW HEAD CONFRONTS A CRISIS IN STUDENT MISBEHAVIOR AND FAULTY TEACHER MANAGEMENT

It's five months into Bella Starr-Singer's tenure as head of Lincoln Fields School, and another week has nearly ended. The trees are beginning to show color, the Fall Festival is on the docket for Saturday, and the grounds crew has the place looking lovely. Bella muses that the "honeymoon" still seems to be on for her.

With a knock at the door, her feelings of tranquility come abruptly to an end. It's the father of Sara Margate, a senior, and he has his daughter in tow.

The previous night, Sara had received a forwarded e-mail from a classmate. The e-mail referred to a letter of recommendation that Millicent Carson, the charismatic chair of the English department, had written on Sara's behalf. Apparently, the contents of the recommendation were well known to the original writer of the e-mail, who not only was the daughter of a Lincoln Fields science teacher but had also added a few choice words herself about Sara.

The parent demands to know what Bella is going to do.

Lincoln Fields is a small, moderately selective independent school located in one of the leafier suburbs of a metropolitan area in the industrial Midwest—bluntly stated, the Rust Belt. Even as the region's economy has declined, Lincoln Fields has prospered, with a surplus of applicants, unflagging support from the city's more clubbable families, and a reputation for high-quality athletic programs and academics. Ten of the 47 students in last year's senior class are attending Ivy League schools, which makes LFS the most prestigious school in the area. Although the school is not notably diverse, an influx of children of academics from several local universities has given the school something of an international flavor.

In recent years, a point of pride at Lincoln Fields has been the work of Millicent Carson. A brilliant, demanding teacher, Millicent has been accustomed to having her strongest senior honors students spend time in her office, which she likes to think of as a kind of salon and where students hold spirited discussions about literature, life, and sometimes even their Lincoln Fields classmates and teachers. The "Carson Crew," as students with "office privileges" have come to be called, occupies a favored spot in the school's academic hierarchy, and, in fact, their intellectual achievements are notable. Some of the less accomplished students—and a few teachers—are at times resentful of the Carson Crew's status. But anyone would have to admit, however grudgingly, that as English students they are pretty formidable.

Among other things, Millicent keeps in her office a notebook of her lecture notes that students are free to borrow and copy to supplement their own class notes. Even non-Crew students are permitted to enter the office for this purpose, and some come by on occasion to make small talk about their weekends or about the amusing gaffes of the latest substitute teacher, a topic in which Millicent takes special delight.

Over the next few days, Bella, along with the upper school director and the dean of students, works to unravel the story of Sara Margate's e-mail. As they do, the following story takes shape:

On the day before Sara Margate and her father came to visit Bella, Millicent Carson had been absent. Jerry Languard, a junior soccer star in Millicent's standard-level course, had stopped by to check the notebook, hoping to find some clues as to the content of an upcoming test on *The Scarlet Letter.*

Jerry was surprised to find under the notebook a pile of papers, on the top of which was clearly Millicent's letter of recommendation for Sara Margate, who is an off-and-on member of the Crew. Jerry looked the letter over, noting with amusement some rather lukewarm things that Millicent had written about Sara. Riffling through the pile, Jerry was surprised to find letters for a number of senior students. Putting the pile down and replacing the notebook, he had run off to tell his best friend. By midday, at least a dozen students had looked at the recommendations.

By that evening, the story had become well known throughout the junior and senior classes. Even Sara had heard rumors, but until the e-mail had arrived, she had not known that her own recommendation had been involved.

When these facts are first presented to Bella, she listens sympathetically to the furious Mr. Margate. Sara sits in a leather easy chair in Bella's office looking small, sad, and afraid. Mr. Margate demands to know what the school is going to do, and Bella Starr-Singer knows that the honeymoon is over.

To be continued....

CASE STUDY ANALYSIS:
NAIS PROFESSIONALS OFFER INSIGHTS

The NAIS Principles of Good Practice for Secondary School Educators focus on relationships between institutions and people: the programs, policies, and practices aimed at reaching students and sustaining communities in which the quality of individual experience and dignity of each person are paramount. At Lincoln Fields, structural failures, arrogance, misjudgment, and omissions in practice have quickly escalated into crisis. Once the facts are known, Bella finds herself living an administrator's worst nightmare: student misbehavior enabled by the school's faulty practice. This bad practice has already tainted the relationship between the school and its constituents and directly harmed individual students and their families.

As Bella and her management team struggle to unravel the situation, they encounter collateral issues relating to some of the Principles of Good Practice that, in a well-ordered school, should be topics of conversation. The teacher's lecture notes, for example, assume special value if they are the teacher's primary or only mode of presenting material. For many adolescents, the lecture is a cognitive challenge in itself, and, so, perhaps Jerry Languard's anxiety over the forthcoming test arises from his struggles in a lecture-based classroom. But Millicent's apparent preference for being "the sage on the stage" is emblematic of other, more insidious problems at Lincoln Fields.

The heart of this case is a longstanding failure in the school's management of a teacher and the equally longstanding poor judgment of this teacher, who has blurred the boundaries between professionalism and something else in her relationship with students. The crisis has come, and with it a host of issues relating to the school's policies and practices. Neil Kramer, dean of faculty at New Community Jewish High School in California, sees these issues as "a problem of school culture"—an "unhealthy culture," in the words of Naomi Norwood, special assistant to the head of the Brentwood School in California.

Lincoln Fields is in a privileged position. Neil Kramer makes the point that "as a prestigious place, it can go forward without attending to any of these matters, and its students will still get into fine colleges." With a sufficient stock of local prestige, Lincoln Fields could probably weather the storm while doing little to address the problems manifest in the case. Stonewalling often works (although it can lead to cracks in the foundation).

But if the school is committed to explicit values and to a sincere educational mission—and to the NAIS Principles of Good Practice for Secondary School Educators—it must address the problems face on. As a new head, Bella Starr-Singer has suddenly had thrust upon her a once-in-a-headship opportunity to address systemic problems she has inherited—and, of course, to bring Lincoln Fields into alignment with the principles.

It is time for self-examination among the good people of Lincoln Fields, as difficult as this will be. There is plenty of crow to be eaten, but a serving now will obviate the need for a whole meal later on. What went wrong? How should the school respond? Most important, what are the lessons in good practice that can be learned from the Lincoln Fields case? These questions will frame our analysis.

What went wrong?

Culpability for the situation at Lincoln Fields is widespread.

In the first place, students have ignited the conflagration by snooping among Ms. Carson's recommendations, by sharing the pilfered information, and by passing along commentary on this information via derogatory e-mails. Regardless of adults' failures, "students' ethical violations cannot be condoned because they were occasioned by adult carelessness," notes Richard Barbieri, author, long-time school administrator, and current interim head of Stone Ridge School of the Sacred Heart in Maryland. Jerry, those who viewed the letters, and any students who shared their content have all "violated the trust that Carson placed in her students"—however misguided or badly motivated that trust was, says Russell Combs, former dean of students at the Albany Academy and Doane Stuart School in New York.

Millicent Carson's negligence in caring for sensitive documents (negligence that is possibly actionable; letters of reference are protected under the Federal Educational Records Privacy Act) has provided the temptation that has drawn Jerry Languard and others into the fire. Simply cleaning up after the security breach will keep people at Lincoln Fields busy for some time, and damage control will have to involve conferences with families, communication with college admission offices, public and private explanations by school administrators, and the preparation of a whole new set of letters—either by Millicent or by other, more responsible teachers.

More seriously, Millicent has permitted and apparently encouraged the growth of a self-styled student elite. However great their strengths as English students, the Carson Crew's separation from the rest of their schoolmates and their reputation for bad-mouthing peers and even teachers—perhaps in the presence of Millicent herself—are inexcusable. If the group has operated under the aegis of Millicent's "charisma," this is surely a case of a teacher failing to use her powers for good. As department chair, she may grant herself the "privilege" of teaching only the most adept students—unwilling to make the effort to develop her craft or to build relationships that would bring every student into her salon of ideas. This self-aggrandizing and selfish behavior, as Naomi Norwood puts it, "conveys to colleagues that Ms. Carson is more worthy than they: 'Let others spend time with the less-talented students.'"

Millicent may simply be oblivious to what the Crew has become, which demonstrates a singular lack of awareness and common sense. If so, professional guidance from administrators will be in order, at the very least. And if Millicent has in fact seen her coterie for what it is and made no effort to curb it, she is guilty of an extraordinary lapse in professional judgment—and perhaps she is also the victim of a neurotic narcissism that manifests itself in a craving for adulation. As Kate Parker-Burgard, dean of students at St. Luke's School in Connecticut, wonders, "Whose needs are being met by the Carson Crew, anyhow?"

It is also hard not to wonder what lies at the heart of Millicent's tepid letter on behalf of Sara Margate. "By her lukewarm comments, she is not affirming the student," says James Holmes, former head of Flint River Academy in Georgia. "When she accepted the invitation, she should have looked within herself to make sure she could advocate." As Naomi Norwood points out, teachers' "obligation to 'affirm and defend the dignity and worth of each member of the community' (Principle 8) should preclude their agreeing to write a recommendation for a student whom they do not intend truly to 'recommend.'" But even beyond the Margate letter, by her carelessness in handling other confidential material, Millicent has failed to support all of the students for whom she wrote.

But it is the administrators of Lincoln Fields who have somehow allowed a deplorable state of affairs to, as James Holmes puts it, "drive wedges among others in the community." No one has stepped up to confront a teacher who, successful as she might be in turning out fine English students, should have been reined in or had her methods questioned long ago. For Russell Combs, "much of the 'blame' here falls on the administration for not squashing this unhealthy relationship between Millicent and her students. If this situation was known throughout the school, someone should have taken it to the academic dean, upper school head, associate head—whatever the administrative structure supported."

To Neil Kramer, the issue is nothing less than a "cowardly failure to manage this talented person." Holmes observes that this "cult of personality reflects artificial power structures that exist in many schools." The management of the prima donna teacher (not a rare creature in independent schools) can be a good indicator of an administration's overall efficacy and of its insensitivity to the health of the community as a whole. Just who matters in the school?

Too often, a charismatic teacher creates a following that is perceived by others as exclusionary, drawing into question issues of fairness and equitable instructional support and enrichment. When students feel "unfavored," they are less likely to advocate for themselves and to trust that the teacher has their best interest at heart. It breeds jealousy that easily spills from the academic arena to the social arena. Even the performance of "favored" students, with regard to intellectual risk-taking or the expression of views opposed to the instructor, may be affected by a gnawing fear of status loss. As Norwood remarks, "Maintaining favored students is not even good for 'the chosen'; it creates a stratification that can lead to a false sense of superior worth and, ironically, to insecurity— that one may lose one's chosen status." The actions of a single teacher and a school's failure to address them can, in the words of Russell Combs, leave the Principles of Good Practice "bludgeoned beyond recognition."

Combs adds that when "key administrators are not willing to address a teacher-turned-institution" or when a teacher is known to be guilty of "condoning students discussing students and teachers," whatever occurs has been given the "tacit consent of the administration." The administration is responsible for the harm done to the Lincoln Fields community by the existence of Millicent's "salon." "This business is about relationships," Combs continues. "We have to prize each relationship and cannot value one over another. You can't develop a sense of community where each member is valued when groups like Carson Crew are allowed to conduct themselves like this."

Both Combs and Neil Kramer look at the head of school as a potential factor in the problem—either because of unwillingness to confront a powerful and popular teacher or because of a bad case of tunnel vision. Even if Bella can perhaps be excused for not having taken up the matter of the Carson Crew immediately upon her installation, her predecessor ought to have done so—and even had a golden opportunity to undertake this as a final act before departing. As Norwood puts it, "The situation presents a real leadership challenge," the first of Bella's tenure at Lincoln Fields.

Although the Carson Crew may be a Lincoln Fields point of pride—an able, intellectually aggressive "dream team" in a school that trades on its academic reputation—the divisive effects of its existence are hard to miss. The harm done by students in Millicent Carson's office started long before Jerry Languard entered the picture, and there is no escaping the conclusion that administrators who have in the past enabled Millicent and the Crew have been remiss.

Last but not least—although perhaps the hardest issue to define and act upon—is the e-mail problem. Lincoln Fields publishes a fairly generic acceptable-use policy, or AUP, that applies only to technology supplied or managed by the school. If messages pertaining to Millicent's recommendations were sent via Lincoln Fields bandwidth or server space, the senders have violated the AUP. If school equipment—either a school computer or a school-supplied laptop—has been involved, the violation is even more egregious.

The real issue, however, lies in the moral dimension, even if school technology is not involved. Principle 9 refers to students taking "responsibility for themselves and the multiple communities in which they live." In this case, Lincoln Fields must consider how it presents and construes the extent of its moral, if not strictly statutory, community.

Some independent schools make sweeping claims for the "reach" of their communities. Students know that their actions in almost any circumstances are subject to review by school authorities. Although the legal aspects of such a claim—based on the notion of "conduct unbecoming"—are complex, a stated policy stakes out the moral high ground in calling students to account for behavior away from the school–student nexus. A compelling argument can be made that the e-mail involving Sara Margate has violated the school community as a whole. If other hurtful communication about the incident has occurred, the harm is even more serious. Defining the nature and extent of whatever "offense" has occurred will be yet another problem facing school officials.

If Lincoln Fields has not previously addressed these issues explicitly in its policy statements or handbooks, or if it has not otherwise made clear among its constituents how it defines its moral jurisdiction—the boundaries of the "multiple communities" in which students live—the school's potential grounds for action will be more narrow, its moral advantage reduced.

There remains, of course, the possibility that the Margates may initiate legal action. If the e-mail message was disseminated widely enough to be considered "published" and if the content is defamatory, or if the whole mess is in fact a FERPA violation, the school and individuals in it are potentially exposed. This extremity lies beyond the scope of this essay, but it does underscore the sobering point that a statement of recommended practice from a governing or representing professional body can be the fulcrum upon which a lawsuit eventually tilts.

In sum, each of the Principles of Good Practice has been assailed. As learners, as members of the broader school community, and as young people working to develop their habits of mind and values as adults in the global community, the students of Lincoln Fields have been let down by their peers, their teachers, and their administration. The relationships among teachers, including Millicent, have been similarly bruised. Parents and college admission offices have also been affected.

The school community is suffering, and Bella must lead a healing process. The cure will not be entirely painless.

CASE STUDY *continued from page 131*

A NEW HEAD CONFRONTS A CRISIS IN STUDENT MISBEHAVIOR AND FAULTY TEACHER MANAGEMENT
HOW THE SCHOOL RESPONDS AND REBUILDS

As Bella Starr-Singer considers how to respond to Lincoln Fields' dilemma, she knows she must first consider many less-than-obvious issues. The case clearly involves violations of good practice with regard to Millicent's relationship with her students, her management of confidential information, and her pedagogy. The case also involves violations of good practice with regard to student conduct within the school community and behavior that occurs beyond school borders, affecting individual students and the school climate in general. Finally, the case violates good practices related to Lincoln Fields' partnerships with families and with colleges to which students are applying. As a response strategy is designed, the head and her team will need to consider all of these constituencies.

Jerry Languard, as Russell Combs points out, "is in a heap of trouble. I would recommend a suspension. When the community has been violated, a student needs to be removed from it for a period of time in order to evaluate his or her place in it and to decide whether he or she wants to remain a part of it." The science teacher's daughter who sent the message to Sara also "has not behaved honorably," says Naomi Norwood, "and should also be admonished."

Neil Kramer sees the other students who saw and shared the letters in Millicent's office as being "whipsawed." He and Combs see the response to their actions as contingent on Millicent's reaction to the incident. If the teacher fails to take ownership of her own role in creating the conditions that have led to this mess, Kramer suggests that "exacting consequences from these students would be hypocritical at best." If Millicent apologizes, then the guilty students "could benefit from some counseling or disciplinary response to their misdeeds." At the very least, says Richard Barbieri, seniors "who were guilty should be asked to seek new references, and perhaps even explain the incident to colleges." Whether the school will notify colleges of disciplinary consequences depends on its existing policy.

Millicent has at the very least failed to live up to Principles 5, 6, and 7, and, as Barbieri points out, she "should be admonished for her errors as a role model" as well as for her negligence. Following the admonitory discussion, it is imperative that Bella file a formal reprimand specifying a required course of action.

Kate Parker-Burgard goes further: "Assuming that Millicent's record is stellar and they want to keep her, a serious conversation regarding boundaries would be in order, and counseling possibly required. If Ms. Carson's record is not stellar, probation would be in order." Naomi Norwood adds, "If Carson cannot adopt a more egalitarian approach to her students, Lincoln Fields will be better off without her." Commentators also agree that Millicent owes a raft of apologies, both for her negligence and for enabling her exclusive and exclusionary following.

Parker-Burgard and Norwood both suggest radical changes for the Crew. Parker-Burgard suggests dismantling the group and charging Millicent with responsibility for "damage control and encouraging the kids toward an understanding and positive spirit." Norwood actually suggests encouraging the continuation of the salon, "but it should be in the cafeteria or student life center and open to students based on their interest in participating." Rather than confine such intellectual discourse to an elite few, Barbieri suggests that, if a chastened Millicent can be persuaded to model open access, other teachers might be encouraged "to emulate her openness"—neatly turning the problem into its own solution.

The problem of the improperly distributed information will necessitate a complex and detailed resolution, requiring—at the very least—apologies from Millicent to all and sundry as well as specific communication with families involved regarding the breach. Here James Holmes sees an important role for Bella as moral leader, including a presentation to students in the upper grades to "address the matter and inform them of the purpose that the letters of recommendation have" and "demystify the letters' importance. Finally," Holmes says, "the head should draft a letter explaining the breach of confidentiality and assuring parents and stakeholders that measures have been taken to make sure that this would not happen again."

Clearly, Millicent owes Sara and the Margate family an apology; the decision to rewrite Sara's letter should be the teacher's. In turn, Sara should be allowed to ask a teacher other than Millicent to endorse her application.

As for the e-mail, if Lincoln Fields' stated policy is that students' actions outside of school may damage the health and wholeness of the community (as well as reflecting poorly on the institution), then the infraction is obvious. Although the legal situation may not be crystal-clear—case law regarding schools and cyber communication is still evolving—ethically the school may look upon the senders as having failed to take responsibility for themselves and their community. At the very least, school administrators must initiate some pointed conversations.

The most important response must come from the very highest offices of the school. Something in the culture and administrative practice of Lincoln Fields has gone amiss. From the board on down, every adult in the school must consider his or her role in creating the circumstances that have led to the situation.

Above all, as Russell Combs observes, "Relationships need to be rebuilt here. Acknowledge, apologize, assure."

Bella, the administration, and even the board must make it clear that the school understands the enormity of what has occurred and that there is a process for making restitution and for ensuring that such a situation will never again arise. There must be administrative accountability, and Lincoln Fields must be strong and honest enough to undertake a systematic analysis of the situation so that the Principles of Good Practice will pervasively inform the school's policies, programs, and practices in the future.

CASE STUDY

A NEW HEAD CONFRONTS A CRISIS IN STUDENT MISBEHAVIOR AND FAULTY TEACHER MANAGEMENT

LESSONS IN GOOD PRACTICE

As Bella and the management team at Lincoln Fields work through the individual elements of the case and begin to determine how to implement the NAIS Principles of Good Practice more effectively, they develop plans for action in the following five areas. Within each category, the way is clear for Lincoln Fields to bring its practices to the most sophisticated level. Improved practice will not only further justify the school's good reputation but, more important, create conditions in which the experience of future Lincoln Fields students will be both excellent and just in all its dimensions.

1. Clarity in the meaning and "jurisdiction" of the school community. Lincoln Fields must clarify to students, parents, and faculty what it expects with regard to behavior. The school will consider the option of pressing the notion of student responsibility and behavior away from school under the doctrine of "conduct unbecoming." If the school decides to move in this direction, the policy will be stated in the school's handbooks and reiterated in the public utterances of school officials. Acceptable-use policies for cyber communication will be clarified and language added to make these as comprehensive as possible.

Although Bella understands that such policies do not have the force of law and may not always stand up to a legal test, they will express the school's expectations and help define the place of the school and its members in the multiple communities that make up the Lincoln Fields world.

Of course, good policies do not guarantee good practice. Lincoln Fields will convene a committee of faculty members to consider ways the school can begin teaching about its policies within the curriculum to familiarize students with the values underlying such policies. (For more on this, see Point 4 below about the academic program.)

2. Professional evaluation and development. From the first, Bella has been keenly aware that a school administration that allowed Millicent's unprofessional behavior to go unchecked must take much of the blame for what has occurred. As Russell Combs states, "Good forest management would have cleared away this underbrush and prevented the fire altogether."

Facing the issue of why Millicent had not previously been confronted has forced Bella to wonder why some administrators resist giving seasoned teachers the feedback they need. In our busy lives, even the best of formal evaluation processes in independent schools are underutilized for all but the most recent recruits. Lincoln Fields has, in the past, been no exception. As a result, the "sage on the stage" has been enabled to maintain her autonomy and her reign as leading lady—even as aspects of her job performance and effectiveness have deteriorated.

Bella appoints a small committee of department heads and faculty leaders to develop a formal evaluation process for Lincoln Fields teachers, including senior teachers. Making sure that the evaluation process contains opportunities for teachers to receive feedback on areas not limited specifically to the classroom will also provide a structure for giving all teachers (including, of course, Millicent) feedback on all aspects of their performance within the school community. Even beyond the evaluation process, Bella knows she must encourage (and train, if need be) administrators to give direct and constructive feedback to their colleagues whenever it is warranted.

Bella realizes that the evaluation issue does not apply only to classroom teachers. She, like her predecessor, has found herself focusing more and more on fund raising and meeting external goals, leaving increasing amounts of supervisory authority resting on the shoulders of "middle managers" for whom a Lincoln Fields evaluation system is practically nonexistent. In her first months, she has begun to see that some of the middle managers at Lincoln Fields are not accustomed to receiving a great deal of support and feedback. At the same time, she has sometimes felt conflicted about how much internal authority she should retain (especially since she enjoys it) and how much she really should delegate.

As a school with relatively few mid-level administrators, Lincoln Fields has an administrative culture that has grown more collaborative than hierarchical—this was one of the things that drew Bella in the first place. But as the Carson case has unfolded, she has observed that the upper school director and the academic dean, in particular, seem to have difficulty believing in and asserting their own authority without the support and affirmation of the head.

Perhaps, Bella muses, these administrators, granted too much autonomy and too little feedback, have affiliated more with the faculty than the larger interests of the school and its students—just as Millicent, a seasoned teacher with too much autonomy, has forgotten her boundaries with students. This affiliation undermines accountability.

Bella makes three notes to herself:
- The Lincoln Fields management team will need some professional development around leadership.
- She will ask the management team to develop an evaluation tool for its own members that can be piloted as soon as the end of the current year.
- She will have to be firm with the school's governing body about the need to provide for a clear line of authority inside the school while her attention and energy are focused outside.

Bella also resolves on a personal level to heed the advice of Russell Combs and attend to, support, and cultivate the management team herself. Creating a culture where direct, respectful feedback is given on a regular basis from the top down would diminish the risk of another Carson scenario.

Bella also sees that it's the right time for focused professional development to support teacher growth and increase institutional capacity in a number of specific areas. If in the end Millicent is retained, she must learn new ways of presenting material and assessing student learning. More expertise in addressing a range of student learning styles and more knowledge of adolescent development might also have helped Millicent

CASE STUDY

A NEW HEAD CONFRONTS A CRISIS IN STUDENT MISBEHAVIOR AND FAULTY TEACHER MANAGEMENT

apprehend the dangers inherent in the growth of the Crew and enabled her to maintain the salon concept within boundaries commensurate with students' developmental capacities and needs. In the future, discussion of the issue of boundaries will form a portion of the new-teacher induction and mentoring program, and all teachers will receive regular reminders of the importance of maintaining appropriate relationships with students.

Bella also asks the college counseling office to include the writing of recommendations in the faculty development program so that as teachers prepare letters of support, they will know how to "affirm and defend the dignity and worth" of each student. Part of this training will involve teaching teachers how to say no when they feel they cannot fairly represent the student in a positive light.

3. Policy development. Along with achieving greater clarity in its policy on behavior away from school, Lincoln Fields will develop an unambiguous written policy on notifying colleges with regard to disciplinary infractions. Having a clear statement in place would simplify, to a degree, the task of those deciding how to inform colleges about an incident involving applicants—a task that Bella acknowledges is never easy, even with the clearest of policies in place.

In terms of broader policy, James Holmes makes the argument for an honor code, since "most high school seniors are still developing their sense of abstract ethics." In his view, a code can be a more reliable moral compass for students than assuming that students possess "inherent understanding that stealing, cheating, and lying carry negative consequences for society." Although Bella herself has no direct experience with honor codes, she asks the academic dean and the dean of students to investigate how such codes are designed and how they operate at a few peer schools.

The simplest action Bella can take is to enunciate, with the help of the dean of students and the department heads, a clear policy about student access to faculty offices: Teachers must be responsible for maintaining confidential materials in a secure manner. A few teachers have to be reminded more than once of the importance of consistently following this policy, and over time it may erode. But, for the moment, everyone gets the point. Teachers will also be reminded (as if they need it for the current year!) of the importance of securing confidential information. Bella has told the business office as well to make certain that all teachers have access to locking drawers or file cabinets so that private material can indeed be protected.

4. Academic program. Here lie some exciting opportunities for Lincoln Fields, both to improve the substance of its educational programs and to become a true leader in establishing good practice. Bella is excited that the Carson situation has spurred this work forward.

At least a part of the Carson case hinges on distinctions made among students by school policy. The culture of Lincoln Fields has, like those of many schools, become replete with honors- and standard-level courses, and Millicent Carson favors her highest-level students for access to the salon. Even Jerry Languard is identified by his star status as a soccer player.

Bella charges the Lincoln Fields department heads with addressing several pointed questions:

- What if Lincoln Fields were to open access to its higher-level or premium-designated (such as AP and honors) courses to any student interested in taking them?
- What if regular attendance at a salon-like event—a series of seminars on special topics or lecture-discussions led by visiting scholars—were to become the factor that allowed students to earn "honors" credit?
- How can the distinctions that characterize the academic culture at Lincoln Fields be erased or modified so that all students can be offered equivalent levels of challenge and equivalent opportunities to earn success, based on their inclinations and passions rather than on invitations by teachers or on invidious distinctions embedded in the school's culture? Such a concept, Bella believes, is merely the logical extension of the suggestions by Norwood and others that access to the heretofore-privileged world of the Crew be granted to anyone with the interest. Even if no concrete changes ensue immediately, it will do Lincoln Fields no harm to begin conversations about these fundamental aspects of its practice.

As some of these directives from the head's office take form, a few teachers become excited about the idea of expanding the curriculum to include opportunities for ethical discussions about the appropriate use of the Internet as well as other student-life issues relating to integrity and community. One group champions the idea of a mandatory "situation ethics" course for ninth-graders, perhaps using case studies derived from situations in the school's recent past, to help guide students toward making better decisions in the future.

The academic dean also waxes enthusiastic about asking Lincoln Fields to rise from its comfortable bed of laurels and engage in some schoolwide, departmental, and individual curriculum planning. This would encompass professional training in pedagogy focused on supporting the development of curriculum based not on the transfer of information (through lectures, for example) but on active, student-centered inquiry. The dean's experience at a workshop on how to design an understanding-based curriculum several years ago made him excited about project-based, constructivist-inspired curricula that would engage all students in their own learning and in the development of active habits of mind. The Carson case has freed him to push this idea as a formal initiative.

The academic dean and the director of technology also see the case as a chance to encourage faculty who keep class notebooks to publish these ideas online. The course-

CASE STUDY

A NEW HEAD CONFRONTS A CRISIS IN STUDENT MISBEHAVIOR AND FAULTY TEACHER MANAGEMENT

management package offered by the developers of the Lincoln Fields website can be modified to handle this easily. In the meantime, a new section is created on the school intranet where class notes can be posted. As Kate Parker-Burgard and Neil Kramer observe, having these notes in a truly public venue means that Jerry Languard need never poke around in a teacher's papers again.

5. School culture. In many schools, fundamental aspects of the Principles of Good Practice are given lip service, and people of good will may assume, correctly most of the time, that colleagues and students generally intend to do the right thing. This has been the case at Lincoln Fields, and for years this has been fine in itself.

But Bella believes that a school that truly realizes the human potential within its gates must possess a culture based not on assumptions but rather on active, continual discourse about practice and about the issues that inevitably arise in the community. Transparency and accountability are essential to this culture; the processes by which issues are addressed and decisions made should be clear to all; and the lines of authority and expectations for performance must be explicit. Layers in the authority structure should not be mirrored by restricted access to knowledge of what is going on or why certain decisions have been made.

Having considered these five areas, Bella takes additional action on two fronts.

For herself, she vows to develop the practice of "management by walking around"—being as much as possible a presence in various aspects of the daily life of the school, including classrooms. She asks her assistant to set aside three 45-minute periods each week that are protected as "walkabout" time—with no appointments, no phone calls, no interruptions. She also encourages her division and department heads to do the same.

On a broader front, Bella works with the management team to develop a schedule of faculty meetings with specific agendas focused on key issues and dilemmas—about curriculum, student life, or school policies—and in which collaboration in problem-solving is invited and even celebrated. This will be a culture shift for Lincoln Fields, but she knows that conversation and collaboration, rather than secrecy and avoidance, are the foundation of a culture in which situations like that of Millicent and her Crew are unlikely to reach a critical point ever again. Russell Combs quotes Judith Schechtman, a consultant specializing in leadership and organizational management who spoke at an NAIS Emerging Leaders program. Schechtman suggested that sometimes, when a situation has become a morass, the only thing to do is "drain the swamp"—exposing hidden issues and shadowy interests to light and oxygen. Bella has begun to pump the water out of the swamp.

Combs also refers to one of Bella's favorite books: Theodore and Nancy Faust Sizer's powerful *The*

Students Are Watching. Lincoln Fields has become a school in which that truth is largely forgotten, and Bella sets out to reverse the situation. Lincoln Fields is a good school, she knows. But she also knows that a great school, a vibrant, equitable, and forward-thinking school, thrives on the awareness that—along with students—teachers, families, and the community at large are watching, too.

Lincoln Fields School has found itself in a difficult place, and unpleasant consequences surely lie ahead for some of its members. But, like all challenges, this one is also an opportunity; Bella believes it is an opportunity as important as any since the school's founding. Sober circumspection and a willingness to embrace change on many fronts can move Lincoln Fields to the leading edge in its implementation of the Principles of Good Practice for Secondary School Educators. ■

DISCUSSION QUESTIONS

1. What challenges does a school face in supporting individual teacher initiative and autonomy while maintaining institutional priorities and values?

2. As the role of head of school becomes more external, in what ways have the needs of middle managers changed, and how can a head support them in assuming and asserting their own authority?

3. How can your school effectively hold senior faculty more accountable and provide them with tools for growth and self-reflection?

4. How do you recognize and address culture and program issues within your school that limit students' access to academic challenge and prestige?

5. In what ways do power and status manifest themselves in your school, and how do you manage these issues to preserve equity and fairness? As you ponder this question, consider faculty, families, and the student body.

EXEMPLARY APPLICATIONS OF GOOD PRACTICE

EXAMPLE 1: Implementing Effective Evaluation
(Relates to Secondary School Principles 1, 2, 3, 4, and 9)

Great teacher evaluation systems abound. Many schools have adopted the Meaningful Faculty Evaluation, or MFE, program developed by Independent School Management (*www.isminc.com*). Based on goal setting, self-evaluation, and reflection, as well as observation and feedback, MFE, like any good evaluation tool, focuses on the individual teacher's professional growth needs. Other systems, like that in use at the Phillips Brooks School in California, focus on collaborative examination of teacher practice. Any effective system would have helped Millicent Carson well before the Margate letter situation arose.

EXAMPLE 2: Battling Senior Slump
(Relates to Secondary School Principle 2)

Some programs aim to make the senior year more meaningful and allow students to focus on their interests and highlight their strengths. These include the Wise Individualized Senior Experience, or WISE, program used at the Milken Community High School in California and Senior Focus at the Dwight-Englewood School in New Jersey. The latter is a year-long elective in which students focus on an area of interest, culminating in a portfolio and presentation on their topic.

Other schools draw on the work of teachers at Central Park East Secondary School as documented in Deborah Meier's *The Power of Their Ideas* (Beacon Press, 2002); they make such an "exhibition" the major experience of senior year for all students. A more student-centered senior year at Lincoln Fields might have given more students an opportunity to shine, broadening the narrow inward focus of the Carson Crew.

EXAMPLE 3: Offering High-level Learning to All
(Relates to Secondary School Principles 1, 2, 3, and 4)

At Beaver Country Day School in Massachusetts, a system of honors seminars is the essence of the history department's honors program. Any student can sign up for the program, and any student who completes the work—specified readings, active participation in a seminar led by a school faculty member or a visiting scholar, and the preparation of a paper—to a high standard receives honors credit for history. All students are invited to participate at the highest level—Millicent's "salon" without the exclusivity.

EXAMPLE 4: Setting High Behavioral Standards Inside and Outside School
(Relates to Secondary School Principle 9)

Greenwich Academy in Connecticut states clearly in its online handbook that "although the school has a limited responsibility for student behavior outside of school during off-school hours, it continues to take the position that should the behavior of any student reflect badly on the school's reputation or represent a danger to herself or others, the school reserves the right to impose disciplinary sanctions." Savannah Country Day School in Georgia includes "behavior that reflects poorly on the school" among infractions of "Major School Rules" in its handbook.

Such ideas may seem old-fashioned, but most schools would wish to make clear that students' behavior away from school is an aspect of their overall moral development. As a result, accountability within the school for "outside" behavior underscores students' "responsibility for themselves and the multiple communities in which they live."

EXAMPLE 5: Encouraging Candid Discussion
(Relates to Secondary School Principle 5)

Effective school management practices include administrative structures in which open, frank, and frequent discussion of major school issues can take place—before such issues become crises. The management team meetings at one school that preferred not to be named include time for each administrator to pose an issue or query and then to hear commentary and suggestions from colleagues. This interaction continues without administrative comment, at least until all ideas have been aired. The team can then problem-solve collectively and give administrators tools they can use right away.

A comprehensive evaluation program that applies to all administrators is also critical to effective school management. Had Lincoln Fields put such a system in place years ago, the head of school's life would be considerably easier.

SUGGESTED RESOURCES AND READING MATERIALS

NAIS maintains a growing library of online resources relating to all aspects of school practice, management, and governance at *www.nais.org.* In addition, NAIS's annual Leading Edge recognition program highlights schools' best practices in a number of areas, including community relations, curriculum innovation, equity and justice, and technology. (Learn more by typing "Leading Edge" into the NAIS search engine at *www.nais.org.*)

The Association for Supervision and Curriculum Development (*www.ascd.org*) generates a wealth of resources—including books, magazines, newsletters, online courses, and conferences—for teachers and administrators on every conceivable subject relating to K–12 education.

More and more interest is being paid to the role (and management) of experienced teachers in independent schools. Regional association workshops, David Mallery's Experienced Pro seminar, and the Westtown School's Experienced Teacher Institute all offer avenues for veteran teachers to explore their own roles in their schools. Peter Gow's *An Admirable Faculty: Recruiting, Hiring, Training, and Retaining the Best Independent School Teachers* (NAIS, 2005) explicitly addresses this issue within an in-depth discussion of practices and elements of school culture that maximize the effectiveness of the teacher–school relationship at all ages and stages.

OTHER ESSENTIAL READING FOR SECONDARY SCHOOL EDUCATORS

The Students Are Watching: Schools and the Moral Contract (Beacon Press, 1999) by Theodore and Nancy Faust Sizer is a profound and powerful meditation on teaching and school culture.

Theodore Sizer's seminal Horace trilogy—*Horace's Compromise* (1984), *Horace's School* (1992), and *Horace's Hope* (1996)—has been reprinted by Mariner Press. These books helped spark a revolution in teaching and school organization; schools remain complacent in the face of Sizer's ideas at their own peril.

Four collections of essays on boarding school issues published by Avocus Publishing will provoke thought among educators in all schools:
- *Casualties of Privilege: Essays on Prep Schools' Hidden Culture,* Louis M. Crosier, ed., 1991.
- *Healthy Choices, Healthy Schools: The Residential Curriculum,* Louis M. Crosier, ed., 1992.
- *Far and Wide: Diversity in the American Boarding School,* Tim Hillman and Craig Thorn IV, eds., 1997.
- *Second Home: Life in a Boarding School,* Second Edition, Craig Thorn IV, ed., 2003.

Although it has a public school focus, *Fires in the Bathroom: Advice for Teachers from High School Students* by Kathleen Cushman and the Students of What Kids Can Do (New Press, 2003) confronts issues of teacher favoritism. It's part of a compelling exploration of teacher efficacy as a function of student–teacher relationships and of student-need-driven curriculum design.

An excellent discussion of aspects surrounding the senior year can be found in Nancy Faust Sizer's *Crossing the Stage: Redesigning Senior Year* (Heinemann, 2002).

Sara Lawrence-Lightfoot, professor of education at Harvard University, has written three books that discuss academic, cultural, and moral issues relating to secondary schools:
- *The Good High School: Portraits of Character and Culture* (Basic Books, 1983).
- *Respect: An Exploration* (Perseus Books, 2000).
- *The Essential Conversation: What Parents and Teachers Can Learn from Each Other* (Random House, 2003).

An outstanding nuts-and-bolts guide to effective teaching is *The Skillful Teacher: Building Your Teaching Skills* by Jon Saphier and Robert Gower (Research for Better Teaching, Inc., 1997).

It's "old school," but Eric W. Johnson's *Teaching School: Points Picked Up* (Association of Independent Schools in New England, revised edition 1993; originally published 1979) contains the wisdom of the ages for teachers at all levels.

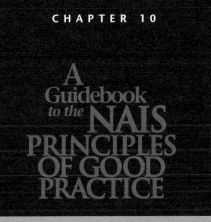

CHAPTER 10

A Guidebook to the NAIS PRINCIPLES OF GOOD PRACTICE

for
PARENTS WORKING WITH SCHOOLS/ SCHOOLS WORKING WITH PARENTS

By Charles Sachs and Linda Alexander

Charles Sachs, who has 10 years' previous experience as a school head, is currently associate head and interim upper school head at Hawken School. He becomes head of Park City Academy in Utah in fall 2007. Linda Alexander is an organizational development consultant and a parent volunteer at Hawken School. Hawken has 950 students in preschool through 12th grade on campuses in Lyndhurst and Gates Mills, Ohio.

NAIS PRINCIPLES OF GOOD PRACTICE for

PARENTS WORKING WITH SCHOOLS/SCHOOLS WORKING WITH PARENTS

Revised and approved by the NAIS board in 2004

Parents and independent schools work together to create and sustain effective partnerships. The following Principles of Good Practice describe the respective roles and responsibilities of both partners. (Although many of the principles apply to this case study, the ones in **boldface** are the most pertinent.)

PARENTS WORKING WITH SCHOOLS

1. **Parents recognize that effective partnerships are characterized by clearly defined responsibilities, a shared commitment to collaboration, open lines of communication, mutual respect, and a common vision of the goals to be reached.**

2. In selecting an independent school, parents seek an optimal match for the needs of the student, their own expectations, and the philosophy and programs of the school.

3. **Parents are familiar with and support the school's policies and procedures.**

4. Parents provide a home environment that supports the development of positive learning attitudes and habits.

5. **Parents involve themselves in the life of the school.**

6. Parents seek and value the school's perspective on the student.

7. **When concerns arise, parents seek information directly from the school, consulting with those best able to address the concerns.**

8. Parents share with the school any religious, cultural, medical, or personal information that the school may need to serve the student best.

SCHOOLS WORKING WITH PARENTS

1. **The school recognizes that effective partnerships are characterized by clearly defined responsibilities, a shared commitment to collaboration, open lines of communication, mutual respect, and a common vision of the goals to be reached.**

2. The school clearly and fully presents its philosophy, program, and practices to parents during the admission process and encourages dialogue that clarifies parental expectations and aspirations for the student.

3. The school seeks and values the parents' perspectives on the student.

4. **Teachers and administrators are accessible to parents and model candid and open dialogue.**

5. The school keeps parents well informed through systematic reports, conferences, publications, and informal conversations.

6. **The school defines clearly how it involves parents when considering major decisions that affect the school community.**

7. **The school offers and supports a variety of parent education opportunities.**

8. The school suggests effective ways for parents to support the educational process.

9. The school actively seeks the knowledge it needs to work effectively with a diverse parent body.

CASE STUDY
THE RISING TIDE

After devoting the majority of his first year as a school head to learning the stories of his new home and building personal relationships with a seasoned faculty and diverse trustees, Terry had found his second year, now rapidly approaching its conclusion, to be an active, rewarding one.

Barrow Academy was perceived as a model of excellence, due primarily to its attractive new facilities and enthusiastic alumni support. Dr. Watson, Terry's predecessor in the head's office, had set the stage perfectly for his retirement. After 15 happy years raising funds and expanding facilities to accommodate a growing and increasingly diverse student body, Dr. Watson had orchestrated a successful leadership transition for Barrow.

In Terry's first year, Barrow's 10-year regional evaluation/accreditation process provided him with the opportunity to devote a year to institutional self-study. In addition to addressing the usual brushfires any school experiences, Terry participated in several joint trustee, parent, student, and faculty committees in the standard self-study process. In so doing, he familiarized himself with the unique aspects of a new school and its constituencies.

As the new head, Terry could probe into processes and programs that the community took for granted but that had become, in some cases, hard to justify. From his valuable grounding at NAIS's Institute for New Heads that first summer, Terry knew to avoid referring to how things had been done at his previous school. However, in the spirit of objective analysis, Terry could ask questions that added to his growing reputation as

a creative thinker and a considerate leader. Dr. Watson's near-mythic reputation—particularly among the faculty—had resulted in burgeoning applications but, over time, had mitigated against critical self-examination among members of the school community.

Some long-tenured trustees and old-guard faculty believed that Barrow's accreditation self-study failed to take full advantage of the opportunity for self-congratulations. However, many parent self-study volunteers and the upper school student committee members took every advantage of the new head's honeymoon period to raise questions about whether Barrow's programs had kept pace with its facilities. In fact, one of Terry's great diplomatic challenges that first year was drafting the "philosophy and mission statement" section of the report. After much discussion and word-smithing, however, he was able to express his committee's question about whether the critical mass of Barrow's academic leaders adequately modeled the mission-statement key concept of "lifelong learning."

The evaluation/accreditation visiting team's stay near the beginning of Terry's second year ostensibly went well. Although the Barrow community felt affirmed and secure in its opinion of itself as an outstanding independent school, Terry was gratified at the visiting team's clear recommendations regarding improvement— particularly in the areas of curricular advancement, technology integration, marketing, and communication. Regarding the parent community, the recommendations included:

1. Offer more substantial opportunities to a diverse range of parents to serve on formal and informal school committees.
2. Take measurable steps to ensure that all parents know they are welcome to join in the full community life of Barrow Academy.

Terry was interested in moving Barrow forward, not marking time as a placeholder. As outlined to him in his first meetings with Dr. Watson, the transitions from the self-study to the visiting-team report to a new strategic plan for charting Terry's leadership objectives seemed to provide natural and seamless opportunities for Terry to learn.

In the winter of his second year, Terry was surprised by the occasionally contentious verbal exchanges unleashed in the early stages of the strategic planning process. The reactions, Terry remarked to his wife, Melissa, reminded him of the paroxysms that traditionally accompany the departure of long-ruling despots in developing countries. In contrast to the period of muted questioning during the self-study process, suddenly it seemed that everything was on the table and up for grabs. Terry was hearing that the mission statement—cursorily reviewed and reaffirmed by the board last year in the self-study—did not embody, for some, a forward-thinking dynamic vision around which the school community could rally.

Terry and his family had just returned from their first real vacation in three years. Scanning his day-timer for the first time in a week, Terry noticed that in his absence Karin, his assistant, had scheduled a meeting for him with Kim and Vanessa, two active mothers in the Parents' Association with whom he had first become acquainted during the self-study process.

With their children in different grades along the Barrow spectrum of preschool through 12th grade, Vanessa and Kim seemed to have little in common other than an evident appreciation for independent schools and successful professional careers previous to full-time parenthood. It wasn't unusual for parents to take advantage of Terry's open-door policy to share their views on matters large and small. But normally Karin noted the primary topic of the meeting in the day-timer so that Terry could ascertain from the most appropriate division director whether a particular problem prompted the visit. For this upcoming meeting, Karin had written only the cryptic words "new models?"

However, refreshed and reinvigorated by his vacation, Terry welcomed Kim and Vanessa with warmth. Their own convivial but clearly sincere greetings suggested that nothing could be too seriously amiss. After a few minutes of banter, Terry asked with a smile, "How can I help you all today?"

He was pleasantly surprised to hear Kim respond, "Well, Terry, we are here to offer you and Barrow our time and experience, and all we really need from you, for the time being, is to listen with an open mind. We love Barrow, but with all due respect, it needs to get over itself if it is to realize its full potential as a learning community."

Terry leaned back in his chair as, across the table, Kim leaned forward. "We thought the world of Dr. Watson as a fund raiser, but he was never much of an educator. We would never have mustered the nerve to request this meeting if we didn't think that you are."

CASE STUDY
THE RISING TIDE

Clearly the leader of the pair, Kim continued, "Your invitation to us and the other parents to participate as full team members in the self-study process allowed us to understand Barrow's challenges and potential in a whole new way. But that wasn't all. We also learned about other benchmark programs and model schools in our regional and national association. Before, we complained about the seemingly never-ending tuition increases. Now, after serving on the self-study committee for budget and financial management, I see how delicately our budget must be balanced."

Vanessa added, "More parents need to have the educational opportunity we did to understand how different independent schools really are from anything we had experienced before coming to Barrow."

Kim nodded and spoke again. "We appreciate the structures and support that you and Barrow's faculty give our children. However, parents need clear structures, too. The guidelines you distributed last spring about hosting student parties, and the information about curfews and teen alcohol use, helped us say no to our kids and to stand up when Mr. and Mrs. Olds intended to allow that keg party after prom. And Ms. Shelton's evening parent information event on Internet dangers was a revelation."

Vanessa interrupted to point out that, before the self-study, she had no idea how much of a resource for parents the NAIS website could be on all sorts of subjects.

Kim and Vanessa were really warming to their topic now, and Terry felt a bit like a tennis fan on a long grass-court rally.

"Although of course Barrow is a much better school for Mark and Daniel," Kim continued, "University Collegiate Academy includes the NAIS Principles of Good Practice for Parents in both its student-parent handbook and in its re-enrollment contract. Some folks may not care for the dress code and may not like rules, but I sure do. The Principles of Good Practice make the rules of the educational marriage between the school and the home crystal clear—and they aren't just rules for Barrow… they have larger social credibility. I'll take clear and up-front over warm and fuzzy any day. "

Apparently the self-study process and the visiting team recommendations had stimulated Barrow parents to consider becoming involved with school life in more meaningful ways. The visioning work that parents, teachers, and trustees had done as part of the accreditation and evaluation efforts provided an unprecedented opportunity to extend, consolidate, and formalize a cultural transformation. Like many other parents on self-study committees with whom they had previously had no contact, Kim and Vanessa had begun to wonder why, with good leadership, such issues-oriented forums could not continue beyond the accreditation and strategic planning cycles.

"In my other life before marriage and my four children, I served as a managing partner at Watson, Morrow, and Duckett," Vanessa said. "I have never regretted giving up that life to become a homemaker. But now that Colin and Justin are pretty much occupied from drop-off until after athletics, I want to use my discretionary time in the best way I can. The array of Barrow

Parents' Association volunteer opportunities—selling wrapping paper and baking for Faculty Appreciation Day—are pleasant and worthwhile for connecting to the life of the school. But, frankly, the volunteer offerings appeal to only a narrow slice of our current parent population. I am able to and want to contribute in other ways, and many in the parent community feel the same way."

Kim continued, "From time to time, particularly when things seem the rosiest, the culture of any organization—educational, corporate, or otherwise—must be honestly assessed. The self-study is a good start and will serve the visiting team well as a reference document. But our culture desperately needs a community structure for both follow-through and proactive troubleshooting. Otherwise, too often, an unanticipated institutional crisis is necessary to counteract the inevitable inertia of complacent success. No one wants that."

Kim spoke of her previous experience in a successful public school system in another state and then added, "Cultural habits can either impede or energize innovation. Barrow has more than its fair share of habits that seem mindless. To fundamentally reconsider our school and its pedagogy requires us to involve all segments of our diverse community in creative thinking."

Having obviously put a great deal of thought and preparation into her impassioned plea, Kim went on to say, "Promoting how solid the school is may have been advantageous when Dr. Watson was soliciting funds from foundations and alumni. However, schools that are truly student-centered—as our mission statement and

marketing materials say Barrow is—must demonstrate that ideas are the commodity of highest value. But ideas must be communicated to have value, and to communicate effectively, relationships must be fostered. If relationships improve, shared trust and collaborative involvement are the byproducts.

"You, Terry, recommended Robert Putnam's book *Bowling Alone* in your most recent newsletter column, so I don't need to preach to you about the importance of social capital. If we can generate social capital in the next few years the way Dr. Watson generated financial capital, Barrow will emerge as an inclusive learning community where everyone, not just select members, may have a voice."

Referring to a three-by-five note card that she had deftly produced in her hand, Kim quoted from a report on the Johns Hopkins University website:

"An emphasis on the social organization of a school… and changes in the structure of an environment will produce changes in attitude, behaviors, and accomplishments of the people in that environment."

What Kim and Vanessa said that day gave Terry much to ponder.

Although he liked Ms. Waskowitz—the longtime head of University Collegiate Academy—he couldn't help resenting the idea that Barrow's friendly rival school served as the model for Kim's point about the NAIS Principles of Good Practice. He remembered the principles fuzzily from his pleasant indoctrination two summers ago at the NAIS Institute for New Heads.

CASE STUDY
THE RISING TIDE

To refresh his memory, he pulled up the NAIS website on his laptop screen and located the principles by conducting a quick keyword search. After skimming them once, Terry went back through more slowly and was gratified to see that many of his first- and second-year initiatives seemed to be referenced.

For example, under his direction, Barrow had made a significant effort to educate parents about parenting. The school placed particular emphasis on issues related to risky student behavior and the pressure to perform that is so prevalent in affluent suburbia.

Through its marketing and branding efforts, the school had also made important headway in better defining what Barrow stood for—and thus what distinguished it from University Collegiate and the many Christian academies that had recently joined the competition and undercut regional tuition averages.

In addition, one of the defining skirmishes of his first year—about crèches, dreidels, and Kwanzaa drums in the front lobby—seemed to be referenced in several of the principles.

After some thought, Terry concluded that the common denominator in all the Principles of Good Practice was communication. And after the initial gratification he had felt subsided a bit, he realized there was much Barrow could do to communicate better. Having heard Kim and Vanessa's fresh perspectives, he inferred that the gradually deteriorating support for his predecessor, Dr. Watson, and his own recent struggles reflected friction among conflicting priorities—priorities including athletics, academics, college guidance, admissions, diversity, dress code, financial aid, student discipline, and scheduling.

The more Terry discussed the mothers' proposal with Barrow's board chair, Robin, the clearer it became to them both that the glossy patina of a highly effective external relations effort—of which they had been so proud—had the possible downside of undermining effective communication.

With Terry's arrival at Barrow had come a leadership change that encouraged more candid conversations within a parent community that was more diverse than it had been 15 years before. Given that the previous administration had placed a premium on stability and tranquility, the school's marketing and fund-raising materials had gradually become Barrow's primary communication vehicles. As the medium became the message, the loyal hype repressed differences of perspective that in time had become seismic fissures in the school's philosophic foundation.

Ultimately, the meeting with Kim and Vanessa proved to be a providential "tipping point" in mobilizing some very talented parents. As a result, Barrow's strategic plan shifted away from clarifying faculty and administrative job descriptions and objectives and toward establishing relationship-building as Barrow's fundamental institutional priority. The term "bottoms up" assumed a new professional connotation for Terry as he solidified his administrative vision.

To be continued....

EXEMPLARY APPLICATIONS OF GOOD PRACTICE

EXAMPLE 1: Using Technology to Promote Open Communication
(Relates to Schools-Working-with-Parents Principles 1, 4, and 5)

At the encouragement of the head of X School in Arkansas, the director of community relations worked with the development office and the health office to establish a database of e-mail addresses. Eventually, they gathered addresses for more than 90 percent of current parents and 50 percent of involved alumni. When a well-known faculty member was arrested, the head used the resulting parent listserve to stay ahead of the innuendo in the popular media. For two weeks after the arrest, daily e-mail updates provided the school community with detailed, accurate information as well as talking points about the situation and the school's position.

Although the matter was difficult for all, the e-mail communication minimized speculation and misinformation and reassured parents that the school was doing everything possible to help students work through their shock and disappointment. Although the situation could have been a public relations catastrophe, the proactive communication actually improved parents' perceptions about the school.

EXAMPLE 2: Making Sure Must-know Information Gets Known
(Relates to Schools-Working-with-Parents Principles 1, 2, and 9)

Y School in Missouri wanted to ensure that everyone was clear about the school's responsibilities to parents and the parents' responsibilities to the school community. To make sure the information got out, the school did two things:
1. With the active involvement, advice, and consent of the parents' association, it created a detailed list of such responsibilities to include in the annual student-parent handbook.
2. Then the school used the list as the basis for the enrollment and annual re-enrollment contracts that both parents had to sign and return to the school with the deposit.

EXAMPLE 3: Setting Aside Time to Listen
(Relates to Schools-Working-with-Parents Principles 1, 3, and 7)

At a Texas school for children in preschool through fourth grade, parents meet for 30 to 45 minutes with their child's homeroom teacher in the days before the school year starts.

The meeting allows parents to bond with the teacher and share their hopes and concerns about the year ahead. Teachers are trained to use this as a listening conference to gather insight about the student and family rather than a time to discuss curriculum and schedules. (Nuts-and-bolts topics like these are covered in a separate intake package.) To help initiate dialogue, the teachers know to use prompts such as, "What did Alex do over the summer?" and "Have there been any changes in your family?"

This school encourages continuity in volunteer activities through a leadership council that brings together past, present, and future parents' association and committee chairs in monthly meetings with key administrators. The leadership council provides training for future presidents and various school committee chairs as well as historical perspective for the incumbents.

EXAMPLE 4: Providing the Resources That Make Roles Clear
(Relates to Schools-Working-with-Parents Principles 1, 6, and 7)

For the sake of clarity and consistency, several schools provide the same resources for parent volunteers as for the board of trustees: clearly defined bylaws and job descriptions for the parents' association, plus flow charts for communicating decisions in various areas of school life in which parents are involved.

CASE STUDY *continued from page 158*
THE RISING TIDE

PROCESS AS PRODUCT

In the late winter of Terry's second year, the Barrow board engaged a retired school-head-turned-consultant to guide the strategic planning process. As the first step, the school convened several focus groups representing the usual suspects: parents, alumni board members, upper school student leaders, and faculty who wanted to participate. The consultant also guided a Saturday morning trustee retreat on strategic planning.

To Terry, the entire process seemed to exist in a vaguely parallel, but sanitized, virtual reality. Identifying opportunities, threats, challenges, and opportunities... riffling through new goals and objectives... then preparing to reassign them in traditional patterns of organizational accountability.... The steps didn't seem to connect a majority of Barrow constituents around a reinvigorated vision of the school.

By using techniques that were time-honored, easily controlled, predictable, but now—in Terry's mind—outmoded, it seemed that Barrow was almost squandering the opportunity to unify the school around his new leadership and define for prospective parents the unique experience Barrow provided to the surrounding community. Any large systemic revisions in who participates, how work is accomplished, and how to empower, rather than impede, organizational progress seemed at best an afterthought—if a thought at all.

Fortunately, Kim's previous human resources experience had taught her a new paradigm—one that linked the strategic planning process to a

critical assessment of structure, work processes, and job design. Moreover, as Terry began to research other models on the Internet, he encountered persuasive educational research that correlated student achievement and parental involvement as well as the association between community involvement and overall satisfaction with the school. Perhaps the welcome mat that Barrow had placed at its selective doors was starting to wear thin—and this was the time to do something about it.

The board responded well to Terry's suggestion that his first strategic plan at Barrow should proceed more slowly. He argued for designing and building it around the relationships that define a school's culture and create either positive or negative associations for parents, teachers, students, and staff. However, trustees expressed concern about shifting the embedded culture. Could they improve established relationships and organizational norms without endangering Barrow's valued traditions?

From that discussion emerged the first of only four interrelated strategic priorities of the new strategic plan: "Strike a balance between Barrow's tradition of cultivating the involvement of individuals... while also building our school's many very different individuals into a strong, cohesive community." This priority focused on new ways to strengthen relationships among all members of the Barrow community.

With that statement as its keynote, the strategic planning process accelerated remarkably. After two more months of hearing diverse voices in open focus groups, the board approved a preliminary draft of the plan at the May meeting.

CASE STUDY
THE RISING TIDE

Soon thereafter, via a summer mailing and the Barrow website, members of the larger community received a copy of the draft for comments. After a few consequent minor modifications, the board formally approved a strategic plan revision in September.

However, the dialogues had really only just begun. The relationships that evolved among diverse parents and among parents, trustees, and faculty may have been the strategic planning process's most important achievement. Gradually it dawned on both Terry, as head of school, and Robin, as board chair, that perhaps they didn't need to hang on to the controls so tightly to do their jobs successfully. With time, a less hierarchical, more inclusive governance model might emerge using the new strategic priorities as the structural foundation.

LISTENING TO LEAD

Terry quickly realized that the overarching Principle of Good Practice for parents and schools working together was, except for the subject, the same first principle in both lists:

"Effective partnerships are characterized by clearly defined responsibilities, a shared commitment to collaboration, open lines of communication, mutual respect, and a common vision of the goals to be reached."

He began to refer to that quote frequently, particularly in relations with Barrow's faculty. With Kim and Vanessa contributing most of the planning time necessary, the really interesting work began for Terry in the fall of his third year.

Over the summer, Terry had reviewed the advice from the various professional gurus on cultural transformation. On the basis of his own recent experience, Terry could agree with some pundits' pronouncement that all lasting organizational change requires three to five years to coalesce. To see beyond their familiar world, a small group of parents and faculty (and Terry, as time permitted) began an external organizational study to evaluate parent involvement in 100 private and public schools. Based on those findings, the group developed four "involvement models":

- **Traditional,** in which parents are engaged primarily in the social and economic dimensions of the school, such as fund raising, homeroom support functions, or short-term, ad-hoc tasks. The traditional model is quite common in education, where organizational silos often occur. For example, parent volunteers typically operate in completely separate spheres from school personnel. Barrow exemplified the traditional model.
- **One-way linkage,** which is typically hierarchical, with restricted leadership opportunities for parents and faculty and limited meaningful interaction with school administration about school policies and procedures. Although a few key issues may create opportunities for interactions among parents, faculty, and school administrators, these issues are usually limited to parent education or child development.
- **Two-way linkage,** whereby mixed teams of various constituents (such as parents, faculty, administrators, and board members) collaborate on key issues. School employees and parents are trained in the dynamics of

project and meeting management, and the teams create rules for interacting and decision-making processes upfront. There is a defined structure around key strategic-plan priorities. The organizational structure itself is less hierarchical, and diverse opportunities are available for parents and school staff to develop leadership skills and take charge of various initiatives.

- **Integrative,** with a culture of shared partnerships and flexible teams advancing strategic plans and priorities. Among the signs of an integrative culture: A dynamic parent homepage lists ongoing volunteer opportunities that are varied and evolving. A new-parent orientation conveys the school's operating philosophy, culture, and key values. School decisions reflect its mission and core values as well as an external awareness of national and international best practices. Parents and school personnel are trained and equipped to represent the school in leadership positions throughout the community. And the organizational structure fosters a flexible learning community that's mindful of the importance of monitoring, assessing, and altering programs and plans.

While also seeking advice from a nationally known consultant on independent school management, Terry worked closely with the division heads to develop a school-culture survey to distribute to the faculty. The survey covered their awareness and appreciation of the Barrow mission statement; their sense of professional collegiality and support in the school; their attitudes toward, and involvement in, student discipline and supporting student success;

effectiveness of faculty meetings; and other, similar systems previously taken for granted. To establish benchmarks the school could use in evaluating progress via future surveys, the culture survey was administered to all teachers in their respective division meetings, and the results were tabulated accordingly.

Thought-provoking differences in perspective arose between divisions around questions such as the relative importance of character education in their work with students. These differences became fascinating topics for later discussion in small faculty groups, in division meetings, and within the full faculty. For example, upper school faculty perceived proactive communication with parents as significantly less important. In fact, one upper school history teacher commented, "I communicate well with those students and parents who merit and appreciate my effort and my time." For Terry, the feedback underscored the need to serve more as a pastoral counselor for his teachers and less as a pit boss.

As Barrow progressed toward the integrative school model, Terry began to find his own unique vision and voice as a head of school. When a shared sense of mission and common goals exists, teachers can work with families more as partners, ideas cross-fertilize, and innovation becomes the norm rather than an exception. As Terry conceived the ideal, a visionary appreciation of the school would emerge as a highly collaborative, team-oriented learning community, with mechanisms in place to monitor, assess, and challenge assumptions through broad-based, objective community data.

CASE STUDY
THE RISING TIDE

With that goal in mind, later that fall Terry worked with Robin, Kim, and Vanessa to develop a steering committee made up of personnel from all three divisions and parents who represented various subgroups in the school community (such as males and parents of minority students). This mixed forum of parents and teachers, dubbed the Community Council, was intended to represent concerns that in the past may have been perceived as peripheral. The concerns included communicating with alumni, new Barrow families, and families unfamiliar with independent schools.

The Community Council's mission was "strengthening partnerships among faculty, families, administration, staff, and alumni to advance Barrow's educational goals for students."

Chaired by Community Council members, design teams emerged to focus on specific issues that Barrow's strategic plan had identified. These design teams offered open opportunities for staff, faculty, administrators, parents, and alumni to come together and share ideas to strengthen teaching and learning opportunities. In the first year, design teams formed around key strategic priorities, such as advancing external relationships/student internships, technology integration, family education, communicating the curriculum, and supporting inclusion.

Many of Barrow's younger faculty members embraced the Community Council from the outset. They saw it as a new opportunity to become involved and to express their views about pedagogy, technology, student discipline, and other topics they'd never been asked about before. In the Community Council's early discussions, several younger faculty expressed concerns about communication that sometimes seemed distant and disrespectful between divisions and Barrow's two campuses, between parents and teachers, and between the old guard faculty and the younger teachers. They expressed concerns as well about too-familiar and perhaps inappropriate communication between some teachers and students.

Now finding a more confident stride, and with a second three-year contract in hand, Terry knew that communication is inevitably the central issue in schools. One can never communicate enough, and the visiting team certainly reflected this concern in its report. Moreover in his three years at Barrow, Terry had learned that criticism about a "poor communicator" often meant that the recipient disagreed with the message being communicated. At one meeting, Kim focused the issue succinctly by commenting, "As Barrow depends upon relationships to thrive, any successful relationship depends upon effective communications. That is the premise underlying the Community Council's mission."

In the wake of the strategic plan, communication had certainly become more regular and consistent. However, judging from how the parents on the council affirmed their concern, the school would soon need to look at the subject of communication from a different perspective.

CASE STUDY CONCLUSION: AN EDDY IN THE STREAM

This year, the drab days of January and February flew by. Terry, his administration, and most of the trustees were uplifted by the fresh enthusiasm that greeted the recent initiatives. The community appeared re-energized by a sense of collective purpose.

However, Terry was not surprised by a counter-reaction to his including parents more openly in school processes. He remembered well Dr. Watson's candid orientation summary of three years before, almost to the day, about Barrow's history, pride of purpose, and reputation as a "faculty-run" school. Consequently, Terry was prepared when he looked at his schedule for a late-spring Friday before Memorial Day and saw that several upper school department chairs from the old guard had requested a meeting. Karin had made a notation in Terry's day-timer that said "institutional direction."

Fred Durham, head of the English Department for more than 15 years and a Barrow teacher for at least 15 years before that, spoke first for the other three.

"Terry, we are here because we are concerned. Collectively, we have more than 100 years committed to this school. For most of us, you are the fourth head of school—some good, some not so good—under whom we have taught a couple of generations of Barrow students, including a few who are now our trustees. We all endorsed the search committee's recommendation for you to replace Peter Watson, and I for one served on the advisory committee. Despite your youth and relative inexperience with the complexities of a school like Barrow, we liked your enthusiasm and energy.

"However, we no longer feel we can stand idly by while the bedrock of our school is undermined by excessive interference by parents. Barrow is not a public school, and we want to keep it that way."

Fred's colleagues echoed those keynotes with minor variations. After listening attentively to their views for about 20 minutes, Terry spoke with a dawning clarity and a passion that surprised him:

"You all are absolutely right in many respects: The academy's current success is in large part a function of your dedicated commitment as Barrow teachers to the highest ideals of our profession. And although my job description these days involves few papers to grade and more adult contact, I am, and will always consider myself, a teacher.

"To be perfectly candid, I am not sure where the recent discussions with parents will lead. Like a great discussion in a thoughtful, well-prepared class of students, the dialogue we have encouraged is not easily predictable. But I am a teacher, not a lawyer, and therefore I am willing to ask questions for which I don't already know the answer.

"It certainly has not made my life as head of school any easier, and sometimes, frankly, that uncertainty awakens me at 3 in the morning. However, the genie is out of the bottle and won't go back in. Fortunately, our genie is a powerful one that wants to do, and can do, great things.

CASE STUDY
THE RISING TIDE

"As a day school, we must be responsible to, and serve, the community in which we live and work. And as our community has changed, you all have seen how our student body has changed as a result. And schools are increasingly serving expanded roles as community centers because we've lost these gathering places elsewhere in society. But has Barrow been as mindful of those changes as it should be? Although we may not like how our students sometimes talk or the values that sometimes they bring with them, Barrow must evolve thoughtfully to remain relevant in our city and for our graduates to retain the respect of the full gamut of colleges to which they matriculate.

"You are concerned that allowing parents more access to information about, and involvement in planning for, our curriculum compromises your professional autonomy. But remember that we were founded in 1922 by parents involved in their children's education and not fundamentally unlike some of the current parents whom you refer to as opinionated and sometimes intrusive.

"As Barrow's current head, I work to find the common ground among the various constituencies to which I am responsible—you, the faculty, the trustees, and the parents—in the best interests of the children we serve. Just as I encourage parents to express their informed opinion, I very much appreciate your taking the time to meet with me today, and I truly value your opinion.

"As head of school, I am challenged to divine the best course among the many worthwhile ideas with which I am presented. Ideas come in many shades of gray. However, I'll take a surfeit of good ideas over a dearth any day. Any process we implement to identify and cull the best ideas is only as good as the people who are involved. I certainly can't do it alone. As leaders of the faculty, I need you to be positively involved. This process is not secondary to our business as teachers, but primary to it.

"However, I must point out that now, as the hour is late and Memorial Day is upon us all, I have a fifth constituency, which ultimately is of the most importance to me: my family. Melissa, the kids, and I are taking off before dawn tomorrow morning for a few days without Internet, phones, or faxes. I would tell you more, but Melissa has sworn us all to secrecy under penalty of death. In any case, I wish you a restful and rewarding long weekend and look forward to continuing our conversation in the future." ∎

DISCUSSION QUESTIONS

1. What are the key advantages of enhancing parent involvement and opportunities for meaningful collaboration?

2. When increasing parental participation, what are some of the issues regarding planning and communication that you must consider to manage new processes and working relationships?

3. How can you use your strategic plan or other school-improvement plans to devise an organizational or team structure?

4. When moving from a traditional model to an integrative or learning-community model, what kinds of training should you consider for parents, faculty, and staff?

5. How can the head balance the need to continually improve with the obligation to protect the traditions that are part and parcel of the fabric of the school?

6. When a collaborative team of parents and faculty is formed, what key topics need to be covered in the first meeting to establish role clarity and appropriate boundaries for all participants?

7. Describe how you could use technology to increase participation among and ongoing feedback from various school constituents (including stay-at-home parents, parents who are employed full time, faculty, staff, etc.).

SUGGESTED RESOURCES AND READING MATERIALS

National Association of Independent Schools: Search "Parent Associations" (*www.nais.org*).

North Central Regional Educational Laboratory (*www.ncrel.org*). See especially "Critical Issue: Constructing School Partnerships with Families and Community Groups."

National Network of Partnership Schools at Johns Hopkins University. See especially "The School Planning and Management Team: SPMT" (*www.csos.jhu.edu*) or (*www.partnershipschools.com*).

Clearinghouse on Educational Policy and Management (CEPM), formerly the ERIC Clearinghouse on Educational Management (*http://eric.uoregon.edu*).

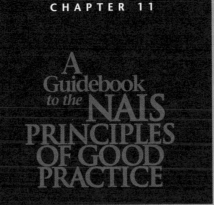

A Guidebook
to the NAIS
PRINCIPLES
OF GOOD
PRACTICE

for

SCHOOL SEARCH COMMITTEES AND SEARCH CONSULTANTS

By Roger J. Bass

Roger J. Bass *is a partner and senior consultant with Resource Group 175, which does executive search and consulting in governance and strategic planning. Formerly, Bass served as head of University Prep in Seattle, president of the Pacific Northwest Association of Independent Schools, and board treasurer of NAIS.*

NAIS PRINCIPLES OF GOOD PRACTICE for

SEARCH COMMITTEES AND SEARCH CONSULTANTS

Revised and approved by the NAIS board in 2003

The following Principles of Good Practice are designed to help search committees as they embark upon the task of selecting a school head. Each school must decide for itself whether or not it will retain a consultant to help with the search. If the school does decide to engage professional counsel, the same principles should be observed. (Although many of the principles apply to this case study, the ones in **boldface** are the most pertinent.)

SEARCH COMMITTEES

1. The board and search committee should devise a search process that is viewed as fair, orderly, and cost-effective by all parts of the school community.

2. The search committee should actively solicit the names of the best available candidates drawn from a broad candidate group without regard to age, race, religion, gender, or national origin unless the school has a religious mission that requires the head to have a particular religious affiliation.

3. The search committee should see pertinent materials related to any and all candidates, including applications that come from outside the consultant's regular network.

4. **The search committee should recognize the sensitivity of visits by trustees to a candidate's present school. The consultant should work with the search committee and candidate to see that such visits are complete and thorough yet at no time jeopardize the relationship of the candidate to his or her present school. School visits should be made only when the candidate and search committee are at a mutually serious stage.**

5. The search committee should make every effort to present the school with a diverse group of candidates. All principles associated with providing equal opportunity should be observed in the process.

SEARCH CONSULTANTS

1. The search consultant should make every effort to present the school with a diverse group of candidates. All principles associated with providing equal opportunity should be observed in the process.

2. In outlining procedures to the search committee, the consultant should provide a full written description of services offered, including expenses and fees. In the case of a consulting firm, the search committee should be told which person in the firm will do the search and should interview that person prior to any contracting for services.

3. **The consultant should make known the names of other schools for which he or she actively is performing a search for persons to fill a similar position.**

4. The consultant should limit searches during any given period to a number that will assure service of high quality to each client school.

5. **The search consultant should make a reasonable effort to understand the school, its mission, its culture, and the nature of the position to be filled.**

6. The school, not the individual candidate, should always be the client.

7. **Both consultant and search committee should check candidates' references with great care. The consultant is responsible for presenting a candidate for consideration by the search committee and for emphasizing the committee's responsibility after that time.**

8. The consultant should respect the confidentiality of each candidacy and impress upon both search committee and candidates the importance of discretion. Any candidate now a head who is seriously exploring other school headships should so inform his or her current board chair in confidence.

9. The consultant should keep the search committee fully informed about the progress of the assignment throughout the search and ensure that each candidate is informed fully and promptly about the status of his or her candidacy.

10. The consultant should refrain from inviting the head of a school placed in that position by the consultant's firm within the past five years to become a candidate for the client school.

11. No consultant or any member of the consultant's firm should be a candidate for a position in which the consultant is conducting a search.

CASE STUDY
A SEARCH COMMITTEE CHAIR CONFRONTS HARD REALITIES

Tom has served on the board of the Extraordinarily Special School for four years. His two children have gained a lot from attending the school, so Tom and his wife are pleased with the program.

Today, Selma, the board president, calls to tell Tom that, after 17 years as head of ESS, Helena Handly has informed the executive committee that she will retire in June. Although Helena has always been controlling about all things related to ESS, she has said the board is on its own with the search process. She is adamant that she does not want to be involved.

After explaining this situation, Selma asks Tom to serve as the chair of the search committee charged with finding Helena's successor. Tom is flattered and accepts immediately. Selma then informs him that, because selecting a new head is such an important decision, she plans to visit the current school of every finalist. These personal visits will make sure that "we leave no stone unturned."

In Tom's business, the human resources department takes care of hiring. Tom simply tells HR what position is open, says yes or no to the HR manager's choice, and waits for the new employee to show up at work. Now Tom learns that he will be expected to "involve everyone in an open and inclusive process." Furthermore, his board president wants to veto the process if she does not like something she learns from her personal school visits.

"What am I to do?" Tom asks his wife that evening. "I never thought I'd have to do this when I joined the board. I'm not even sure where to begin. What in the world have I gotten myself into?"

Early the next morning, Tom calls NAIS and asks for help. NAIS suggests he order a copy of the recently revised *NAIS Head Search Handbook* and suggests that he go to *www.nais.org* and review its listing of search consultants. Tom checks the website immediately and reads the book as soon as he receives it. Although he feels reassured that he's capable of handling this important job for ESS, he realizes that to serve the school's best interests, the committee will need guidance. He subsequently phones several search consultants to see how they might help with the ESS search.

To be continued....

EXEMPLARY APPLICATIONS OF GOOD PRACTICE

EXAMPLE 1: Careful Reference Checks Prevent a Hiring Disaster
(Relates to Search Consultant Principle 7)

At a school in the West, the members of the search committee identified their first-choice candidate for head of school. Following the usual practice, their consultant did extensive reference checking but found he could not recommend the candidate. By this time, however, the school's search committee had already "fallen in love" with the candidate. He was bright, had good academic credentials, looked the part, and interviewed well.

At first, the search committee chose to ignore the reference report indicating that the candidate was high risk. The consultant reminded the search committee of the Principles of Good Practice, which indicate that both the search committee and the consultant are obligated to check references carefully. The search committee finally heeded the consultant's warning about red flags and offered the position to another candidate.

Two years later, the members of the committee learned that their original candidate had been hired and soon dismissed by another school over the very concerns their careful reference checks had identified.

EXAMPLE 2: Careful Reference Checks Confirm a Candidate's Viability
(Relates to Search Consultant Principle 7)

Another school's search consultant found through reference checking that a candidate's school had been involved in a serious legal case. A student indicated that she had been abused by her uncle while boarding with the school's receptionist. The abuse did not take place on school property nor at the home of the receptionist, but the consultant found the information troubling. After getting permission from the candidate, the consultant talked with the attorney who had represented the girl's school.

The consultant revealed what he learned to the school's search committee. Committee members discussed the situation, decided the case had not been the result of negligence on the part of the head (their first-choice candidate), and agreed to hire the candidate.

Thanks to the thorough reference checks, the school was able to move forward with confidence. Everyone involved in the hiring felt fully informed and prepared to knowledgeably dismiss questions that might arise from any rumors. The search committee and board had all the needed facts to ask questions, make a sound judgment, and prepare a formal communication plan that proactively addressed the issue.

EXAMPLE 3: Schools Feel Pressured to Short-circuit the Process
(Relates to Search Consultant Principle 7)

A small school's search committee was unanimous in its approval of one candidate for head. The candidate, a charismatic gentleman, persuaded the search committee that he had just received an offer from another school. Saying that he had to decide quickly, he gave the school only one day to make a final decision. Against the consultant's advice, the board decided to hire the candidate immediately without reference checks.

Only after all parties signed the contract did the school discover that its charismatic new head had actually been fired from his previous position. The new head lasted for only one year. The school then had to repeat the arduous search process.

Another school faced a similar situation when a candidate pressured the search committee for an immediate answer. This school, however, did not give in and instead followed the Principle of Good Practice stating that the search committee must share responsibility for rigorous reference checking. The reference checks took place and did reveal serious inconsistencies between the resume and reality—thus helping the school avoid serious problems in the future.

EXAMPLE 4: A Candidate Misrepresents His Credentials
(Relates to Search Consultant Principle 7)

One school hired a head who said he had completed his doctorate. In truth, he had never passed his final exams and was misrepresenting himself. This school failed to realize that college credentials should always be verified as part of reference checking, and details of the resume should be checked against an official, sealed college transcript.

EXAMPLE 5: A Board Learns to Confront Its Own Shortcomings
(Relates to Search Consultant Principle 5)

Sometimes schools try to put forward only the best view of themselves. The real stories are left for new heads to discover after they have been hired. This creates a difficult start for the heads and hurts morale throughout the schools.

Search consultants can help present a realistic picture by following Search Consultant Principle 5. It states that a consultant must understand the school's true nature and encourage everyone to be forthcoming about the circumstances that necessitated a leadership change. By being honest with each other, the consultant and the school can shape the background story, thereby creating an accurate understanding of issues the new head will face as well as a learning experience for the board.

In one instance, a school in California had a strong desire to complete its search speedily. After selecting a consultant, the search committee revealed that the board was unclear about what it wanted and, lacking adequate leadership from the board, faculty members felt they should write the job description and hire the head.

When the consultant expressed alarm, the search committee insisted on pressing forward with all haste. The consultant notified the school in writing that he felt the search was in trouble. He suggested that the board have a retreat, the goal of which would be a better understanding of the board's role. The consultant also advised doing extensive work with the faculty to clarify that hiring the head was the board's responsibility. Finally, to alleviate the time pressures, the consultant suggested hiring an interim head and slowing the process in order to make the best selection.

This advice ultimately proved acceptable to board members. They were then able to proceed with a successful search in a more deliberately paced and organizationally appropriate manner.

EXAMPLE 6: A Consultant Avoids a Conflict of Interest

(Relates to Search Consultant Principle 3)

Search consultants themselves must be completely honest in avoiding conflicts of interest, or the appearance thereof.

One consultant had a candidate who was being considered by two schools within the same geographic region. Following the Principles of Good Practice, this consultant fully disclosed involvement in multiple searches to both schools. With their approval, the consultant then timed the searches so that the candidate was able to see both schools, after which the candidate made a decision about which school was the best match. After that, the candidate remained in only one search.

The ground rules were clear for all parties from the beginning: This excellent candidate should have an opportunity to see both schools but could not become a finalist in more than one search represented by a single consultant.

CASE STUDY *continued from page 172*
A SEARCH COMMITTEE CHAIR CONFRONTS HARD REALITIES

MAKING BEST PRACTICE THE TOP PRIORITY

Tom calls several individuals for initial information about their firms and their approaches to conducting searches. After interviewing their top choices, the search committee selects Henry Holden of Quality Consulting Services. Henry begins by spending several days at ESS getting information about the school, its challenges, and the qualities the school needs in its next head.

While talking with Tom, Henry hears about Selma's desire to visit the schools of all finalists. This is not the best practice in a search, Henry says. It is very disruptive for a school to contemplate losing one of its valued employees. And for candidates who do not become ESS's final choice, Selma's visit to their current schools will put them in an extremely uncomfortable position.

Tom has never considered these possibilities. But, for the moment, his main concern is this: Selma is a formidable board president. How can Tom convince her that her "interrogation plan" may be destructive rather than helpful?

Henry refers Tom to the NAIS Principles of Good Practice for Search Committees and Search Consultants. In particular, Henry points out this principle:

"The search committee should recognize the sensitivity of visits by trustees to a candidate's present school. The consultant should work with the search committee and candidate to see that such visits are complete and thorough yet at no time jeopardize the relationship of the candidate to his or her present school. School visits should be made only when the candidate and search committee are at a mutually serious stage."

"So," Tom asks, "exactly what does all that mean?"

It means the ESS representatives should visit only the final candidate's school and plan that visit very carefully, Henry replies. The visiting committee needs to agree in advance on the answers to questions like these: What types of questions are appropriate? How deeply should these questions delve? Who will be asked these questions?

Tom sighs. He foresees a battle with his board president.

Henry emphasizes that the search committee must understand that its mandate is to bring forth one final candidate for the board to consider. Allowing the board president to veto this process would be entirely inappropriate. As a member of the board, Selma would, of course, be welcome to participate in discussions about the candidate. But if she were to visit the final candidate's school, she would need to be teamed with a member of the search committee, and their findings and opinions would have to be forwarded to the search committee for consideration.

After Tom sighs again, Henry offers to go with him to speak with Selma. Tom feels greatly relieved to have Henry's additional support. At the subsequent meeting, Selma listens carefully and, though she is not pleased, agrees to forgo her visits to each candidate's school.

The search moves forward with a less-anxious chair and a consultant who works in tandem with the committee. Henry adds value to the search in several ways. Because of his experience with many different schools, he is able to anticipate issues that typically arise around governance, founders, and finance. He offers an objective view on issues facing ESS. In addition, since most members of the search committee have never done anything like this before, he helps them create an effective structure and realistic schedule for the search. Thanks to his access to relevant networks, he brings forth a wide and diverse pool of candidates.

Like all searches, ESS's has its ups and downs. But by combining the NAIS principles with Henry's guidance and their own growing insight into what the school really needs, the members of the search committee are able to recommend a well-qualified candidate. Eighteen months after Tom first took Selma's call, the new head is warmly received by the school community. ■

DISCUSSION QUESTIONS

1. What is the appropriate role of the chair of the board of trustees in the search for a new head of school?

2. What is the best way for search committees to check references? Who should do the checking, and what types of questions should be asked?

3. What types of conflicts of interest might arise during a search, including conflicts involving trustees, faculty, committee members, or the consultant?

4. How can a search committee conduct a search that is open and inclusive but does not get stalled in endless process?

SUGGESTED RESOURCES AND READING MATERIALS

Adams, A. "How to Keep Your Head: Great Schools and Long-Term Headships," *Independent School Magazine* (Fall 2002).

Albert, Sheila. *Hiring the Chief Executive: A Practical Guide to the Search and Selection Process.* Washington, DC: BoardSource, 2000.

DeKuyper, Mary H. *Trustee Handbook: A Guide to Effective Governance for Independent School Boards,* Ninth Edition. Washington DC: NAIS, 2007.

Dowdall, Jean. "The Right Search Committee," *Chronicle of Higher Education* (July 30, 2004).

The NAIS Head Search Handbook: A Start-to-Finish Guide for the Search Committee. Washington, DC: NAIS, 2006.

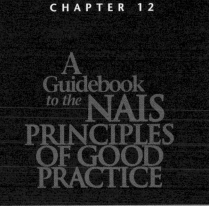

CHAPTER 12

A Guidebook to the NAIS PRINCIPLES OF GOOD PRACTICE

for
TEACHERS
AND
SUPERVISORS OF
TEACHERS

By Steve Clem

Steve Clem is executive director of the Association of Independent Schools in New England, located in Braintree, Massachusetts.

NAIS PRINCIPLES OF GOOD PRACTICE for

TEACHERS AND SUPERVISORS OF TEACHERS

Revised and approved by the NAIS board in 1990

Entrusted with the education of children, the independent school teacher promotes the best interests of the child within the context of the school's philosophy. Those who supervise teachers are responsible for the quality of teaching and for promoting growth in those who teach. The following Principles of Good Practice provide guidelines for teachers and for supervisors of teachers in their joint efforts to educate children. (Although many of the principles apply to this case study, the ones in **boldface** are the most pertinent.)

PRINCIPLES OF GOOD PRACTICE FOR TEACHERS

1. **The teacher has a thorough knowledge appropriate for his teaching assignment and stays abreast of recent developments in the field.**

2. The teacher uses a variety of teaching techniques suitable to the age and needs of the students and subject matter being taught.

3. The teacher establishes positive relationships with students, which, while recognizing the differing roles of adult and child, are characterized by mutual respect and good will.

4. The teacher collaborates with colleagues and the school's leadership in the design and implementation of curriculum within the context of the school's overall program and mission.

5. The teacher initiates growth and change in her own intellectual and professional development, seeking out conferences, courses, and other opportunities to learn.

6. The teacher is self-aware and self-monitoring in identifying and solving student, curricular, and school problems. At the same time, the teacher knows the mission and policies of the school and, when questions or concerns arise, raises them with appropriate colleagues and supervisors.

7. The teacher serves his school outside the classroom in a manner established by the individual school and consistent with the responsibilities of a professional educator. For example, teachers often serve as advisers, coaches, or activity sponsors.

8. **The teacher participates in the establishment and maintenance of an atmosphere of collegial support and adherence to professional standards.**

9. **The teacher welcomes supervision in the context of clearly defined and well-communicated criteria of evaluation.**

10. The teacher models integrity, curiosity, responsibility, creativity, and respect for all persons as well as an appreciation for racial, cultural, and gender diversity.

PRINCIPLES OF GOOD PRACTICE FOR SUPERVISORS OF TEACHERS

1. **The supervisor has thorough knowledge appropriate to her supervisory assignment and stays abreast of recent developments in the field. The supervisor also exemplifies in her own work with faculty members the qualities that she hopes to develop in the faculty.**

2. The supervisor develops and administers a comprehensive system of hiring, consistent with the policies of the school, which results in the appointment of the best-qualified candidate and a well-informed match between school and teacher. Throughout the hiring and supervisory processes, the supervisor values racial, cultural, and gender diversity.

3. The supervisor ensures that faculty members new to the school receive orientation and support sufficient for them to work effectively and with confidence that they are carrying out the educational mission, policies, and procedures of the school.

4. **The supervisor ensures that teachers are informed of both praise and criticism of their work and that useful**

support and assistance are available to each teacher to improve the quality of teaching.

5. The supervisor makes available to all faculty members on an equitable basis whatever resources the school can provide for professional growth and development, both inside and outside the school.

6. The supervisor encourages and challenges teachers to initiate curricular improvement by providing the necessary time and resources and by creating structures to foster faculty collaboration on curriculum development.

7. The supervisor leads faculty members in upholding high standards of professional behavior and responds immediately when behavior occurs that is harmful to children or harmful to the school community.

8. The supervisor evaluates and works to improve teaching through classroom visits, discussions with teachers, and other methods that are fair and consistent with the practices of the individual school. Evaluation is based on clearly articulated criteria that teachers have helped define and occurs in a context of respect for the teacher's professional knowledge and decision-making capability. The supervisor also monitors her own work by inviting suggestions and critiques from teachers.

9. When a faculty member's future in the school is in question, the supervisor devotes sufficient attention and resources to ensure that the situation is resolved or that the faculty member's departure from the school is handled with attention to due process and the dignity of the individual.

10. The supervisor ensures that all personnel policies are clearly articulated to faculty members and makes every effort to promote the establishment of salaries and benefits commensurate with the professional responsibilities of teaching.

CASE STUDY

A DEAN OF FACULTY CONFRONTS A TROUBLING LACK OF STANDARDS

The March meeting of the professional development committee had just broken up 10 minutes early. As Juliette, the dean of faculty, gathered her papers and shut down her laptop, Pat stopped by to say how much she had enjoyed the conversation about curriculum mapping. She wanted to volunteer to be on the study group that would do some research about mapping and report back to the committee later in the year.

Pleased and not a little surprised, Juliette took Pat up on her offer. They scheduled a meeting for the following week to discuss next steps. Pat left the conference room, waving and smiling, and Juliette sat back down and allowed herself an all-too-rare moment of reflection and satisfaction.

Things had not always gone so well. Looking back from the vantage point of almost two years, Juliette remembered the problems she confronted when she first took on this new job.

****

More than two years before that committee meeting, the head of Fredonia Country Day School realized she had less and less time to devote to hiring and working with faculty. So, with board approval, she created the position of dean of faculty in early April. Juliette applied for the job after considerable thought. As much as she enjoyed her work in the classroom, she had begun to think that she might enjoy working with adults even more. And it was time for a new challenge; she wasn't sure she could make it through another year of teaching *Lord of the Flies*.

Juliette got the job in May and officially started in August. By the next February, she was finally starting to feel less clueless, if not competent. Despite having been at the school for eight years, this new job was a revelation. The hardest part was the apparent expectation that anyone who had been a successful teacher would know how to be a successful administrator without any particular training and mentoring—just as independent schools in general seemed to think that being a successful college French student meant you could teach French. The head was too busy to give her much time beyond the weekly admin team meetings, and Juliette was reluctant to ask for help. In this school, people didn't readily admit they didn't know how to do something.

On top of feeling a bit at sea professionally, she had to deal with the emotional complexities of being the supervisor of people who had been her peers for more than eight years. Although she knew she was the same person, the new title seemed to be a distorting lens through which people now viewed her. Colleagues she knew and admired seemed to be making a lot of assumptions about her based solely on her new position in "The Administration."

Working with adults turned out to be a lot more complicated and frustrating than she had anticipated. The adults didn't feel obliged to do what she suggested, and sometimes they even seemed to take a perverse pride in non-compliance. Gandhi was definitely right about the power of passive resistance, thought Juliette. Had he worked in a school?

CASE STUDY
A DEAN OF FACULTY CONFRONTS A TROUBLING LACK OF STANDARDS

Navigating by trial and error, Juliette had made her way through her first year feeling pleased that she had at least managed to put out most of the fires. Then two drop-ins in a single week—one from the head and one from Pat—challenged her to move beyond fire control and begin to resolve the dissonance she was experiencing.

First, around 8:30 on a Tuesday morning, the head stopped by to tell Juliette about the previous night's board meeting. The trustees had voted to put into place an evaluation system that would "hold people accountable," "get rid of the dead wood on the faculty," and serve as the basis for a "long-overdue system of merit pay." And, to boot, the new system was supposed to be up and running a year from the coming September. Although the head had protested both the charge and the time constraints, the board was adamant and suggested she turn this over to "that new dean of faculty you were so anxious to hire." This suggestion made eminent sense to the head, so she came down the hall, popped into Juliette's office, and proceeded to transfer the proverbial monkey to Juliette's back.

Now, like many schools, FCDS did in fact have an evaluation process on the books. Six years before, a visiting committee had pointed out that FCDS was in violation of a standard by having no process at all. The school then hired a consultant to create a system, and there was a brief flurry of activity.

But the system was too complicated, and soon the faculty was in an uproar. The division heads and department heads (Juliette among them) were bearing the brunt of the faculty's pique and convinced the head to let the process wither and die, which it promptly did. The failed evaluation process quickly passed into the school's mythology and became a reliable topic of mirth as well as a powerful confirmation that the school's administration was, as the more polite put it, "out of it." As things stood, teachers at the school were getting virtually no professional feedback, and most people seemed to think that was just fine—their attitude was "Leave me alone and let me teach." But Juliette wasn't so sure anymore.

Although every accreditation process requires schools to have a process in place for teacher evaluation, the process is most often honored in the breach. As a consequence, most school teachers do not get the regular professional feedback they need. Why, Juliette wondered, is this so often the case? She concluded that the reasons are legion: time constraints, lack of training, and, more than anything, the tendency to avoid the anxieties stirred up by the prospect of actually talking about and evaluating the effectiveness of teaching. Professional feedback enhances teacher effectiveness, and that enhances student learning. The process of observation, evaluation, feedback, and goal setting must become a natural, integral part of the ways adults interact in schools. We can't imagine a school where students don't get feedback. Why do we accept being in a workplace where adults get no feedback?

Trying to work through some specific problems with several teachers left Juliette questioning this laissez-faire approach to supervision. She had become particularly aware of the near-total absence of any kind of written standards or expectations for teachers at the school; there was actually even less guidance for administrators. So it felt to her sometimes that she was operating in a vacuum, making things up as she went along. The absence of professional points of reference seemed to imply an atmosphere of "anything goes" in the classroom, as long as the parents didn't go ballistic and nothing made it to the front page of the local paper.

As overwhelming as the task of defining and implementing an effective process of faculty evaluation and supervision seemed to Juliette, there was a part of her that understood the need and welcomed the challenge. What with the claws, the smell, and the constant jabbering, monkeys on the back aren't much fun, but they do serve to focus the mind—plus, there's the fruit and the grooming.

Then there was Pat.

Pat had been at FCDS for 12 years and had always been a vocal champion of "high standards" for the school. Pat's teaching quickly became known as very demanding—unfairly so to some people—but students seemed to see having Pat as a kind of rite of passage, hard to cope with at the time but oddly satisfying in retrospect. Some colleagues, and Juliette herself, privately complained about how Pat's students often seemed to have little time or enthusiasm for other work. But even the complainers begrudgingly respected how much the students learned, particularly the really bright kids who were well prepared for the next year.

It was also true that in the past, Pat stood out because the rest of the middle school faculty was not particularly strong when she arrived. But a number of key hires over the next five or six years had brought in teachers of equal talent, two of whom had a stronger understanding of current educational theory and practice.

When Juliette was Pat's peer, she chose to stay away from the situation. But she no longer had that luxury. By late winter, nearly a year after Juliette became dean, colleagues she valued (including the school counselor), students she cared about, and parents she respected were seeking her out more and more frequently to tell her about their problems with Pat. Juliette was starting to feel some pressure as dean of faculty to "do something," but she didn't know where to start. Pat's prickliness was legendary; she could wear anyone down. Pat was, as the counselor put it, "heavily defended."

On the Thursday afternoon after the head had dropped in, Pat walked into Juliette's office at the end of the school day. She sat down, sighed deeply, and launched into a five-minute exegesis of exactly why Monday's faculty training on learning styles (which Juliette had planned) was an ill-advised (if not downright dumb) waste of time—time that could have been much better spent grading papers and responding to parent e-mails, which were, incidentally, also a waste of time.

CASE STUDY
A DEAN OF FACULTY CONFRONTS A TROUBLING LACK OF STANDARDS

Pat had a definite knack for making abstract problems very real.

Juliette spent 10 minutes trying to explain the importance of understanding the implications of different learning styles, and although Pat grudgingly conceded that there might be something to this, it was probably just for inexperienced teachers. She knew, after 20 years of teaching, that the best thing to do was to treat everyone the same and make sure everyone followed her methods. "It must be working," she said. "I haven't had any complaints, and the head always tells me what a good job I'm doing."

Juliette knew Pat was right. Pat had been, in a sense, teaching in a vacuum, given that there were no clear expectations, no standards for professional behavior, and essentially no feedback from colleagues and supervisors. So naturally Pat had filled that vacuum with her own ideas, assumptions, and methods, just as every other teacher had. And Juliette had to remind herself that talented, interesting teachers doing their own thing had always been, for better or for worse, a hallmark of FCDS in particular and independent schools in general.

Juliette was going to bring up the complaints she had been hearing with Pat but decided that conversation would be much more fruitful if there was more of a context for professional feedback. And the school had survived 12 years with Pat, not to mention some other folks who presented even greater challenges. Whatever mistakes Pat had made, she had also been aided and abetted by the institution.

Faced, then, with both a systems challenge and an individual challenge, Juliette was casting about for some way to get a handle on these problems, some kind of fulcrum to give her leverage.

As she was explaining these issues to a friend at a school across town, the friend suggested she take a look at the Principles of Good Practice on the NAIS website. As an athletic director, the friend had found the Principles of Good Practice for Athletics helpful when she was restructuring the department and looking for some outside reinforcement for her ideas. She said it had also been very helpful to have the principles in hand when she and the head had met with the board to discuss some major changes.

After reviewing the Principles of Good Practice for Teachers and Supervisors of Teachers, Juliette reflected further on both the general challenge (reanimating the evaluation process) and the specific problem (how to work with Pat and other teachers). Juliette then came to realize that the principles could help.

She was struck by how the double set of principles highlighted the idea that the relationship between teacher and supervisor is very much a two-way street. The school had professional obligations to the teacher that mirrored in many ways the teacher's obligations to the students and her supervisors. Good supervision wasn't just about telling people what to do.

What FCDS lacked most were clear professional standards for teaching. Absent standards, anything goes. Every school had to be able to articulate a set of principles about what makes for effective teaching, and teachers had to be fully engaged in—and, in fact, had to drive—the process for defining those standards. At the same time, to honor the interdependent relationship of teacher and supervisor, the school also needed to define what constituted effective administration and involve teachers in giving professional feedback to supervisors. For Juliette, defining these standards seemed to be the very best place to start.

As she talked to friends and began reading, she realized that there is a knowledge base about effective teaching and supervision of which she and most of her colleagues were relatively ignorant. Independent schools have for too long operated on the assumption that the only way to learn about being a teacher is to teach. Schools clung stubbornly to this trial-and-error approach, choosing not to consult the research on teaching and learning that has been built up over the years. In this way, sometimes independence mutated into arrogance.

Although teachers and supervisors wanted to be treated as professionals, they had sometimes been reluctant to take on some of the obligations of most professions, such as defining standards, keeping up with new developments, and peer monitoring of performance. Thank God, thought Juliette, my gynecologist doesn't operate the same way.

Bringing folks together to talk about effective teaching would almost certainly lead to the realization that they ought to at least be reviewing some of the literature. Creating standards for effective teaching was also the necessary first step in designing and implementing a process of supervision and evaluation that would meet the needs of the teachers and the institution.

Juliette knew she couldn't do this on her own. It would be crucial to ensure that the head of school bought into this approach. Enlisting the active, public support of the head of school was the sine qua non for making progress. Everybody knew that what the head thinks is important, and what the head doesn't care about isn't. The head would also have to be willing to go back to the board to convince its members that the time frame for its initial request was unrealistic.

To be continued....

EXEMPLARY APPLICATIONS OF GOOD PRACTICE
(School names are fictional)

EXAMPLE 1: **Making a Mentoring Program Truly Effective**
(Relates to Supervisor Principle 3)

To attract and retain beginning teachers, a well-thought-out mentoring program is essential. At many schools, experienced teachers are designated as "mentors" and paired off with new teachers, but there is no structure to the program and no training for the mentors. To improve the effectiveness and job satisfaction of new teachers while improving the odds that they'll stick around, supervisors must devote time and resources to creating a real mentoring program.

At Waterloo Academy, every aspect of the mentoring program is carefully designed. Mentors go through a selection and training process before starting to work with new teachers, and not everyone becomes a mentor. The goal of the program is to get beyond simple orientation (the point where many schools stop) and create an ongoing professional dialogue. Every new teacher has, in fact, two mentors with whom to meet regularly. As a group, the new teachers gather monthly to cover specific topics and provide mutual support and feedback. At the end of the year, mentors and mentees evaluate the program.

EXAMPLE 2: Making Time for Meaningful Professional Development
(Relates to Teacher Principles 1 and 5 and Supervisor Principles 3, 5, and 6)

Schools that are serious about professional development must give faculty and staff the time and resources to do meaningful work.

Castor Prep approaches professional development for all faculty in a holistic and purposeful way. Teachers new to the school get a four-day introduction to Castor Prep, its culture, its progressive educational philosophy, and the concrete implications of that philosophy for teaching and learning.

Over the years, the school has also worked in depth with different outside institutions and individuals to broaden people's perspectives and has made good use of tools such as curriculum mapping. Castor publishes a *Professional Development Handbook* that offers a menu of possibilities for professional growth, including a local program that allows public and private school teachers to enroll in college- and graduate-level seminars. In addition, the school sets aside significant funds for summer curriculum development projects, with special preference given to collaborative proposals. Working together, people can retool existing curricula or create new units and approaches—things they just don't have time for during the school year.

To get people out of the building to see other campuses and attend workshops, a school has to make it easy for them to do so. Castor uses an employment service to ensure a steady, reliable source of good substitute teachers. Other schools hire "permanent substitutes," full-time teachers whose job is to fill in for people who will be away.

CASE STUDY *continued from page 187*
A DEAN OF FACULTY CONFRONTS A TROUBLING LACK OF STANDARDS

THE DEAN SEEKS TOP-TO-BOTTOM BUY-IN

At the June board meeting, the head succeeded in getting the board to revise its timetable for the implementation of an effective evaluation process. Because the two trustees who had brought up merit pay before weren't there, there was no more talk of it. The board asked for a full update at the December meeting.

Juliette formed a faculty committee of volunteers to work over the summer on defining the characteristics of effective teaching. The group met for a week in June, with each member getting a small stipend from the school for this additional work. The committee members made a presentation to the faculty in late August and, with feedback from their colleagues, went to work on a final draft of standards of effective teaching for all teachers in the school. A subsequent step would have each division add its own unique expectations for its teachers. The NAIS Principles of Good Practice for Early Childhood and for Elementary, Middle, and Upper School Educators would be a good place to start.

With agreed-upon standards in place, the next task would be to define a holistic process of goal setting, feedback, and professional development of which the evaluation process would be a key element. Before the end of the year, Juliette would form another faculty work group to get this going.

Juliette went to the December board meeting to update the trustees on progress. Although there were certainly some skeptics, most seemed to approve of the directions the head and she had taken. In fact, they immediately approved the head's request for a 20-percent increase in the professional development budget for the next year to support the ongoing initiatives.

The Principles of Good Practice were important in winning over the trustees. Juliette reviewed the Principles of Good Practice for Teachers and Supervisors of Teachers with them and explained how the principles had provided a framework for institutional and individual reflection. The trustees seemed taken with the idea of national standards for independent schools. The head mentioned at that point that the Committee on Trustees might want to look at the Principles for Boards of Trustees and Independent School Trustees.

Juliette stressed to the board that creating an effective evaluation and supervision process, testing it out, and fully implementing it would take three to four years. Sensing some incipient grumpiness, she quickly added that, although in one sense this might seem like a long time, transforming a major part of the school's structure, policies, and culture had to be done carefully and thoughtfully, with each step building on the preceding work. Three or four years is not a long time in the context of the school's history to accomplish something so important.

Juliette went on to explain how at each faculty meeting, 20 minutes were set aside to discuss one of the Principles of Good Practice for Teachers. Two teachers led each discussion and encouraged their colleagues to test their own assumptions against the principles and explore how the principles might play out in the classroom. For the first time in a long time, teachers were talking about teaching with each other on a regular basis—and talking about practice is something professionals do. In parallel fashion, the academic administrators were doing the same with the Principles of Good Practice for Supervisors.

The principles also stressed the importance of supporting new teachers. Although FCDS had always been good about providing some kind of initial orientation for new teachers, once the year began, support and guidance became sporadic and reactive. There had never been a true mentoring program of ongoing support and feedback. This would be a priority for the next three years, Juliette said. Strong mentoring programs are an excellent way to smooth the induction process and help schools keep promising new teachers. One valuable bonus to such a program was that the experienced teachers acting as mentors would find the work stimulating and rewarding.

All in all, the board was satisfied that the school was making progress, being thoughtful and purposeful, and making good use of a nationally recognized set of expectations.

Nevertheless, not everything was so positive for Juliette. In the fall after that encouraging board meeting, it became clear to her that a teacher named Gene, who was mediocre at best in the classroom, was so resistant to change and growth and so toxic to the atmosphere that he would have to go.

It had taken Juliette a while to get to this point. Just as teachers sometimes avoid confronting colleagues or students, supervisors may be reluctant to respond to inappropriate or harmful behavior on the part of teachers. In such cases, supervisors convince themselves that either (a) "It's not so bad," (b) "Maybe it will all just go away," or (c) "This can wait until next year." Again, the principles provided real support and encouragement for what had to be done: As one of them noted, the supervisor "responds immediately when behavior occurs that is harmful to children or harmful to the school community."

Gene's behavior at a parent conference Juliette sat in on was so egregiously inappropriate that she knew she had to deal with it immediately, particularly since he had been put on notice that such behavior would not be tolerated and any reoccurrence would lead to non-renewal for the following year.

Situations like this can be devastating both to the individuals involved and to the institution as a whole. They absorb enormous amounts of time and energy; and the aftershocks can continue for years, especially when they're handled badly. Just

CASE STUDY
A DEAN OF FACULTY CONFRONTS A TROUBLING LACK OF STANDARDS

as individuals reveal who they really are by the way in which they leave a school, a school's true nature and values can be deduced from what happens when someone is let go. The Principles for Supervisors stress that a faculty member's departure must be "handled with attention to due process and the dignity of the individual."

Juliette was determined to manage this carefully and thoughtfully. After several conferences with her and the head of school, Gene decided that this would be his last year and he, himself, made the announcement, stressing his desire to seek out new challenges. Part of his agreement with the school was that he would be professional and positive over his remaining time at the school; so far, he was doing just that.

Juliette hadn't mentioned Pat to the board, but in a way, the changes in Pat were the very best sign that the school was on the right path.

The two of them had met several times since the previous spring, and as the personal relationship deepened, Juliette had seen the defenses come

down somewhat. She gave Pat the Principles of Good Practice for Teachers, mentioned she was thinking of using them with the faculty, and said she would be interested in the reactions of an experienced teacher. Pat was intrigued by the principles, seemed to enjoy talking about them, and volunteered to serve on the group that would later build discussion of the principles into faculty meetings. Juliette still needed to find a way to talk with Pat about the complaints, but the prospect felt more doable since she could use some of the principles to start the conversation.

And then, just now, Pat had volunteered to help work on exploring the possibility of curriculum mapping.

There remained a lot of work to do. But Juliette had the sense that, with the support of the head and the board, the active participation of the faculty, and the guidance of the Principles of Good Practice, this important work would get done over time, making the school a better place for students and adults. ■

DISCUSSION QUESTIONS

1. What does your school's mission say, either outright or by implication, about the work of teachers and supervisors?

2. What are the most important implications of this chapter in terms of possible changes for your school? What steps will you take to act on these implications? How will you know if you've made progress?

3. Why is it so important to have clear standards and expectations for all of the adults in schools?

4. Describe and comment on Juliette's evolution over the course of this case.

5. Why have schools in general done such a poor job of providing professional feedback to teachers and supervisors?

6. Define and comment on the respective roles of the dean, the head of school, and the board in the case.

7. How will you ensure that teachers and supervisors have the time and resources they need to grow professionally?

8. What kind of training and professional development do new supervisors need? How will they get it?

9. Why is it that success in working with students does not always translate into success working with adults?

10. How do you change a school culture that seems to posit and even nurture a divide between teachers and supervisors?

SUGGESTED RESOURCES AND READING MATERIALS

Barth, Roland. *Learning by Heart.* San Francisco, CA: Jossey-Bass, 2001.

Brooks, Jacqueline, and Martin Brooks. *In Search of Understanding: The Case for Constructivist Classrooms.* Alexandria, VA: Association for Supervision and Curriculum Development, 1999.

Evans, Robert. *The Human Side of School Change.* San Francisco, CA: Jossey-Bass, 1996.

Gow, Peter. *An Admirable Faculty: Recruiting, Hiring, Training, and Retaining the Best Independent School Teachers.* Washington, DC: NAIS, 2005.

Martin-Kniep, Giselle. *Becoming a Better Teacher: Eight Innovations That Work.* Alexandria, VA: Association for Supervision and Curriculum Development, 2000.

Saphier, Jon. *How to Make Supervision and Evaluation Really Work.* Acton, MA: Research for Better Teaching, 1993.

Saphier, Jon, and Robert Gower. *The Skillful Teacher.* Acton, MA: Research for Better Teaching, 1997.

ABOUT THE EDITOR

James Tracy has devoted his entire career to education at independent schools and universities. Since July 2006, he has served as head of Cushing Academy in Ashburnham, Massachusetts. Before that, he was head of Boston University Academy for six years and a history teacher at The Hotchkiss School in Lakeville, Connecticut, for six years. At the university level, he has taught at Stanford University, the University of Massachusetts-Boston, and Boston University, among others. He has also been an assistant to Boston University's chancellor and a visiting professor in Yale University's history department.

Tracy is the author of the 1996 book *Direct Action,* a history of pacifism in the United States from World War II to the civil rights movement. He has also published several articles in NAIS's quarterly magazine, *Independent School,* and made many presentations at conferences sponsored by NAIS and others.

A native of Boston, Tracy earned his bachelor's degree in history and religion from UMass-Boston in 1984 and his Ph.D. in American history from Stanford University in 1993. He earned his MBA, with a certificate in nonprofit management, as well as his Ed.M. in education administration from Boston University in 2003 and 2006, respectively.

ZENGA
Brushstrokes of Enlightenment

Catalog Selections, Entries and Essay
by
JOHN STEVENS

Catalog Essay and Organization
by
ALICE RAE YELEN

NEW ORLEANS MUSEUM OF ART

1990

Cover Illustration
HAKUIN Ekaku, *Blind Men On a Log Bridge*

Back Cover Calligraphy by John Stevens

4000 copies of the catalog were published for the exhibition
Zenga: Brushstrokes of Enlightenment

Exhibition Schedule

New Orleans Museum of Art	July 15-August 20, 1989
Mint Museum of Art	April 1-May 27, 1990
Seattle Art Museum	October 4, 1990-January 13, 1991
Los Angeles County Museum of Art	March 26-May 26, 1991

ISBN 0-89494-032-5
Library of Congress Catalog Card Number: 90-53276

Designed by Thomasgraphics, Baton Rouge, Louisiana
Produced and Typeset by Skip Brown, New Orleans, Louisiana
Photographs by Owen Murphy, New Orleans, Louisiana, except where otherwise credited
Printed by Dai Nippon Printing Company, Ltd.

CONTENTS

FOREWORD AND ACKNOWLEDGEMENTS

E. John Bullard, Director

For nearly twenty years, the New Orleans Museum of Art has been increasingly interested in the art created in Japan during the Edo Period from 1615 to 1868. This interest was initiated by a trustee, Dr. Kurt A. Gitter, for many years one of the major American collectors of Edo painting. With his generous support and encouragement, the Museum has built a large and varied collection that surveys all of the diverse styles that flourished during the Edo Period, including Zenga—painting and calligraphy by Zen monks. *Zenga: Brushstrokes of Enlightenment* is the latest in a series of exhibitions of Edo painting organized by the Museum.

Several earlier exhibitions, including the first in 1976, *Zenga and Nanga: Paintings by Japanese Monks and Scholars*, drawn from the Gitter collection, were curated by Professor Stephen Addiss of the University of Kansas, who served for several years as our Adjunct Curator of Japanese Art. Through research, publications and exhibitions, Professor Addiss has greatly expanded the knowledge and appreciation of Zenga in the West and has even focused attention in Japan on many previously overlooked or undervalued artists. His work on Zenga culminated in 1989 with the publication of the definitive study, *The Art of Zen: Painting and Calligraphy by Japanese Monks 1600-1925*, which accompanied an exhibition he organized with loans from American, European and Japanese collections.

The current exhibition, *Zenga: Brushstrokes of Enlightenment*, was in part inspired by Stephen Addiss' book and exhibition. Due to scheduling conflicts, we were unable to present *The Art of Zen* in New Orleans. With a sudden opening in our schedule in the summer of 1989, we decided to organize our own exhibition of Zenga drawn from collections just in New Orleans, including the Museum's. As the exhibition developed and we realized the quality and depth of material available locally, we were fortunate to engage as our guest curator John Stevens, Professor of Buddhist Studies at Tohoku Social Welfare University in Sendai, Japan. Professor Stevens, an American who has lived in Japan for many years, is an ordained Zen priest. Working closely with Alice Rae Yelen, Assistant to the Director for Special Projects, Professor Stevens approached the organization of the exhibition from a fresh perspective, utilizing his extensive knowledge and practice of Zen. Rather than presenting the exhibition in a traditional art historical manner, arranging works chronologically or by schools, Professor Stevens divided the works thematically, to inform the viewer about Zen theology and iconography.

Although Zenga has always been appreciated in Japan for its religious content, it has not received appropriate recognition from

7

collectors and art museums until recently. For the Japanese who value great craftsmanship and aesthetic refinement, the bold, often roughly brushed works by artistically untrained Zen monks can appear amateurish or naïve. During the past thirty years, it has been art collectors, scholars and curators in the United States, such as Stephen Addiss, Kurt Gitter, Peter Drucker and John Powers who have recognized the unique aesthetic qualities of Zenga. The great success of abstract art in the West also has contributed to an appreciation of Zenga, separate from its original theological function. That Westerners, who can not read Japanese and have no knowledge of Buddhism, are moved by Zenga attests to the universality of art.

We are most grateful for Professor John Stevens' enthusiastic participation and his willingness to devote a much greater amount of time to the project than originally planned. He not only devised the exhibition concept, he also wrote all of the individual catalog entries and the insightful essay, "The Spiritual in Zen Art." As an American-born Zen priest living in Japan and teaching Buddhist theology to the Japanese, Professor Stevens has made a unique guest curator.

Alice Rae Yelen ably coordinated the organization of the exhibition and the production of the catalog, as well as wrote the essay "Looking at Zen Art," based on her experience as an art historian and museum educator. Other members of the New Orleans Museum of Art staff made special contributions to this exhibition. Darrell Lee Brown, Assistant to the Curators, worked in all areas of the organization, particularly in typesetting and formatting the catalog. Daniel Piersol, Curator of Exhibitions, and Paul Tarver, Registrar, provided essential services in preparing the exhibition to travel. Curatorial secretary Joyce Armstrong prepared the manuscript, while volunteers Oscar Frishoff and Virginia Dupuy assisted in proofing. Ms. Yelen gratefully acknowledges the hospitality of Daizaburō Tanaka, who guided her to Hakuin's hometown and temples in Japan, as well as Professor John Stevens, Dr. Frederick Baekland and Dr. Roger Green who aided in editing her essay from different points of view.

Finally I wish to recognize the participation of the three American museums hosting *Zenga; Brushstrokes of Enlightenment.* I thank our colleagues at these institutions who assisted in circulating the exhibition, particularly Charles L. Mo, Mint Museum of Art, Charlotte, North Carolina; William J. Rathbun, Seattle Art Museum; and Robert Singer, Los Angeles County Museum of Art. The support of these three museums made possible the exhibition tour and the publication of the catalog, thereby allowing New Orleans to share its public and private collections of Zenga with other American cities.

8

THE SPIRITUAL DIMENSIONS OF ZEN ART

by John Stevens

The Zen tradition traces its origin back to the enlightenment experience of Gotama, the historical Buddha who was born over 2,500 years ago in India. After first living as a prince and then as a religious seeker, one day Gotama sat resolutely in the meditation posture beneath a large tree, vowing to be enlightened or die. Following a night of the most intense contemplation, the inner and outer workings of the universe suddenly became clear to Gotama and he attained enlightenment. Gotama was thereafter called the "Buddha," one who is perfectly awake.

Zen represents the contemplative tradition of Buddhism. Meditation masters carried the Zen tradition from India to China and then it was transmitted to Korea, Japan, and, in the twentieth century, to the West. In Japan, painting and calligraphy became a primary teaching vehicle of the Zen masters from the sixteenth century onward, and Zen art is now recognized as being one of the glories of world culture. Devotees of Zen art, both in Japan and in the West, have uncovered and lovingly restored hundreds of magnificent pieces during the past fifty years; indeed, this exhibition largely consists of such newly discovered treasures. Significantly, these pieces—some unseen for centuries but still bearing a message as fresh and forceful as when first delivered—are appearing just when it is possible, for the first time, to display them throughout the world in exhibitions and by means of modern print technology.

Although permeated with humor, joy, and unrestrained freedom, Zen painting and calligraphy is comprised of far more than lighthearted cartoons, witty sayings, and delightful abstract images. True Zen art always imparts a deep message, a message as profound and universal as that revealed in the most venerable religious text or the most challenging philosophical treatise. It is a misconception to think of Zen art as a pleasant diversion from more "serious" forms of religious and artistic expression, on the contrary, a single Zen brushstroke by an enlightened master can reveal a new reality to the viewer.

PAINTINGS OF THE MIND:
THE DEVELOPMENT OF ZEN ART IN CHINA

The origin of ink painting in China is lost in antiquity but by the eighth century there was a definite shift from the formal, linear style of brushwork that characterized early Chinese painting to a more expressive, natural calligraphic style. Detailed, well proportioned and brightly colored painting gradually gave way to impressionistic "paintings of the mind," monochromatic representations of the essence, rather than the form, of things.

One reason for this change was the influence of Ch'an (Zen) ideals. Classical Buddhist art, the dominant force in Chinese art from the third to seventh centuries, was highly structured and strictly dictated. An image was thought to lose its spiritual efficacy if it deviated in the slightest from the iconographically correct form. Preliminary sketches, for example, were carefully constructed with compass and ruler. Such art reflected the canons of Buddhist scholasticism, tremendously complex and minutely detailed. Bodhidharma, the legendary Indian monk who personified Ch'an philosophy, came to China in the sixth century, it is said, in order to overturn the elaborate superstructure of doctrinal Buddhism. Bodhidharma symbolizes the rejection of all externals, and the demand for direct and immediate realization of the Buddha-mind in the here and now. Combined with the ancient Taoist principles of spontaneity, harmony and non-action, Ch'an teachings inspired Chinese artists to break free of confining rules, allowing them to portray the heart of things dynamically with a few vital strokes.

Perhaps the earliest reference to Zen, as opposed to regular brushwork, occurs in the *Platform Sutra of the Sixth Patriarch*, a text which relates the life and teaching of the illustrious Chinese master Hui-neng (638-713). Buddhist scenes, composed in accordance to canonical dictates, were to be painted on the walls of the monastery in which Hui-neng was laboring as a lay monk. Before the paintings could be executed, the abbot's top disciple Shen-hsiu sneaked into the hall one night and expressed his understanding of Zen by brushing this verse on the white wall:

> *The body is the tree of enlightenment,*
> *And the mind, a bright standing mirror;*
> *Keep it polished continually,*
> *And never let dust collect there.*

After viewing the calligraphy the next morning, the abbot dismissed the commissioned artist with these words: *"I have decided not to have the walls painted after all."* As the *Diamond Sutra* states, *"All images are unreal and false."* Evidently fearing that his disciples would adhere too closely to the realistic pictures, the abbot thought a stark verse set against a white wall better suited to awaken the mind. When Hui-neng heard the content of Shen-hsiu's verse, however, he thought it too rigid and orthodox. The poor lay brother had never learned to read or write, but Hui-neng's intuitive understanding of Zen was profound; he asked one of the monks to inscribe this poem next to Shen-hsiu's verses:

> *Enlightenment is not like a tree,*
> *Nor is there a mirror standing*
>   *anywhere;*
> *Originally not one thing exists,*
> *So where can dust alight?*

Upon seeing Hui-neng's "enlightenment poem," the abbot determined that he, and not Shen-hsiu, truly understood Zen. (Even today, Hui-neng's poem, especially the third line, is a favorite theme of Zen artists.)

Thereafter, art was used by Chinese and Japanese masters to reveal the essence of Zen through the use of bold lines, abbreviated brushwork, and dynamic imagery.

VISUAL ENLIGHTENMENT:
ZEN PAINTING IN JAPAN

Although the seeds of Zen painting and calligraphy were sown in China, this genre attained full flower in Japan. Masterpieces of Zen art by such monks as Ch'an-yueh, Lian-K'ai, Yu Chien, Mu Ch'i, Chi-weng, Yin-t'o-lo, and I-shan I-ning were enthusiastically imported to Japan during the twelfth and thirteenth centuries and a number of native artists, for example, Kao Shonen and Mokuan Reiun, studied on the mainland.

It was the outstanding artist Sesshū Tōyō (1420-1506) who established the independence of Japanese Zen painting. Sesshū's paintings were technically superior, of course, but his brushwork additionally displayed a freshness and directness largely absent in the works of professional and literati artists. Sesshū had only the most tenuous relationship with the academy of professional artists, and he was among the first to open his commissions to anyone who asked. Furthermore, his paintings were original interpretations, not merely imitations of classical subjects, based on careful observation of—and deep insight into—the natural world. Tradition has it that Sesshū would begin a painting session by first contemplating the sea and mountains from his studio window. After a cup of rice wine, he would play his bamboo flute until his mind was properly composed. Only then would he put brush and ink to paper.

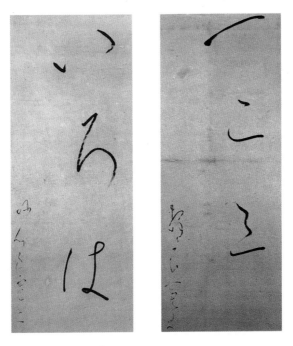

figure I-a & b.
I-ro-ha Ichi-ni-san.
Ryōkan, 1758-1831.
(Private Collection)

11

During the first three centuries of its existence in Japan, Zen was primarily a creed for samurai and cultured aristocrats, but by the sixteenth century Zen masters began to take an active interest in the material and spiritual welfare of ordinary folk. The emphasis on "People's Zen" dramatically expanded the scope of Zen calligraphy and painting. Previously, Zen calligraphy consisted primarily of difficult Buddhist verse, sayings of the Patriarchs, and selections from ancient texts. Painting centered on portraits of the Buddha, Bodhisattvas, Bodhidharma and the Chinese Patriarchs, and famous events in Zen history. In People's Zen, however, painting and calligraphy became a kind of ultimate folk art—one of the most famous examples of Zen calligraphy is a set of scrolls brushed by Ryōkan (1758-1831) for an illiterate farmer: *i-ro-ha, ichi-ni-san,* "A-B-C, One-Two-Three" (fig. I). Other masters such as Hakuin, Sengai, and Tesshū employed brush, ink and paper to create enlightened art which illuminated every aspect of the human experience.

HAKUIN, SENGAI, TESSHŪ: MASTERS OF ZEN ART

Hakuin (1685-1769) was adept at brushwork in his youth but painted almost nothing for forty years after viewing a totally unselfconscious piece of Zen calligraphy by the master Daigū (or, according to other accounts, by Ungō). Thinking to himself, *"This is the result of true enlightenment,"* Hakuin burned his brushes and calligraphy manuals, dissatisfied with the pretense of his own efforts; it was not until his mid-fifties that he felt confident enough of his own insight to paint seriously again. In the last three decades of his life, Hakuin produced a vast number of pieces on an extraordinary variety of subjects, ranging from full-color "visual operas," with a large cast of characters and various themes and sub-plots, to roughly drawn cartoons.

Along with traditional themes brushed in a strikingly fresh, highly personalized manner, Hakuin drew inspiration from other schools of Buddhism, Confucianism, Shintōism, Taoism, folk religion, and scenes taken from everyday life; his calligraphy, too, encompassed more than the words of the Buddhas and Patriarchs—it embraced nursery rhymes, popular ballads, humorous verse, and bawdy songs from the geisha quarters. Hakuin's paintings were, as one of his seals reads, "paintings that liberate beings" *(hōjō-e),* works of art to bring the viewer to a deeper understanding of his or her own nature and the world at large.

In a sense, Hakuin's work was "anti-art," that is, not consciously created to be "beautiful" or "decorative." In fact, Hakuin never corrected mistakes or omissions in his calligraphy and if the pieces had drips or catpaw tracks on them so much the better! On large pieces, Hakuin frequently did an outline first but instead of erasing it, he drew over the outline, creating a kind of "3-D" effect.

figure II.
A Single Arrow Shatters
Three Barriers
Hakuin, 1685-1769.
(Eisei Bunkō)

An example of Hakuin's distinctive brushwork is shown in figure II. Waste is abhorred by Zen masters, and ink would never be thrown away. In this calligraphy, Hakuin used old ink that had partially congealed. With tremendous power and extension, Hakuin slowly brushed a visual *kōan*—"*A Single Arrow Shatters Three Barriers*"—with the leftover ink. The ink splotches give the characters a three-dimensional quality, and when the ink happened to run when the piece was being lifted, that drip became a part of the creative process. Incredibly robust, this piece illustrates the Zen approach to art: bold, forceful, and free of artifice.

Sengai (1750-1838) led a happy-go-lucky life, freely associating with all manner of people, ranging from mighty lords to vagrants, from aristocratic ladies to lowly pleasure girls, instructing all, mostly through the medium of Zen art, with a delightful combination of worldly and transcendental wisdom.

As with Hakuin, it is not clear where Sengai developed his skill as an artist; he, too, probably studied informally with artist friends and disciples. Also similar to Hakuin, Sengai did not devote himself to Zen art until he was in his sixties.

Sengai wrote this about his brushwork: *"Worldly painting has a method: Sengai's paintings have no method. As Buddha said, 'The True Law is no Law.'"* That is, each piece was created in the here and now in response to a particular situation, just as Buddha tailored the content of his talks to the ability of his listeners, speaking to the moment rather than reliance on sermonizing. Zen art is never drawn after abstract models or ideal forms: it is always centered in the present reality.

Since Sengai's art addressed the realities of life he produced an enormous number of pieces on every imaginable subject—name it and there is probably a Sengai painting of the theme. (Sengai received so many requests that he complained on one of his paintings: "People must think that my study is some kind of toilet, they bring so much paper here.") Perhaps Sengai's supreme contribution to the perfection of Japanese Zen art was his insistence that Buddha-nature has a physical as well as a spiritual side that cannot be ignored or explained away. Hence, Sengai did cartoons of people (and Buddhas!) passing wind and answering the calls of nature. One such self-portrait shows Sengai squatting in a field relieving himself. The inscription jokes, *"I hope no one comes!"* Even distinguished abbots have to answer nature's calls; without their fancy titles and magnificent garments our leaders are the same as any other human being. Nor did Sengai avoid the question of sex. Sengai's attitude towards human emotions is summarized by this Zen verse:

> *Falling in love is dangerous,*
> *For passion is the source of illusion;*
> *Yet being in love gives life flavor*
> *And passions themselves*
> *Can bring one to enlightenment.*

translated by John Stevens

This Zen master's "visual sermons" have a powerful effect and it is said that a greedy merchant mended his ways after viewing a painting of Kannon, the Goddess of Compassion, by Sengai.

Sengai's "joy of enlightenment" can be sensed in his humorous portrait of Sen no Rikyū, founder of the tea ceremony (fig. III). While standard portraits of Rikyū show him in strictly formal dress against a meticulously ordered background and with a dignified expression, here Sengai captures Rikyū at his leisure. Notice how Rikyū's utensils are scattered about in delightful disarray; the tea master is obviously enjoying himself in an unbuttoned manner. An occasional lapse in procedure is permissible—in fact, necessary, for nothing should be taken too seriously. The inscription, too, indicates that each person must walk to his or her own drummer: *"Shaka was a Buddha (in India), Confucious was a sage (in China), and (here in Japan) we have Rikyū, a great tea master."*

Tesshū (1836-1888) was a layman

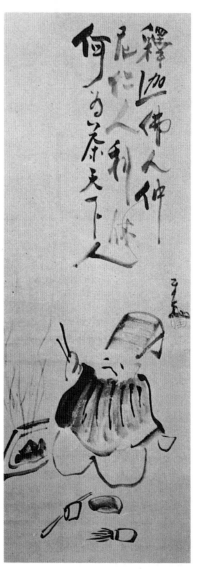

figure III.
Tea Master Rikyū.
Sengai, 1750-1838.
(Private Collection)

14

who combined Zen enlightenment with family life, public service (he was Emperor Meiji's most trusted aide), and social welfare. Tesshū's output of Zen art is truly staggering—conservatively estimated at a *million* pieces. The primary reason for such astounding productivity was to raise money for the restoration of temples, for disaster victims, and other worthy causes.

During the last eight years of his life Tesshū averaged five hundred pieces of Zen art a day; if necessary he could turn out more than a thousand pieces in twenty-four hours (his record was 1,300). On those occasions when Tesshū needed to brush a large amount of calligraphy to be donated to charity, he would begin right after morning *kendō* training (Tesshū was one of Japan's greatest swordsmen). Five or six assistants would prepare the ink, set up the paper, dry the finished sheets, and so on, while Tesshū wielded the brush. Except for a few minutes break to have a simple meal of rice and pickled plums, Tesshū would continue well past midnight. *"Gather all things in heaven and earth in your brush and you will never tire,"* Tesshū told his disciples as they dropped, one by one, from exhaustion.

Tesshū's calligraphy was in such demand that to maintain order his disciples had to hand out numbers to scores of people who came daily to ask for a piece. One day his disciples were so angered by a butcher's request for a signboard they refused to let him in. (In those days, most Japanese Buddhists were vegetarian.) Tesshū overheard the commotion and came out. *"If it helps his business, that will be fine,"* he lectured them sternly. *"My calligraphy is not for sale, nor is it a commodity to be bartered; anyone who comes here with a request, regardless of what it is, should not be turned away."* Even today, there is a well-known bakery on the Ginza in Tokyo that proudly displays a reproduction of the signboard that Tesshū wrote for the original shop over a hundred years ago.

Although there was no charge for Tesshū's brushwork, most petitioners offered something, either a gift or money. Whenever Tesshū received a money envelope he placed it, unopened, in a special box. When a needy person or persons appeared, Tesshū would rummage through the box and pull out the necessary amount. The sale of Tesshū's Zen art raised a fortune for others but not a yen for himself.

Each time Tesshū brushed a piece, he would silently recite a Buddhist vow: *"Sentient beings are innumerable, I vow to save them all."* When an acquaintance commented, *"You certainly have brushed a lot of pieces,"* Tesshū replied, *"I've just begun. It will take a long time to reach thirty-five million"*—the population of Japan at that time.

One day a noted calligrapher visited Tesshū. After outlining his elaborate preparations, his careful selection of instruments and paper, and his special techniques, the calligrapher asked Tesshū the method the Zen master followed.

"The method of no-method," Tesshū told him.
"I don't understand," the puzzled calligrapher said.
*"Which do you think is the better carpenter: one who
can only work with exactly the right tools, or one
who can make do with whatever is on hand?"*

Looking at an example of Tesshū's calligraphy (fig. IV-a&b), we can see how the spirited brushwork seems to flow up and down the paper in an unbroken stream. It has a vitality that almost crackles with energy. Unlike many Zen artists, Tesshū was a master of technique as well as a spiritual giant, and his work is considered to be the finest Zen art of the modern era.

VISUAL ENLIGHTENMENT:
THE CONTEMPLATION OF ZEN ART

Zen art is meant to be contemplated rather than merely viewed. Originally, each piece of Zen art was reverently displayed in the alcove of a temple or in the rooms of a master's disciples and parishioners, speaking silently but eloquently to every person who sat before it. In modern Japan, exhibitions of Zen art are sometimes held in a meditation hall, allowing one to sit quietly and gaze calmly at a piece. Zen art hangs today in homes all over the world, bridging cultural and conceptual barriers, proclaiming a message of liberation from pettiness, greed, and delusion.

The creation of Zen art depends on two essential factors: state of mind *(shinkyō)* and level of enlightenment *(gokyō)*. Indeed, in Zen art, one has to be a masterpiece in order to create a masterpiece—Zen art is an expression of the Buddha-mind. The depth and breadth of a master's enlightened vision is revealed through the medium of brush, ink, and paper as "Zen activity" *(zenki)*. The freedom, naturalness, profundity, vitality, power, stability, warmth, and refinement that we sense in a genuine example of Zen art all derive from Zen activity. A master's spirit permeates, and radiates from, a work of Zen art and each viewer can actually encounter a living presence in the brushstrokes.

While the primary purpose of Zen brushwork is to instruct and inspire, it does have a distinctive set of aesthetic principles. In his book *Zen and the Fine Arts*, Shin'ichi Hisamatsu distinguished seven characteristics of Zen art: asymmetry, simplicity, austere sublimity or lofty dryness, naturalness, subtle profundity or deep reserve, freedom from attachment, and tranquility. Zen, however, cannot be so easily characterized; there are, for example, paintings of perfectly symmetrical Zen circles, highly complex "visual operas" by Hakuin, and a number of erotic works by Zen artists. Actually, the most important element in Zen art is *bokki*, the flow of energy *(ki)* in the ink *(boku)*.

16

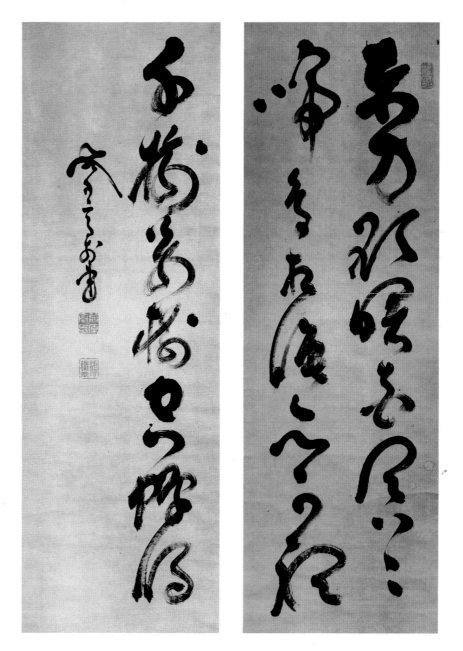

Bokki is the vibrant force we perceive when we contemplate a piece of Zen art. It is the *anima* of the work, the heart and soul of the brushstrokes. *Bokki* is as much felt in the pit of one's being as perceived with the eyes. Each line of a work of Zen art must manifest clarity, liveliness, intensity, gravity, sensitivity, suppleness, extension, and, lastly, technical competence. In short, the best Zen art is true *(shin)*, beneficial *(zen)*, and beautiful *(bi)*.

It is well understood in the Orient that contemplation of art fosters awakening no less than sitting in meditation, studying a sacred text, listening to a sermon, or going on pilgrimage. Zen masters applied their insight to painting and calligraphy to inspire, instruct, and delight all those who choose to look.

figure V.
Circle, Triangle, Square.
Sengai, 1750-1838.
(Idemitsu Museum)

CIRCLE, TRIANGLE, SQUARE
BY SENGAI

This is likely the most famous Zen painting in the world (fig. V). Various interpretations of this enigmatic work have been put forth over the years, including one that holds that the painting means nothing at all—Sengai drew the three shapes to give children who flocked to his hermitage a geometry lesson. Others view the work as an abstract representation of the Zen life: the mind of enlightenment (the circle) is expressed through *zazen* (the triangular meditation posture) within the temple walls (the square). Or perhaps the circle symbolizes infinity, the triangle the human world, and the square myriad phenomena. Or maybe the circle stands for formlessness, the triangle the three aspects of human existence (body, speech and mind), and the square the four elements (earth, water, fire and air). Or could it be that the circle represents the "empty" teaching of Zen, the triangle the mysteries of Shingon esotericism, and the square the ordered philosophy of Tendai Buddhism? Or is this a diagram of the universe's physical composition: "liquid body" (circle), "vapor body" (triangle), and "solid body" (square)? Sengai had some knowledge of Christianity—he read the works of the early Jesuit missionaries and visited churches in Nagasaki—so this Zenga could even be interpreted in Christian terms: the circle represents the perfection and eternal existence of God, the triangle stands for the Trinity, and the square is an emblem of the confines of earthly existence.

What do you see?

by Alice Rae Yelen

ZENGA:
BRUSHSTROKES OF ENLIGHTENMENT

The artistic and spiritual strength of Zenga—Japanese for Zen painting—is powerfully demonstrated by seventy masterworks in the exhibition *Zenga: Brushstrokes of Enlightenment*. Primarily from the Edo Period (1615-1868) but extending through the mid-twentieth century, this collection of paintings was inspired by the experience of Zen Enlightenment. While the majority of Zen painters were Zen Buddhist monks, the exhibition also includes works by laymen embued with the Zen spirit, and by monks and a nun from other Buddhist sects. Zenga's energetic action-packed brushstrokes, giving simplified visual form to Zen concepts, find a sympathetic reception in Westerners accustomed to modern abstract painting. Yet, a majority of the works in the exhibition predate non-representational art by one to three centuries. Moreover, Zen masters never considered their painting to be either abstract or "art for art's sake," as it is the Zen masters' spiritual zeal which is expressed in their brushstrokes. Reflecting the unique Zen Buddhist vision, spontaneous brushwork can be a path to enlightenment.

Designed to appeal to the connoisseur and the general public, this exhibition introduces over fifty previously unpublished images by acclaimed Zenga masters, recognized disciples and yet unstudied artists. The latter are included to increase public awareness, scrutiny, and scholarship of later Zen painting.

Artworks are presented in a thematic arrangement of subjects typically found in Zen painting in order to familiarize the viewer with the religious and cultural significance of each work, as described in the catalog entries and essay, "The Spiritual Dimensions of Zen Art." The grouping of like subjects in chronological order, by varied artists, encourages a comparative aesthetic judgement of these images. Usually without understanding the meaning of the religious iconography and often unable to decipher calligraphy, the Western viewer approaches Zenga from a purely aesthetic perspective, perhaps based on exposure to twentieth-century abstract painting. This is in contrast to the Japanese who, by understanding the religion, culture and language of Zenga may appreciate these works differently. While this essay places Zenga in historical perspective, it emphasizes aesthetic appreciation of Zen painting in its thematic context.

Zenga: Brushstrokes of Enlightenment is the first Zen painting exhibition in the United States to be organized by placing works in their cultural and religious context, rather than in the traditional art historical format. In this arrangement, Zenga emits a remarkable power based on its completeness, in which art and spirituality emerge triumphantly and simply as one.

HISTORICAL OVERVIEW

Zen Buddhism was brought to China from India in the sixth century by the Indian monk Bodhidharma, known to the Japanese as Daruma, the Grand Patriarch. Later, in the thirteenth century, Zen was transmitted to Japan. Although all Buddhists seek enlightenment, Zen differs from other Buddhist sects in its belief that individual enlightenment is achieved through discipline, *zazen* (meditation), and understanding of one's inner self rather than through rote intellectual study of Buddhist *sutras* (texts). Historically, the strict beliefs of traditional or doctrinal Buddhist sects were reflected in their stylized paintings which can be termed "mainstream Buddhist iconography." The tightly composed *sutra* cover (fig. I), which serves as a decorative illustration to the religious scriptures, exemplifies highly defined Buddhist philosophy and its related painting style from which Zen Buddhism deviated. Fashioned of cut-gold applied to an indigo background and decorated with symbolic lotus flowers (which signify purity amidst corruption), this cover displays recognizable Buddhist deities, with elegant refinement. Such stylized artistic renderings of the Buddhist pantheon are depicted within the canons of religious painting, canons in which digression from the exact formula represents a divergence from the doctrinal Buddhist ideal. Concurrence with prescribed form and controlled technique requires disciplined artistic training. Formal Buddhist iconographic painting, which often employs brilliant colors and precious metals, has remained the predominant form of Buddhist painting from its sixth-century inception in China to the present day.

Zenga represents the spiritually and artistically expressive art of Zen masters whose free, personal interpretations, contrasted in style with the rigidity of traditional Buddhist painting. Zen painting and calligraphy, emphasizing spontaneous, individual expression, are primarily monochromatic, achieved through the application of *sumi* (black ink) onto paper or occasionally silk. Zen masters were not trained officially as artists. They attended no painting workshops or schools and thus subscribed to no predetermined canon of proportions or style. Artistic expression of their Zen beliefs in a free style of their own choice not only was acceptable, but encouraged as a method of increasing self-awareness.

Zen masters believe in the direct transmission of the Buddha-mind from teacher to pupil. Some teachers relied on enigmatic philosophical questions known as *kōans* (cat. no. 70) to jolt their students into achieving their most important goal, self-realization and insight into their own inner natures. These paradoxical *kōans* defy logic and serve as a mentor's aid to direct his student to deep, unanticipated insight. One famous but puzzling *kōan* used by the great Zen master Hakuin was *"What is the sound of one hand clapping?"* Unlike other Buddhist sects whose route to enlightenment is gradual and based on pursuit of graded knowledge, Zen enlightenment is sudden and spontaneous, often a startling

response to a simple event, such as the ringing of a bell. The moment of enlightenment cannot be calculated, measured or predicted; it comes unexpectedly after years of training and commitment, when the individual is ripe for the experience. It is the expression of this Zen spirit which is captured in the vibrant, spontaneous brushstrokes of Zenga.

During the Muromachi Period (1392-1568), shortly after the introduction of Zen Buddhism into Japan, Zen became the principal religious and cultural influence in the country, affecting education, government and the arts. This resulted in commissions for Zen painters by the chief patrons of the time: the aristocracy, government officials, feudal lords, wealthy samurai and temples. The major Muromachi Period art forms were Zen-inspired. Many of these professional artists were also monks, whose primary commitment was to painting rather than Zen teaching. They excelled in *suibokuga* (ink painting) often of landscapes, and displayed more individual expression in their brushwork than had previously appeared in traditional Buddhist painting. Muromachi Zen artists also signed their paintings and calligraphic inscriptions, unlike doctrinal Buddhist painters who often left their works unsigned.

In the subsequent Momoyama (1568-1615) and Edo Periods (1615-1868) the influence of Zen Buddhism declined in aristocratic and government circles. Thus, the prestige confirmed upon Zen affiliates also deteriorated, and eventually altered the future direction of Zen art. Zen masters began to internalize, practicing Zen and simultaneously creating art solely from within, for their parishioners and priestly students. This resulted in a more instructive, individualistic and expressive art. Unlike their Muromachi predecessors, Edo Period Zen monks no longer received patronage and commissions, as the officials and newly arisen merchant patrons transferred their support to artists of the many other established and new painting schools such as *Kanō, Tosa, Shijō,*

Rimpa, Ukiyo-e and *Nanga* which flourished during the approximately 250 years that Japan remained closed to the outside world. While much of Muromachi Period painting was Zen-inspired, Zenga represented only a small fraction of the varied artistic output of the Edo Period.

Edo Period Zen masters were not professional artists; they painted solely in pursuit of their Zen beliefs. They almost never sold their works nor sought artistic acclaim from the outside world. Individual artistic expression in the early Edo Period emerged within the framework of the diverse life styles of the Zen masters and their affiliation with the three main Zen sects. For example, Fūgai (1568-1654) of the Sōtō sect, the earliest artist represented in the exhibition, largely avoided temple life, living as a hermit, following his own Zen style. Fūgai's brushwork, usually depicting traditional Zen subjects (cat. no. 3), is delicate, refined, poignant and penetrating.

By contrast, Sokuhi (1616-1671), came as part of a delegation of Chinese monks who introduced the Ōbaku sect to Japan. He chose to live like the majority of Zen monks, as a temple abbot, propagating Zen beliefs to the common people. Ōbaku monks were noted for their bold calligraphy, exemplified by Sokuhi's *Dragon and Tiger* (cat. no. 1).

A totally different expression is seen in the tight, refined quality of the Rinzai monk Daishin's work (cat. no. 39). From Kyoto's famous Daitoku-ji, Daishin's painting and calligraphy represent the well defined style of his illustrious temple predecessors.

This exhibition focuses on the work of Hakuin (1685-1769) and his followers, as well as other individual post-Hakuin Zen painters of the Edo Period, with selected examples extending into the mid-twentieth century. Hakuin revitalized Zen Buddhism in Japan through his writings and teachings, and became recognized as the most influential Zen teacher of his era. Abbot of Shōin-ji and Ryūtaku-ji, small temples at the foothills of Mt. Fuji situated far away from metropolitan centers, Hakuin's religious impact was spread throughout Japan by his numerous religious followers. Hakuin had three main disciples: Suiō (1716-1789); Tōrei (1721-1792); and Reigen (1721-1785). Other followers and their disciples also disseminated his teaching (fig. II). The great master became a Zen monk at the age of fifteen, but did not begin painting in what art historians today call his early period until after age sixty. Hakuin never devoted himself exclusively to painting; his chief concern was always Zen study. Nevertheless, by the time he attained his fullest artistic expression in his eighties, he was a painter and calligrapher of the highest order. Today, Hakuin is considered the most important Zen monk and Zen artist of the last three centuries.

Another important Edo-period Zen master was Sengai (1750-1838), figure II.

**GENERATIONAL CHART OF
HAKUIN SCHOOL ARTISTS
REPRESENTED IN THE EXHIBITION**

HAKUIN Ekaku (1685-1769)

SUIŌ Genrō (1716-1789
TŌREI Enji (1721-1792)
REIGEN Etō (1721-1785)

GAKO Tangen Chiben (1737-1805)
KŌGAN Gengei (1747-1821)
SHUNSŌ Jōshū (1750-1839)
TAKUJŪ Kosen (1760-1833)

SOZAN Genkyō (1799-1868)
TSU'Ō Sōtetsu (1801-1854)
HŌJŪ Zenbyō (1802-1872)

Yamaoka TESSHŪ (1836-1888)
Nakahara NANTEMBŌ (1839-1925)
SANSHŌKEN Yūzen Gentatsu (1841-1917)
Matsubara BANRYŪ (1848-1935)
Ashikaga SHIZAN (1859-1959)

compiled by John Stevens

a prolific artist from the southernmost island of Kyūshū, who created many cartoon-like, Zen inspired paintings (cat. no. 27). Some noted Zenga artists were not members of the Zen sect. Jiun (1718-1804), of the Shingon sect, created strong, bold calligraphy replete with the Zen spirit (cat. no. 64), and Gōchō (1749-1835), of the Tendai sect, frequently depicted traditional Zen themes in his painting and vibrant calligraphy (cat. no. 29).

Zen art is part of Zen training. The practice of calligraphy is an important part of the disciplined Zen life. Calligraphy is considered to be active meditation by the painter, while the visual depiction serves as a teaching tool for others. Paintings often were given as gifts to students and parishioners to serve as a source of Zen inspiration. Thus, Zen masters quite naturally selected subjects and characterizations of Zen life as themes for their work. It is through such iconography that this exhibition explores the artistic accomplishment and spiritual impact of the Zen master's brush.

DARUMA

Zenga: Brushstrokes of Enlightenment is organized thematically into five sections designed to introduce viewers to the subjects and ideas central to Zen thought and life: "Daruma: The Grand Patriarch of Zen;" "Zen Heroes;" "Zen Teachings;" "Zen Calligraphy;" and "Zenga: The Contemplative Art." Each category is presented chronologically. The first section presents twenty-two images of the most frequently represented Zen figure: Daruma, The

Grand Patriarch, who brought Zen teachings from India to China. Daruma embodies the Zen spiritual quest, the search for and knowledge of the inner mind, and the rejection of externals. As no one knew what Daruma actually looked like, Zen paintings of Daruma are not historical portraits; rather, they reflect each master's perception of his or her own spiritual experience.

Daruma is presented here in his four traditional poses: Half Body; Side View; On a Rush Leaf; and Wall Gazing (seen from behind while meditating against a wall). Each form symbolizes a special aspect of the patriarch. The combination of clearly delineated facial features and elusively suggested robes in Daruma's depiction emanates from the Chinese visual tradition. By omitting detailed depictions of his robe and underlying anatomical structure, the Zen artist encourages the viewer to look beyond the obvious, the tangible and material and to concentrate instead on the spiritual.

Although united by motif, each Zen artist records his own interpretation of Daruma. Comparison of this subject in similar poses as portrayed by artists spanning three centuries (the early seventeenth through the mid-twentieth) reveals the uniqueness of each master's hand. The range of variety in Half Body Darumas is dramatic. Instructive examples include: Fūgai's deliberating depictions, (cat. nos. 3 & 4); Hakuin's simple, yet profound and serene *Giant Daruma* (cat. no. 2); Shunsō's severe and penetrating image (cat. no. 7); and Hōjū's jocular, pirate-like portrayal (cat. no. 10). Modern renderings, more free-spirited and loosely defined, include Kokai's peaceful, dreamlike depiction (cat. no. 9), Nantembō's whimsical interpretation (cat. no. 23) and Banryū's humorous Daruma (cat. no. 13). The individuality of each artist is apparent, but it is difficult to distinguish the century in which a work was created by examining the image alone.

As the viewer compares these similar images and absorbs the diverse personalities, the subtle differences in style which make

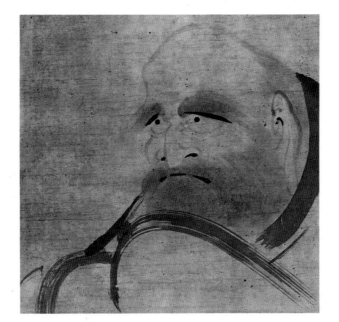

figure III.
Half Body Daruma
Fūgai, 1568-1654.
(detail, cat. no. 3)

24

figure IV.
Half Body Daruma
Sanshōken, 1841-1917
(detail, cat. no. 12)

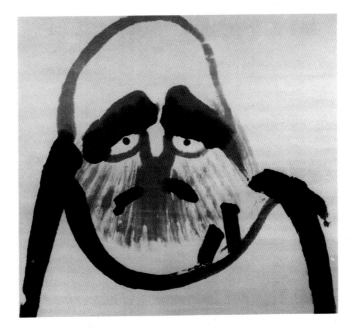

each work distinctive become noticeable: ink tonality, ranging from white to grey to black; textural variation; thinness and thickness of brushstroke; and varied compositional use of space for positioning of the painting, calligraphic inscriptions, artist's signatures and seals. What do these works and the manner in which they were executed reveal about the Zen master as a teacher, as an artist, and as a human being?

A juxtaposition of Fūgai's seventeenth-century *Half Body Daruma* (fig. III), the earliest work in the show, and Sanshōken's twentieth-century *Half Body Daruma* (fig. IV), one of the latest works included, reveals the expressive and stylistic differences in paintings of the same figure, in similar formats, with analogous meaning. The two artists had very different careers. Fūgai was a recluse, who lived mostly in caves; Sanshōken by contrast was abbot of one of the largest temples in Kyoto. Fūgai's Daruma is a piercing portrait while Sanshōken's is a humorous caricature. Seemingly contrasting characteristics, both are typical of Zen painting.

Fūgai's depiction is characterized by finely drawn, pale grey lines which outline Daruma's eyes, eyebrows, ears, nose, mouth and beard, realistically portraying facial features, knitted in a stern, poignant expression. A few thin, precise, black lines describe his eyelids, mouth, inner ear and nostrils, while two black dots portray his intense, penetrating eyes. Daruma occupies the bottom half of the composition where Fūgai employed delicate lines and precise brushstrokes to create an image of spiritual refinement. The depth and severity of Fūgai's Darumas reflect his own reclusive, yet contemplative existence.

Painting on silk, Sanshōken relied on minimal broad strokes of a wet brush to create a Zen-like cartoon. The facial features of his

Daruma are rendered in thick, rough grey strokes contrasted with wide, black strokes for the lower eyebrows, nostrils and robe. The thick eyebrows, a skillful melange of wet, black and grey brushstrokes, illustrate the visual effect of ink bleeding into the silk background and reveal the woven texture of the shiny fabric. As in all Zenga, the color and texture of the material on which the simple ink is brushed is incorporated into the painting's composition. Daruma's robe is larger in proportion to his face in the Sanshōken painting, but is suggested by only three connecting strokes. Here maximum expression is achieved with minimal brushwork, a characteristic of Zenga. Sanshōken's reputation as a big-hearted and humorous monk is reflected in his joyous, playful, loosely brushed rendering of Daruma.

In Zenga the transmission of enlightenment from master to pupil often is referred to as "a doctrine beyond words." It is fitting that a doctrine beyond words employs visual imagery as a key component. Visual imagery sparks the imagination beyond the limitation of words and can expand the boundaries of concepts and ideas. Zen images are intuitive, simultaneously introverted and extroverted, controlled and yet spontaneous—qualities descriptive of and necessary to Zen enlightenment.

Zen masters selected disciples, and students sought mentors on the basis of spiritual enlightenment, not artistic ability. Spiritual lineage can thus be clearly defined by the relationship of a pupil to his mentor as shown in the Generational Chart of Hakuin School Artists (fig. II). Yet visual exposure to the legacy of Zen art came to the practitioners in many forms: through works Zen masters did for students and parishioners; through works done by teachers other than their own (whom students sometimes met on pilgrimages); and through the Zen paintings which temples received as gifts from patrons and visiting masters. Students often learned calligraphy in their early years of education, prior to becoming monks. In the monasteries, there were no classes in painting, no institutionalized, one-to-one transmission of artistic technique to parallel the spiritual transfer, and no designated temple hall in which to regularly view or discuss paintings. Painting was an expression of faith, but not necessarily an established part of spiritual training. Although disciples were spiritually influenced by their mentors, they were often artistically influenced to a lesser degree. Each monk's work reflects his own artistic hand. This may be due to the fact that enlightenment, their primary goal, came through individual pursuit, despite a mentor's guidance. The independence of the process required to achieve Zen enlightenment also encouraged monks to seek individuality in creative self-expression.

The artistic influence of a spiritual mentor on his pupil can be evaluated by comparing paintings of similar subjects by master and disciple. Hakuin's *Half Body Daruma* (fig. V-a) and his student Reigen's work (fig. V-b) on the same theme have much in common: general appearance of the Patriarch; shape and position of the line

figure V-a & b.
Half Body Daruma
Hakuin, 1685-1769
(detail, cat. no. 5)

Half Body Daruma.
Reigen, 1721-1785
(detail, cat. no. 6)

suggesting his robe; and the presence of three dark strokes connecting Daruma's head to the robe. However, Reigen's Daruma is by no means a copy of Hakuin's. It has a more elongated head, utilizes softer greys, a different calligraphic inscription, and less-jagged lines than Hakuin's rendering. Hakuin uses diffused ink to create a fuzzy edge which blends into the paper near Daruma's shoulder. Hakuin's robe line has a greater range of ink tonality whereas Reigen's is consistently darker and the brush skips across the paper surface to incorporate the light background into the brushstrokes. This technique is known as "flying white." Reigen's calligraphy is placed above Daruma's head reaching to the top of the scroll, whereas the head of Hakuin's Daruma is connected to the top of the scroll by a tall vertical line. Although a high degree of influence from Hakuin does exist, a connoisseur can readily distinguish each Zen artist's hand.

Comparison of Hakuin's *Side View Daruma* (fig. VI-a) with the same subject by another of his disciples Suiō (fig. VI-b) also shows the master's influence functioning in tandem with the student's individuality. The general configuration and position of the figure in the picture's format, as well as the facial expression appear similar. Yet in Hakuin's Daruma the nose is more protruded and the light-grey facial strokes are pale in comparison to the medium-grey of his student's darker ink tones; moreover, Hakuin's Daruma is seated on a mat depicted in an array of lines, whereas Suiō's figure indicates no such seat. The shoulder of Hakuin's Daruma again has a skillful interplay of grey and black brushstrokes. Suiō's shoulder and robe show an interplay of short black lines punctuated by black circles—ink seepage from a consistently abrupt brush stoppage indicative of his painting technique. This distinctive line formation is characteristic of Suiō and is unlike Hakuin. It can also be seen in Suiō's *The Chinese Patriarch Rinzai* (cat. no. 36) and *Zen Landscape* (cat. no. 50).

Although the work of Hakuin's two students, Reigen and Suiō, closely reflect their master's visual influence, their respective brushwork, tonality and line quality are distinctively their own, and different from that of one another. These differences demon-

figure VI-a & b.
Side View Daruma.
Hakuin, 1685-1769.
(detail, cat. no.14)

Side View Daruma.
Suiō, 1716-1789.
(detail, cat. no. 15)

strate that Zenga reflects the inner vision of each Zenga master.

In their disciplined quest for spiritual excellence, Zen masters repeatedly brushed the same images. Eventually, such spiritual focus led to creative artistic spontaneity. Just as their disciplined meditation resulted in sudden enlightenment, so did their repetitive, simple (minimal) painting become and appear spontaneous. Achievement of this dexterity took years. When the master Hakuin was asked how long it took to paint a Daruma, drafted in just a few major strokes he said, *"Ten minutes and eighty years."* The "eighty years" refer not only to the time needed to develop the artistic ability of the painter, but the time required to attain the necessary spiritual self-realization of the Zen practitioner. Since the spirit speaks through the brush, a person who had not achieved inner spiritual development could not paint with the power of an accomplished Zen master.

ZEN HEROES AND TEACHINGS

Section two of the exhibition is an array of "Zen Heroes," role models for enlightenment and, thus, a pattern for attaining Zen ideals. It concentrates on three Zen favorites: Hotei, a legendary, happy-go-lucky Chinese monk of the eleventh century who is said to have roamed the countryside carrying a huge bag of presents; and Kanzan and Jittoku, a pair of Chinese eccentrics. Kanzan, a poet, usually is shown with a scroll, while Jittoku, a kitchen sweeper in a mountain temple, is depicted with a broom. Other important Zen Heroes, such as Tenjin, the Japanese God of Knowledge, Hitomaro, the God of Poetry, and Kannon, the Goddess of Compassion, are also represented. The latter three personages are used in many other schools of Japanese painting and are not subjects limited to Zenga.

As in the study of Daruma, comparison of the character and brush-strokes of the same subjects, (Hotei, Kanzan and Jittoku) reflect a wide variety of individual expression through the centuries. For example, Fūgai's fine-lined, vertical *Hotei Pointing at the Moon* (cat. no. 24) seems precise, simple and serious when contrasted with Sengai's thicker brushed, humorous, joyful and horizontal rendering of *Hotei Waking from a Nap* (cat. no. 27). As poignancy is consistent in Fūgai's work, so humor characterizes Sengai's renderings in curvilinear whimsical lines.

While some monks such as Fūgai depicted primarily traditional Zen subjects, Daruma and Hotei, others like Sengai established a varied repertoire of themes including those appropriated from sources other than Zen, such as *Lao T'zu Riding on an Ox* (cat. no. 35), *Three Gods of Good Fortune* (cat. no. 49), and *Zen Landscape* (cat. no. 51). Any subject relating to the life of a Zen-inspired master was considered an acceptable painting theme. It was the special interpretation of an image that gave it a Zen quality, not just the subject itself.

Thus the third section of this exhibition explores "Zen Teachings" in renderings of a wide variety of themes—Practice and Enlightenment, Visual Sermons, Zen and Nature and Mt. Fuji.

Visual sermons are portrayed through a mixture of Zen imagery. Although all Zen works were designed to impart Zen principles, this selection provides visual clarification of Zen beliefs. For example, the painting *Blind Men on a Log Bridge* (cat. no. 46) by Hakuin may be philosophically linked to man enduring the tasks of daily life without the advantage of enlightenment.

Treasure Boat by Hakuin (cat. no. 48), reflects both the symbolic and visual depth of Zenga's seemingly minimal brushwork. The boat is piloted by Fukurokujū, God of Longevity, and is outlined in dark brushstrokes formed by the Chinese ideographic character for "long life." The boat contains four symbols of good fortune: a lucky raincoat, a wide hat, the magic mallet (the Far Eastern version of Aladdin's lamp) and a good-luck bag filled with riches. Zen paintings are often accompanied by a *san* (a poetic inscription), written either by the artist or by some other individual, but always designed to clarify the meaning of the central image and enhance its composition. The *Treasure Boat* inscription prepared by Hakuin reads:

> *"Those who are loyal to their lord and devoted to their elders will be presented with this rain coat, hat, mallet and bag."*
>
> translated by John Stevens

In other words, one who is sincere and considerate in his or her dealings with fellow human beings will be blessed with wealth and good fortune. Disregarding the feelings of others will eventually lead to ruin. The message is deep and universal, whereas the painting's composition is light and buoyant. The *san* positioned in the upper left corner is brushed with soft thin lines which balance the thicker and darker strokes of the boat in the picture's bottom right.

ZEN CALLIGRAPHY:
AESTHETIC ARRANGEMENTS AND MEANING

An examination of Zen calligraphy constitutes the fourth section of the exhibition. While Zen masters rarely had formal instruction in painting, their extensive experience with calligraphy as part of their Zen training familiarized them with brush, ink, and paper. They painted monochromatic and dynamic calligraphic statements, which expressed their Zen doctrines and beliefs. For example, single and double-line calligraphic characters centrally positioned as the subjects of works may implore the viewer to "Always Remember Kannon," Goddess of Compassion (cat. no 33).

Historically, calligraphy has had a significant presence in Japanese painting. Originating in China, in Japan from the Heian Period (794-1185) to the present, it has been considered one of the four arts of the cultured person, along with poetry, painting, and music. Calligraphy plays an important role, too, in the overall design and meaning of Edo Period Zen painting, where there is more visual interplay between calligraphy and image than in any of the other painting schools which flourished simultaneously. To the present day, calligraphy in Japan popularly retains the stature of a greatly appreciated fine art form, and is thus perceived differently than calligraphy currently is in the West.

As a key compositional element, calligraphy can be used in three ways. It can be the central image and subject, exemplified by all the eighteenth to twentieth-century works in the calligraphy section of this exhibition. Calligraphic centerpieces often appear unadorned by other inscriptions, with devotion of the entire picture plane to the artists' configuration of characters. Examples include Jiun's eighteenth-century *Two Line Calligraphy* (cat. no. 64); Tōrei's eighteenth-century *Calligraphic Talisman* (cat. no. 63); and Rengetsu's nineteenth-century *Tanzaku Poems* (cat. no. 65). Calligraphy can serve as an inscription included to enhance a painting's central pictorial image, visually and substantively, as seen in Hakuin's *Treasure Boat* (cat. no. 48); or it can serve as both, when a calligraphic arrangement acts as the work's main image embellished by another calligraphic inscription, as in Hakuin's *Virtue* (cat. no. 61). In unusual instances there is an absence of any inscription and only the artist's signature and/or seals accompany the visual depictions. Examples include Shunsō's nineteenth-century *Mt. Fuji* (cat. no. 55), Kōgan's eighteenth-century *Arhats, Buddhist Saints of India and China* (cat. no. 34) and Ōnisaburō's twentieth-century *Side View Daruma* (cat. no. 17).

30

Photograph by Kurt A. Gitter

Pure calligraphy was the most prevalent Zen painting format, as all monks were trained in such writing. Yet pictorial images with a calligraphic inscription are also quite common. Zenga calligraphic inscriptions usually were brushed by the image maker, although traditionally in Japanese painting, inscriptions could be added by colleagues at the time the painting was made, or even years or centuries later to enliven, strengthen, comment on, authenticate or enhance the work. With the exception of Fūgai's *Daruma on a Rush Leaf* (cat. no. 22) and Chingyū's and Shunsō's *Kanzan and Jittoku* (cat. nos. 28 & 31) all inscribed works in this book were drafted by their image makers. Generally the central image was drawn first, and the poetic inscription added.

The artistic interchange between calligraphic inscription and pictorial image appears gracefully intertwined in a variety of creative spatial arrangements which balance content and composition, and thus confirms the artistic sensibility of the Zen master. Image and inscription may be spatially separated or, less frequently, physically connected. Ideally, the image and inscription are balanced but occasionally the image dominates; more rarely the inspiration predominates. In Fūgai's *Hotei Pointing at the Moon* (cat. no. 24) the rounded happy eccentric's figure is positioned in the bottom left corner of the scroll, juxtaposed to the rectangular poetic inscription placed diagonally and separately in the scroll's upper right corner. The central vertical section of the background negative space separates the equally weighted image and inscription, which are stylistically similar and contribute to an aesthetically balanced work. In Daishin's *Wall Gazing Daruma* (cat. no. 18) a two-line vertical inscription in the top right center half of the work is brushed in small, precisely drawn characters placed

31

parallel to the artist's signature and seal in the scroll's top left. Centrally positioned in the scroll's bottom half directly beneath the inscription and signature, yet separated by negative space, is an outline of Daruma gazing at a wall. Although equal space is allocated to both the image and inscription, the shape and richness of ink which create the image make it appear as the dominant feature of the work. A more exaggerated example of image dominance over inscription exists in Sozan's *The Japanese Patriarch Daitō Kokushi* (cat. no. 37), where the begging monk occupies three quarters of the scroll and is crowned by a small delicate inscription. Inscription dominated by image is far more common than image dominated by inscription, the latter as exemplified by Nantembō's *Half Body Daruma* (cat. no. 11). Nantembō's broad, bold, black calligraphic inscription runs energetically and diagonally from the top right corner to the left center of the scroll where it meets a characteristic heavy black line splashed in ink. This thick, eruptive brushstroke traces the side and bottom of the Patriarch's face, delicately painted in pale greys, and becomes the line suggesting Daruma's robe. It is the forcefulness of the dynamically drawn inscription, here physically joined with and emphasized by the lower robe line, which suggests that the inscription dominates the image. This is not achieved by excessive allocation of space, rather it results from the qualities of the highly powered application of thick dark ink strewn across the scroll. This highlights the inscription and creates a strong contrast with the very pale grey portrayal of Daruma's facial features.

Calligraphic inscriptions may be placed in less geometrically predictable positions in order to flow gracefully with the design of a painting's central image. For example, a two line vertical inscription paralleling Nantembō's twentieth-century *Zen Staff* (cat. no. 42) echoes the staff's length, which extends vertically nearly the entire length of the scroll. Calligraphy in Gōchō's *Kanzan and Jittoku* (cat. no. 29), vertically-positioned and softly balanced between the top and bottom of the diagonally placed image, is an integral part of the composition. The diagonally-positioned trees on a mountain top in Reigen's eighteenth-century *Shrine of Tenjin* (cat. no. 52) are visually paralleled by a soft delicate diagonal arrangement of calligraphic characters subservient to the pre-eminent image of the Shintō shrine. Hakuin's eighteenth-century *Hotei's Bag* (cat. no. 26) encircles the inscription written in equally pale, but thinner, strokes than those describing the Zen hero's bag. Placement of image and inscription reflects the individual Zen artist's personal expression and is not a function of the artistic style of the century in which he lives. The many asymmetrical solutions we have observed can be viewed within the context of the traditional Japanese aesthetic, which stresses asymmetry in the design of gardens, architecture and tea-ceremony ceramics.

Despite the Zen monk's achievement of high aesthetic standards it must be remembered that he painted primarily to express religious beliefs and never considered his work as art. The substantive function of calligraphic inscriptions and subject configurations is mutual reinforcement and enhancement. Reinforcement occurs through the inclusion of a *san* which expands or elaborates the concept of the central image, both when the calligraphy is a direct commentary on the painting and when the image and calligraphy are the same. In Zen art, the central image (pictorial or calligraphic) and the *san* are meant to work as an organic whole. Take, for example, Hakuin's *Virtue* (cat. no.61) calligraphy in which the subject is a single large character meaning "Virtue." The *san* clarifies the Zen master's view of that attribute:

> *If you pile up money for your descendants*
> *They will be sure and waste it;*
> *if you collect books for them*
> *they probably will not read a word.*
> *It is better to pile up virtue unobtrusively—*
> *such a legacy will last a long, long time.*
>
> translated by John Stevens

In Sokuhi's seventeenth-century pair, *Dragon and Tiger* (cat. no. 1) the bold single character above each image directly names them. The unified meaning of image and calligraphy contributes to the presentation of a stronger message. Tesshū's nineteenth-century *Dragon* (cat. no. 66) further simplifies the issue of reinforcement of image and inscription, as the subject is a visual pun. The character for dragon is simultaneously presented as a pictorial abstraction of a dragon. What is a calligraphic character if not an arrangement of the same brushstrokes that create pictorial imagery? The figures

Photograph by Jan E. Watson.

figure VII.
Process of brushing
calligraphy with
John Stevens.

of Daishin's *Hitomaro* (cat. no. 39) and Hakuin's *Tenjin* (cat. no. 38) are created entirely out of calligraphic characters representing the names of the gods, whom they describe pictorially.

ZEN CALLIGRAPHY: TECHNIQUE AND BRUSHSTROKE

The Zen master's technique employs the application of freshly ground ink mixed with water onto absorbent paper, allowing for little error and no overpainting. He paints with brushes of varying widths on sheets of paper placed on the floor (fig. VII). Seated on his knees, the artist's flexible position allows him to incorporate body force, proper breathing techniques and intense concentration into the execution of brushstrokes. Typically, he paints many works in a session. This method is in marked contrast to the traditional Western process of painting, where an artist paints on an easel, at eye level, one painting over many sessions.

Works made in the beginning of the session, when a brush wet with water was first mixed with the freshly ground *sumi*, tend to be lighter in color (pale greys), while works made toward the session's end, when the wet brush had been repeatedly applied to the rich ink in the stone, tend to be of thicker and deeper ink tone (dark grey to black). Extreme dilution of ink with water creates a paler, washier look no matter when applied. The wetness or dryness, speed and motion of a brushstroke determine the width, tonality, and quality of the line.

The calligraphy style varied widely from formal *Kanji* (Chinese ideograms) executed in a style close to the standard printed form, to a loosely defined cursive style, which is sometimes difficult to read because of the abstraction of the individual Japanese characters.

Zenga masters incorporated the texture and tint of the paper upon which they worked into their compositions. Often images were constructed by just a few strokes, as in Chūhō's *Mt. Fuji* (cat. no. 53) where the background negative space is an integral part of the visual presentation. Shunsō's *Mt. Fuji* (cat. no. 55) reveals the silk woven fabric which absorbed the ink and showcased the visible geometric texture of the work. Ōnisaburō's *Side View Daruma* (cat. no. 17) has a ruffled pattern of black *sumi* and light paper background reflecting the texture of the *tatami* mat floor upon which the paper was placed for painting.

The monk's calligraphic expertise prepared him to depict pictorial subjects, for dextrous brushwork was the basis of both. It is through the Zen master's disciplined but varied application of ink that he establishes his individuality, an external artistic expression of a deeply developed internal vision.

figure VIII-a & b.
Flying white brushstrokes.
Dragon and Tiger
Sokuhi, 1616-1671
(detail, cat. no. 1)

The distinguishing characteristics of each artist are seen in a surprising range of tonal and textural variation in brushstrokes, ranging from black through all shades of grey to "flying white," and executed in thin-to-thick as well as wet-to-dry ink applications. The Zen master's ability to capture and portray an extraordinary spectrum of lights and darks is so superbly and subtly executed that the viewer must accustom his eye to experience these nuances, in order to reap maximum appreciation of the artistic virtues and spiritual depth of Zenga. Consider, for example, the technique "flying white" (fig.VIII-a & b). This distinctive calligraphic stroke is achieved when the calligrapher anchors his brush to paper and moves his arm so quickly that the brush briefly flies off the paper surface, allowing the background paper color to become an integral part of the continued brushstroke. It thus appears as a black line of varying width in which areas of the paper's color shine through. The relative dryness or wetness of the brush and the swiftness of the stroke dictate the degree and quantity of flying white.

Flying white is seen predominantly in broad strokes of calligraphy as noted in Sokuhi's seventeenth-century *Dragon and Tiger* (cat. no. 1) and Jiun's seventeenth-century calligraphic centerpiece (cat. no. 64). It also can be part of an energetically broad sweeping line depicting a non-calligraphic subject such as Chūhō's nineteenth-century *Mt. Fuji* (cat. no. 53). Not all Zen masters employed the technique of flying white. Yet some, like Nantembō, exhibited a propensity for it, as can be observed throughout his work, regardless of theme, in *Half Body Daruma* (cat. no. 11), *Wall Gazing Daruma* (cat. no. 20), *Zen Staff* (cat. no. 42), and *Pair of Two-Panel Screens* (cat. no. 68 a & b).

Each dynamic flying white stroke reflects the artist's arm, body and soul rapidly and vigorously moving through the pictorial plane. Concentrate for a moment on Sokuhi's *Dragon and Tiger* (fig. VIII-a & b), and imagine the amount of physical energy and psychological intensity it takes to create such an image. Flying white does not appear in the thin, fine lines that create the facial features of either Sokuhi's dragon or tiger, or in those lines which create the small tightly drawn calligraphic *san* of Daishin (cat. no. 18). These thinner, greyer and wetter lines often create a striking contrast in tone, texture and tonality with adjacent flying white lines.

The effects of flying white on the picture plane reveal variety in an artist's skill with the brush. Tesshū's *Dragon* (cat. no. 66) is painted with a single, quite varied brushstroke. The dragon's perky head, facing upward, is composed of thick black strokes and ink splashes, while the central rising loop of the body, brushed in flying white, lends pleasing light coloration to the painting's central composition. The blunt terminating brushstroke of the dragon's tail, a broader, darker and fairly thick stroke, manifests the lines of the brush bristles showing minimal flying white. Variety in the closure of flying white lines can also be seen in the robe lines of Shizan's *Side View Daruma* (cat. no. 16), energetic to the end, and in Chūhō's *Mt. Fuji* (cat. no. 53) which floats onto the white paper background suggesting the vastness of Fuji. The skill with which the Zen artist terminates his varied broad lines of flying white suggests his dexterity in controlling the seemingly spontaneous rapidly moving brush.

The use of brushstrokes to create light, medium and dark grey or black compositions in a wide range of contrasting shades of light and dark is further evidence of the Zen master's capability with brush and ink. Wet washy greys are used to create recognizable forms such as a dancer's costume in Shunsō's *Noh Dancer* (fig. IX). These broad, overlapping horizontal and vertical strokes of varying light-to-medium grey gradations depict a frozen moment in the dancer's movement. Implied by minimal dark accents suggesting

figure IX.
Washed grey brushstrokes.
Noh Dancer.
Shunsō, 1750-1839.
(detail, cat. no. 40)

36

the motion of his underlying bent elbows and raised knees, these tonal gradations accentuate the costume enveloping the dancer. His tight belt is suggested by exceedingly light grey tones drawn in contrast to the darker ones which highlight the costume. In keeping with the spirit of Zen art there is little delineation of the dancer's underlying anatomy. The only black lines in the composition outline the dancer's hat and facial features.

Grey washes of middle tone range describe Reigen's *Mt. Fuji* (cat. no. 54) in three simple strokes, complemented by an eggplant and a leaf. The image shows no major contrasting gradations of black or grey ink. This fairly monochrome tonality contrasts markedly with Suiō's *Zen Landscape* (cat. no. 50) where multiple, dark grey to black, circular, vertical and horizontal applications of ink denote trees and rocks, overlying lighter grey mountain peaks. The combination of non-uniform, irregular, and varied shapes creates an unusual landscape.

Achieving extraordinary tonality, Hakuin's work exemplifies an entire range of ink usage from the lightest greys to the deepest blacks. *Blind Men on a Log Bridge* (cat. no. 46) is created with a wide range of greys and blacks. The bridge of muted grey wash is visually balanced by the grey wash of the mountains, whereas the dark tones of the caricature-like blind men identify them as the subject. Hakuin's ability to depict imagery through gradations of ink is further demonstrated in the central character of his *Virtue* (cat. no. 61), composed of varying shades of thick strokes ranging from bold black to dark grey. Examination of the painting reveals a vast range of light and dark nuances confined to a deep dark palette. A textured ink splotch is prominent on top of the virtue character. This interesting effect, unique to the work of the Zen monk, results from his use of left-over, partially dry, congealed ink.

Zen monks worked within the confines of their philosophy. Spartan by discipline, with a disdain for waste, they used supplies which were given to them, in contrast to professional calligraphers who purchased and employed only the best-quality ink. For a Zen artist, painting represents the mind; the spirit of the creator rather than the quality of the materials was important. A Zen master never discarded the unused wet ink remaining at the conclusion of a calligraphy or painting session; rather he would frugally preserve it as a resource for future use. The professional calligrapher, in contrast, would discard it and start again with fresh ink. This is an example of a philosophical restraint which created an aesthetic opportunity for the Zenga master.

The artistic strength of Zen painting can be evaluated within the context of art in general. The final works of a master are generally considered to be the best because they represent a more fully developed spirit; old age provided the benefit of experience and insight. Hakuin's *Always Remember Kannon* (cat. no. 62) was done at age eighty-four, in the last year of his life. The strength of this work, completed from top to bottom in one vigorous breath and deliberate brushstroke, required tremendous energy of body and mind. At the time when his physical prowess was greatly diminished, his spiritual strength was at its peak and provided him sustenance to complete the task.

Zen artists were committed to the study and transmission of Zen, not to art. It is the modern viewer, particularly in the West, who tends to respond to this one-dimensional aesthetic aspect of Zenga. Zen masters never considered their work as objects to display solely in the interest of art. This is best expressed by the Zen master Sengai:

> *"My play with brush and ink*
> *is not calligraphy nor painting;*
> *yet unknowingly people mistakenly think:*
> *this is calligraphy, this is painting."*
>
> translated by John Stevens

CARE OF PAINTINGS

Zen paintings were executed with deep spiritual commitment and disciplined experience. Zen art contains the essence of the master, and Zen practitioners lovingly preserved their teachers' brush-work. The condition and longevity of these works were considered in each aspect of their mounting, handling, storage and display. This is the custom and tradition with all Japanese painting.

Two-dimensional Japanese artworks can be presented in a number of formats: hanging scrolls, hand scrolls, album leaves, fan paint-ings, folding screens, and sliding or stationary panels. Most Zenga are hanging scrolls (cat. nos. 1-66, 69 & 70) and less frequently screens (cat. nos. 67 & 68). The scrolls could be placed in the *tokonoma* (alcove) in a house or temple room for private viewing and meditation (fig. XI).

The mounting of paintings in different formats is an historically important and respected art form in Japan, dating back to the eighth century. Just as monks studied Zen under the tutelage of masters, so students of mounting were apprenticed to master craftsmen for a decade before being considered qualified mounters.

Typical Zenga mountings echo Zen philosophy in their austere, simple use of unadorned paper materials. The feeling of an original Zen mounting becomes an integral part of the art work, designed to enhance it rather than to emerge as a notable element on its own. Often mountings are made of inexpensive materials available to the monk or student at the time of the work's creation. Although spartan, original-style Zen mountings may vary from a thin marbleized paper in deep-blue with beige-like swirls, as surrounds Kogan's *Daruma on a Rush Leaf*, (cat. no. 21) to a simple

beige paper background similar in color and quality to that on which Tesshū's *Zen Calligraphy* (fig. IV, p.17) is brushed.

Each painting has a mounting style which was originally considered most appropriate. Whereas basic, frugal mountings suit the goals and imagery of an Edo Period Zen artist, colorful decorative Rimpa paintings of the same period were originally mounted on bright silk-brocade fabrics in concert with the elegant, highly decorative qualities of the artworks. As Zen paintings became considered more precious and valued by their owners in the last two generations, some chose to remount the pieces in more elaborate gold brocade and silk, while others continued to select simple papers in the original style.

Scroll mountings are designed to both enhance the aesthetics of the artwork and provide protection of the painting. They consist of several elements: paper backings adhered to the artwork, textiles or paper which surround and frame the painting and, for hanging, a wooden rod with ivory or lacquered wood knobs around which the painting can also be conveniently rolled for storage. In this regard, the Japanese scroll mounting made of paper and fabric differs from the western painting frame often made of wood or metal, in that it is less rigid and more flexible for easy movement and storage. Yet because of the time-consuming and delicate process, remounting is usually done only when necessary, in contrast to the western frame which can be easily changed. An expert mounting can last two hundred years or more depending upon the condition and care of the object.

Japanese paintings are usually shown for only short amounts of time, a few days to a few weeks, in honor of special occasions or seasons. When not exhibited, they are conveniently rolled and

figure XI.
The late rōshi of Ryūtaku-ji seated in front of an alcove with a painting by Tōrei, *Buddha Descending the Mountains Following His Enlightenment.*

Photograph by Kurt A. Gitter

placed in an individual *hako* (box) for storage. In the damp climate of Japan, these *hako* (fig. X) were essential for the preservation of scrolls which, left unprotected, might be ruined by mold and insect damage. In the past each box was typically made of *kiri* (paulownia) wood, and was individually handcrafted by special artisans to specifically fit the painting. Often, specially valued scrolls like Hakuin's *Giant Daruma* were contained in double boxes for extra protection.

The tradition of box storage created an environment whereby box inscriptions and seals by previous owners, famous scholars, tea masters, Buddhist priests and other outstanding figures were prized in themselves, and served as historical confirmation about the artist. For example, when the original box for Fūgai's *Hotei Pointing at the Moon* was beyond repair, the scroll was refitted with a new *hako*, but the box maker carefully preserved the old lid, inscribed in excellent seal script, by inlaying it into the new top.

The interior of the lid sometimes contains an elaborate inscription giving details on the artist, comments on the painting and similar information. During hard times (or if the abbot was dissolute), temple treasures were sometimes sold off after the name of the temple was effaced from the box's inscriptions as shown in the lid for Shunsō's *Half Body Daruma.*

Boxes inscribed subsequent to the death of the artist also confirm the authenticity of the enclosed work. The box for Sengai's *Three Gods of Good Fortune* is inscribed and signed by Awakawa Yasuichi, a modern connoisseur and writer about Zen art who "guaranteed" that the scroll was genuine. The box for Hakuin's *Three Shintō Deities* bears the inscription of a recent abbot of Shōin-ji, Hakuin's temple, who guaranteed the authenticity of the work. Such guarantees usually were based on careful scrutiny and comparison of the seals on the scroll with the master's seals preserved by the temple and accessible to the abbot for study.

The individual care for the preservation of Zen painting continues today in the homes of collectors, in museums and Zen temples where works are often contemplated, as described in the final section of the exhibition. A recent visit by this writer to Hakuin's temple Ryūtaku-ji confirmed that Zenga is still treasured and preserved. This personal experience provided a much-cherished human perspective and response to Zen painting. Daizaburō Tanaka, a major collector of Hakuin paintings arranged for a special audience with the *rōshi* (abbot). The *rōshi* sat on a *tatami* mat adjacent to the *tokonoma* (alcove) in which a painting by Tōrei, *Buddha Descending from the Mountain Following His Enlightenment* (fig. XI), was hanging. Through opened *fusuma* (sliding doors), the beauty of the autumn red maples and the wonderful sound of garden waterfalls permeated one's senses.

The abbot served cakes, tangerines and *saké*, and presented a calligraphy by his own hand. The setting was timeless: the traditional architecture of the room and temple grounds, the calming sounds of visible nature and the *rōshi's* crossed legged seated

Photograph by Kurt A. Gitter.

figure XII.
A view of *mushi boshi* at Ryūtaku-ji Temple.

41

position. The small Seiko clock, the only modern element in the room, confirmed this observation.

It was *mushi boshi*, the day each year when the temple's entire holdings of painting and calligraphy are displayed for public viewing while they are simultaneously opened to air. This tradition, dating back hundreds of years, deters insect infestation of the scrolls and their storage boxes. November 23 is the annual observance at Ryūtaku-ji, selected no doubt for the crisp, dry autumn air quality.

The paintings were displayed throughout the temple, side by side, in no particular historical order, attached to beams, covering all available wall space and closed *fusuma* (fig. XII). This is in direct opposition to the typical Japanese-style of displaying only one object at a time.

The majority of the paintings were Zenga painted by Hakuin or his followers who had lived at this temple or had brought gifts during pilgrimages. The storage boxes were neatly placed in front of each work on a broad strip of red felt cloth which served as a division between artwork and viewer. The visitors, mostly local parishioners, respected the necessary distance one needed to keep from the paintings. Unlike museum displays, there were no plexiglass covers or wooden barriers, and no labels or explanations. The works were there for one-to-one communication.

Mushi boshi is a special experience reflecting both a religious and artistic reverence for the fragility of the temple's art treasures. Amidst the large crowd of engaged viewers a young monk sat deeply centered in *zazen* (meditation) suggesting simultaneously past, present and future Zen experiences. For this writer, in this environment, the aesthetic and spiritual magic of Zenga was clear.

A ZEN KŌAN

A monk asked his master to express Zen on paper so that he would have something tangible to study. At first the master refused saying, *"Since it is right in front of your face why should I try to capture it with brush and ink?"* Still the monk continued to plead with the master for something concrete. The master drew a circle on a piece of paper and added this inscription: *"Thinking about this and understanding it is second best; not thinking about it and understanding it is third best."* The master did not say what is first best.

WORKS IN THE EXHIBITION

1 a & b Ōbaku SOKUHI (1616-1671), *Dragon and Tiger*

DARUMA: THE GRAND PATRIARCH OF ZEN

2 HAKUIN Ekaku (1685-1769), *Giant Daruma*
3 FŪGAI Ekun (1568-1654), *Half Body Daruma*
4 FŪGAI Ekun (1568-1654), *Half Body Daruma*
5 HAKUIN Ekaku (1685-1769), *Half Body Daruma*
6 REIGEN Etō (1721-1785), *Half Body Daruma*
7 SHUNSŌ Jōshu (1750-1839), *Half Body Daruma*
8 TAKUJŪ Kosen (1760-1833), *Half Body Daruma*, 1832
9 KOKAI Jikō (1800-1874), *Half Body Daruma*
10 HŌJŪ Zenbyō (1802-1872), *Half Body Daruma*
11 Nakahara NANTEMBŌ (1839-1925), *Half Body Daruma*, 1917
12 SANSHŌKEN Yūzen Gentatsu (1841-1917), *Half Body Daruma*
13 Matsubara BANRYŪ (1848-1935), *Half Body Daruma*
14 HAKUIN Ekaku (1685-1769), *Side View Daruma*
15 SUIŌ Genrō (1716-1789), *Side View Daruma*
16 Ashikaga SHIZAN (1859-1959), *Side View Daruma*
17 Deguchi ŌNISABURŌ (1871-1948), *Side View Daruma*
18 DAISHIN Gitō (1656-1730), *Wall Gazing Daruma*
19 JIUN Onkō (1718-1804), *Wall Gazing Daruma*
20 Nakahara NANTEMBŌ (1839-1925), *Wall Gazing Daruma*, 1909
21 KŌGAN Gengei (1747-1821), *Daruma on a Rush Leaf*
22 FŪGAI Ekun (1568-1654), *Daruma on a Rush Leaf*
23 Nakahara NANTEMBŌ (1839-1925), *Snow Daruma*, 1921

ZEN HEROES

24 FŪGAI Ekun (1568-1654), *Hotei Pointing at the Moon*
25 HAKUIN Ekaku (1685-1769), *Hotei's "Fuki"*
26 HAKUIN Ekaku (1685-1769), *Hotei's Bag*
27 SENGAI Gibon (1750-1838), *Hotei Waking from a Nap*
28 Zuikō CHINGYŪ (1743-1822), *Kanzan and Jittoku*, 1818
29 GŌCHŌ Kankai (1749-1835), *Kanzan and Jittoku*, 1834
30 a & b KŌGAN Gengei (1747-1821), *Kanzan and Jittoku*
31 a & b SHUNSŌ Jōshu (1750-1839), *Kanzan and Jittoku*
32 a & b GAKO Tangen Chiben (1737-1805), *Kanzan and Jittoku*
33 REIGEN Etō (1721-1785), *Kannon, Goddess of Compassion*
34 KŌGAN Gengei (1747-1821), *Arhats, Buddhist Saints of India and China*
35 SENGAI Gibon (1750-1838), *Lao-T'zu Riding on an Ox*
36 SUIŌ Genrō (1716-1789), *The Chinese Patriarch Rinzai*

44

37 SOZAN Genkyō (1799-1868), *The Japanese Patriarch Daitō Kokushi*
38 HAKUIN Ekaku (1685-1769), *Tenjin*
39 DAISHIN Gitō (1656-1730), *Hitomaro*
40 SHUNSŌ Jōshu (1750-1839), *Noh Dancer*

ZEN TEACHINGS

41 HAKUIN Ekaku (1685-1769), *Monk on Pilgrimage*
42 Nakahara NANTEMBŌ (1839-1925), *Zen Staff*, 1923
43 KŌGAN Gengei (1747-1821), *Procession of Monks*
44 TŌREI Enji (1721-1792), *Zen Circle of Enlightenment*
45 TSU'Ō Sōtetsu (1801-1854), *Enlightenment Certificate*
46 HAKUIN Ekaku (1685-1769), *Blind Men on a Log Bridge*
47 HAKUIN Ekaku (1685-1769), *Bonseki*
48 HAKUIN Ekaku (1685-1769), *Treasure Boat*
49 SENGAI Gibon (1750-1838), *Three Gods of Good Fortune*
50 SUIŌ Genrō (1716-1789), *Zen Landscape*
51 SENGAI Gibon (1750-1838), *Zen Landscape*
52 REIGEN Etō (1721-1785), *Shrine of Tenjin*
53 CHŪHŌ Sōu (1759-1838), *Mt. Fuji*
54 REIGEN Etō (1721-1785), *Mt. Fuji*
55 SHUNSŌ Jōshu (1750-1839), *Mt. Fuji,*
56 Ōtagaki RENGETSU (1791-1875), *Drying Persimmons*, 1868
57 HAKUIN Ekaku (1685-1769), *Monkey*

ZEN CALLIGRAPHY

58 HAKUIN Ekaku (1685-1769), *Two Line Calligraphy*
59 HAKUIN Ekaku (1685-1769), *Three Shintō Deities*
60 HAKUIN Ekaku (1685-1769), *Death Kōan*
61 HAKUIN Ekaku (1685-1769), *Virtue*
62 HAKUIN Ekaku (1685-1769), *Always Remember Kannon*
63 TŌREI Enji (1721-1792), *Calligraphic Talisman*
64 JIUN Onkō (1718-1804), *Two Line Calligraphy*
65 a & b Ōtagaki RENGETSU (1791-1875), *Tanzaku Poems*, 1870
66 Yamaoka TESSHŪ (1836-1888), *Dragon*
67 a & b Yamaoka TESSHŪ (1836-1888), *Pair of Six-Panel Screens*
68 a & b Nakahara NANTEMBŌ (1839-1925), *Pair of Two-Panel Screens*, 1923

ZENGA: THE CONTEMPLATIVE ART

69 Nakahara NANTEMBŌ (1839-1925), *Zen Circle*, 1923
70 REIGEN Etō (1721-1785), *Kōan*

Instead of hanging up fancy pictures in your homes, display paintings of Zen teachings in you favorite place. Honor that tradition with respect and you will be free from all distress.

Hakuin Ekaku

1 a & b Ōbaku SOKUHI, 1616-1671
Dragon and Tiger
sumi on paper
44 1/2 x 20 1/8 inches each (113.0 x 51.1cm)
The Gitter Collection

Sokuhi, a Chinese emigre monk of the Ōbaku Zen Sect, portrays here the dragon and the tiger in both pictorial (concrete) and calligraphic (abstract) forms. The dragon, symbolic of spiritual power and enlightened wisdom, commands the heavens while the tiger, the embodiment of physical strength and courageous living, rules the earth. In Zen art, the pairing of the dragon and the tiger—representing the two great forces of the universe—signifies the harmonization of the spiritual and material. Sokuhi's delightful work is a splendid example of Zen brushwork—bold, dynamic, vivid, profound and yet enlivened by subtle playfulness. These two paintings serve as a dramatic introduction to the exhibition.

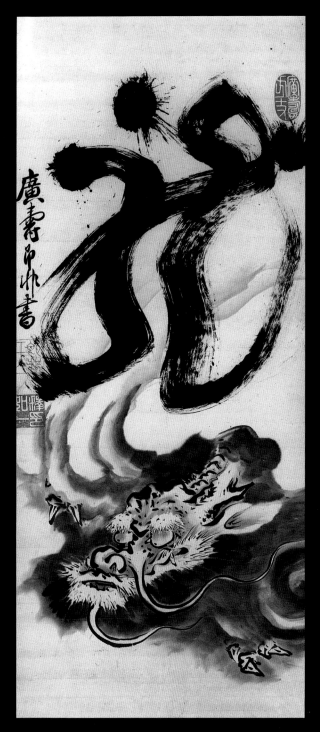

DARUMA, THE GRAND PATRIARCH OF ZEN

The foremost symbol of Zen is its first patriarch Daruma (Sanskrit, Bodhidharma), the legendary meditation master who traveled from India to China in the sixth century to overturn the top-heavy superstructure of doctrinal Buddhism that was being erected in the Middle Kingdom. Daruma's famous encounter with the Emperor of China went like this:

> *"I've constructed dozens of Buddhist temples, supported hundreds of monks and nuns, and sponsored countless religious ceremonies,"* the proud emperor informed Daruma. *"How great is my merit?"*
> *"No merit at all,"* Daruma replied bluntly.
> *"Tell me then,"* the emperor wanted to know, *"What is the first principle of Buddhism?"*
> *"Vast emptiness, nothing holy!"* Daruma shot back.
> *"Who are you?"* the thoroughly perplexed emperor demanded.
> *"I don't know!"* Daruma announced, departing as suddenly as he had appeared.

Daruma's teaching is often summarized as, *"Enlightenment is not found in books or in the performance of empty rites; Zen is none other than your own mind so look within and wake up!"* In Zenga, the artist is not painting Daruma as an historical figure (or even a saint) but as a symbol of penetrating insight, self-reliance, ceaseless diligence, and the rejection of all externals. Furthermore, in order to bring the image of Daruma alive with brush and ink, the artist must become Daruma. Thus, a Daruma painting is a spiritual self-portrait, based on the individual experience of each Zen master.

2 HAKUIN Ekaku, 1685-1769
Giant Daruma
sumi on paper
51 1/2 x 21 3/4 inches (130.8 x 55.2 cm)
The Gitter Collection

This massive image by Japan's great master Hakuin epitomizes Zen art—
unadorned, direct, substantial and bristling with spiritual force. Free of
embellishments and elaboration, the painting presents Buddhism in its most
concentrated form. In the inscription on the painting, Hakuin challenges us:

> *(Zen) is a direct pointing to the human heart;*
> *See into your nature and become Buddha!*

HALF BODY DARUMA

As an embodiment of universal truth— *"unable to be contained by heaven and earth"* —Zen artists generally refrained from depicting Daruma's full form. Also, by revealing only the upper half of Daruma's body, Zen artists challenged the viewer to look beyond the surface in order to grasp the Patriarch's essence. Although seemingly hidden from view, Daruma's core—the Buddha-mind— can be discerned if one contemplates the painting as an organic whole rather than trying to analyze it from historical, aesthetic, or philosophical perspectives.

In half body Darumas, the face and head are brushed ·first (the heavy beard and exotic earring denoting Daruma's Indian origins), then the robe, and finally the eyes are dotted in to animate the image. Indeed, the eyes are Daruma's most prominent feature, for *"One who is wide awake has no fear or doubt."* Regarding the length of time it takes to compose a Daruma painting, Hakuin said in reply to that question, *"Ten minutes—and eighty years."*

3 FŪGAI Ekun, 1568-1654
Half Body Daruma
sumi on paper
25 x 12 inches (63.5 x 30.5 cm)
The Gitter Collection

Free-spirited Fūgai, who spent most of his days on the road or hiding out in caves, actually lived much like Daruma. Fūgai exchanged his paintings for provisions from the local villagers and his artworks were treasured for generations by country folk prior to being "discovered" by scholars and collectors. Firmly constructed and finely textured, the brushstrokes of Fūgai's Daruma are clear and luminous. Still radiant after four centuries, this Daruma remains a living presence. (Until recently, the value of Zenga was not recognized by many dealers, and on this particular piece, Fūgai's original seal—on the right above Daruma's head—has been effaced and a fake "Nobutada" seal added in a foolish attempt to increase the value of the painting.)

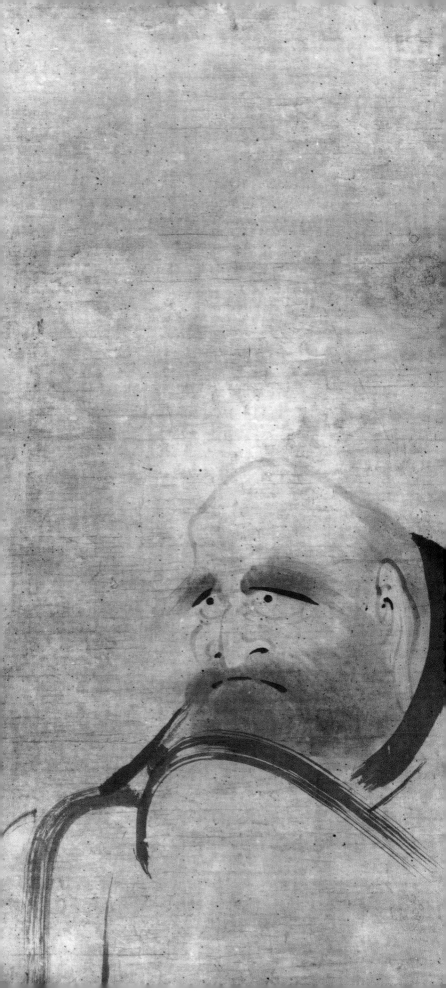

4 FŪGAI Ekun, 1568-1654
Half Body Daruma
sumi on paper
19 x 13 inches (48.3 x 33.0 cm)
The Gitter Collection

A single hawk soars through the sky,
Sparrows cower but there is no escape!
Swooping down as swiftly as a falling stone,
Talons bared, it launches an attack in all directions!

Blackened by several centuries of soot accumulated from the hearth of the
farm house in which it once hung, this Daruma is more roughhewn than
Fūgai's other versions, and the eyes more penetrating than usual. The
dynamic imagery of the inscription well conveys the intention of a Zen
master to shake lethargic human beings out of their complacency.

54

5 HAKUIN Ekaku, 1685-1769
Half Body Daruma
sumi on paper
32 1/4 x 10 1/4 inches (81.9 x 26.0 cm)
The Gitter Collection

> *Bamboo rustles in the cool freshness,*
> *Shattering the golden shadows of the moon.*

Typical of most masters, Hakuin did not start painting until he had been well seasoned by Zen training (in his case at age sixty). This Daruma, likely dating from Hakuin's mid-seventies, has a softer, more reflective cast than his Great Darumas which can be overwhelming. The brushstrokes are bright, rich and vibrant. The Patriarch's robe is skillfully formed by the character for "heart" and the inscription, too, identifies Daruma with the spirit of things. When we are one with the universe, all of nature becomes our meditation hall.

6 REIGEN Etō, 1721-1785
Half Body Daruma
sumi on paper
26 1/2 x 11 inches (67.3 x 27.9 cm)
New Orleans Museum of Art:
Gift of Dr. and Mrs. Kurt A. Gitter, 82.146

Son of an Indian prince,
Disciple of a meditation master from Central Asia
(Daruma has ended up here...)

Not much is known about Reigen, who once lived as a hermit for more than a decade. Reigen was a disciple of Hakuin, and even though his Daruma is based on the style learned from his master, it is hardly a copy—Reigen's unique vision of Daruma is clearly evident. The thick, black brushstrokes of the Patriarch's robe are particularly impressive and the simple paper mounting suits the painting perfectly. The inscription alludes to the transmission of Zen from East to West. Daruma was born in India, studied Zen in Central Asia, carried it to China, and his descendants eventually transmitted his teachings to Japan. From Japan, this painting has been brought to the West to proclaim Daruma's message in modern times.

7 SHUNSŌ Jōshu, 1750-1839
Half Body Daruma
sumi on paper
41 3/4 x 15 7/8 inches (106.0 x 40.3 cm)
Private Collection

Shunsō studied under Reigen as well as several other of Hakuin's direct disciples. His straightforward Daruma seems to have a slightly harder edge to it than the others, and we can sense the fierce determination of the Patriarch. Shunsō's Daruma, with his stern eyes fixed on the viewer confronts us directly, *"Well, how about it?"*

60